HAIT

THE BREACHED CITADEL

HAITI
THE BREACHED CITADEL

Revised and Updated Edition

PATRICK BELLEGARDE-SMITH

Canadian Scholars' Press Inc.
Toronto

Haiti: The Breached Citadel, Revised and Updated Edition
by Patrick Bellegarde-Smith

First edition published in 1990 by Westview Press, Inc.

This edition published in 2004 by
Canadian Scholars' Press Inc.
180 Bloor Street West, Suite 801
Toronto, Ontario
M5S 2V6
www.cspi.org

Canadian Scholars' Press gratefully acknowledges financial support for our publishing activities from the Government of Canada through the Book Publishing Industry Development Program (BPIDP).

National Library of Canada Cataloguing in Publication Data

Bellegarde-Smith, Patrick
         Haiti : the breached citadel / Patrick Bellegarde-Smith. -- Rev. and
updated ed.

Includes bibliographical references and index.
ISBN 1-55130-268-3

         1. Haiti--History--1804-. I. Title.

F1928.2.B44 2004   972.94   C2004-901878-7

Cover art: Cameau Rameau, *Les Dieux Vaudou se penchant sur le destin d'Haiti (The Vodou Gods Considering Haiti's Fate)*. Oil on canvas, 102cm x 76cm. Reproduced by permission of the artist.
Cover design by George Kirkpatrick
Text design and layout by Brad Horning
Photograph of author by Pat A. Robinson

04   05   06   07 08   5   4   3   2   1

Printed and bound in Canada by AGMV Marquis Imprimeur Inc.

Canadä

Dedication

Pou tout fanm vannyan peyi m:
Ewo nan lit la ak nan goumin; pa pèdi fwa pitit
mwen.

For all the women of my homeland:
Heroism is in the struggle; do not lose heart, dear child.

> Legba
> sòti lan Ginen,
> (that came from Africa)
> Legba
> ouvri baryè-a pou nou
> (open the gate for us)
> pou nou pase.
> (so we can pass)

Table of Contents

List of Maps and Photographs   / ix
Preface to the New Edition   / 1
Introduction   / 5

Chapter 1 The Nature of Haiti: Land and Society   / 13

The Land, the People, and Natural Resources   / 13
Vodou Cosmology: World View at the Crossroads   / 21
Women and Society   / 36

**Chapter 2 The Context of Haitian Development and
Underdevelopment   / 47**

Saint-Domingue: Wealth Amid Poverty   / 47
The Haitian Revolution (1791–1806): Economic and
Social Dynamics   / 53
Postindependence Crises: Structures, Institutions, and
Development   / 67
Early Foreign Policy: Diplomatic and Trade
Relations   / 70
Haitian Social Thought and Literature   / 78

**Chapter 3 Modernization and Dependence: Twentieth-
Century Haiti   / 89**

Caudillism and Modernization   / 90
The U.S. Occupation, 1915–1934   / 95
The Caco Wars   / 105

The Aftermath of the U.S. Occupation: Stability
    and Turmoil, 1934–1956   / 114
Prelude to Dictatorship: The Elections of 1957   / 123
Dynastic Dictatorship: The Duvalier Years,
    1957–1986   / 128

**Chapter 4 The Haitian Economy and the National
    Security State   / 143**

Applied Economics: The Puerto Rican Model
    of Development   / 145
The National Security State   / 157

Chapter 5 Politics and Government   / 173

The Constitution of 1987 and National
    Institutions   / 174
The Military Dictatorship and the Electoral
    Campaigns of 1987–1988   / 180
Peasant Organizations, Structures, and
    Institutions   / 207

**Chapter 6 Heralding the Bicentennial: Breaks and
    Continuity   / 221**

Three Generals and a Lady   / 228
The Failed Era: Aristide and the Anatomy of
    a Coup   / 234
On Wings of Eagles: Continuity and
    Uncertainties   / 247

Conclusion   / 257
Appendix   / 267
Notes   / 271
Bibliographical Essay   / 281
Index   / 299

List of Maps and Photographs

Maps

Map 1   Haiti   / 11

Map 2   Central and Middle America and the Caribbean   / 12

Map 3   Carte de la partie de Saint-Domingue habitée
             par les François, Janvier 1731   / 51

Map 4   Peasant movements against the United States,
             1911–1929   / 109

Photographs

Citadelle Laferrière   / 15

Fishermen, sailboats, and dugout canoes   / 17

A Haitian *manbo*   / 23

Rigaud Benoit, "The Recall of the Dead"   / 27

Gérard Valcin, "Loge Bleue"   / 32

The Ligue Féminine d'Action Sociale   / 39

Rural market   / 43

Significant historical Haitian leaders   / 61

Haitian architecture: An upper-class mansion   / 94

President Dartiguenave and U.S. bodyguards   / 100

Corpse of Charlemagne Péralte   / 110

U.S. troops protecting Haitian-American Sugar Co.   / 112

Philominé Obin, "The Crucifixion of Péralte"   / 113

Three mulatto sisters   / 118

Haitian mulatto upper class in Paris   / 120

Mme. Michèle Bennett Duvalier and Mgr. François
    Wolff-Ligondé   / 138
President and Madame Jean-Claude Duvalier   / 141
The National Palace   / 148
Baseball factory in Port-au-Prince   / 154
"Slavery" of young children   / 167
Pharmacy in Les Cayes   / 197
Peasant family in their kitchen   / 209
President Aristide in Washington   / 248

Preface to the New Edition

THE CITADELLE LA FERRIÈRE STANDS VIGIL, ALONE, ATOP THE BONNET-À-l'Evêque (Bishop's Miter), at 945 metres (3,100 feet). It is said that perhaps 20,000 men and women built it, and that thousands died in its construction. It is said that human blood cements that edifice to nationality as in the days of yore in the Kingdom of Abomey. It is said that a Vodou priest—male or female, it isn't said—helped select the site amongst several others in the neighborhood.

In an article published in the *New York Times* dated September 21, 1991, "Haitian Fortress Saved from Nature's Onslaught," it is said that "an elaborate water collection and drainage system, for example, was discovered [within the Citadel] that would enable a 5,000-man garrison to withstand siege for a year. Without a navy to ward off Napoléon's forces, whose defeat had won independence in 1804 for a nation of slaves, Haiti's early rulers conceived a large network of internal defenses to repel invaders ...."

Napoléon Bonaparte never came. In fact, no one came at all, and Haiti suffered international ostracism. Dozens of fortresses built by Haiti's new military rulers in the north, west, and south punctuate the landscape. They remain silent, foundations worn tired for two-hundred years. The cannons acquired at great cost from a plethora of places—Haiti was the original terrorist state—remain unused, wondering perhaps if their rusty mouths could now belch these cannonballs nestled at their feet. These cannonballs now appear, in two neat piles, in the Republic's coat of arms and on the national flag.

As Haiti prepared to commemorate its bicentennial—to celebrate might be too strong a word, unless mere survival is a virtue—the silence continues... The Louisiana Purchase celebrations, 1803–2003, did not address officially the role of Saint-Domingue/Haiti, or that of its Revolution led by 500,000 insurgent slaves, or again that of Toussaint Louverture. The Haitian Revolution remains the most neglected of all major revolutions in the teaching of history. But what is history? At its most pedestrian, it is akin to "he said, she said," but she is silenced. It is the multifaceted interpretation of facts, mythologies as building blocks for nationality, facts chosen or ignored, with the latter unceremoniously "dumped" as so many enslaved bodies, at the bottom of a brooding and dark ocean—zombies awaiting resurrection.

Contemporary history is difficult to write. How might one anticipate the trends and broad themes that survive the moment to become relevant in the distant future? That quest for relevance might be answered in anchoring one's thoughts and analyses on shifting sands of earlier histories, aware of lacunae and new interpretations, from within the undercurrents, the shoals, the reefs that give that history heft, without drowning in the minutiae. Indeed, what is important today may not be remembered in the morning.

Contemporary history might be more formidable and arduous under Haitian conditions perhaps, since history, in the words of Mexican philosopher Leopoldo Zea, remains unresolved. "Our past"—he says—"has not yet become a real past; it is still a present that does not choose to become history." The Haitian historian Beaubrun Ardouin added, logically, "The past regulates the present as it does the future." These declarations, in tandem, allow us to glimpse at constitutive Haitian (and Latin American) realities in which we see ourselves. History is everpresent when so few issues have been resolved, when it undergirds assumptions in present-day ideological and political discourse.

Additionally, on a personal note, one tries to be dispassionate but not neutral, when one finds sustenance, the meaning of one's life and raison d'etre, definitions of self, in a *large* Caribbean country called Haiti, a part of *small* worlds getting smaller. This "acte de foi," profession of faith, is neither xenophobia nor nationalism, but a mere "nod" to what creates human beings out of the constitutive parts of culture and ancestry.

If the Haitian response to itself and the world is not unique, though particularized, it is tethered to larger Caribbean, African, and Latin American worlds, and an international system to which that country belongs. There is no escape.

This book completes a circle started in the mid-1980s; it is a rare privilege to be allowed to revisit old grounds. This work is an act of piety toward the not-so prominent women of my country, all of them, the prominent women who have survived historians and history, now into the collective memory, and to all Haitian girls wizened by an arduous life. Honor and respect come from the struggle for a just society, or for at least trying.

I am most grateful to my editor at Canadian Scholars' Press (CSPI), Althea Prince, for her unstinting support and kindness. The staff at CSPI was hard working and beyond reproach, notably Rebecca Conolly, Rachel Sheer, and freelancers Alban Harvey and Jennie Rubio. My heartfelt thanks go to the Milwaukee Art Museum, CIDIHCA (Centre International de Documentation et d'Information Haïtienne, Caraïbéene, et Afro-Canadianne), the Embassy of Haiti in Washington, DC, Howard Goldbaum, and the United States National Archives for the generous use of the photographs that grace this book.

Additionally, I thank my sisters Claudine Michel, Marlène Racine-Toussaint, Florence Bellande-Robertson, Viviane Nicolas, Marie-Claude Malebranche, Kyrah Daniels, Jacqueline Epingle (and her spiritual progeny), Ferne Y. Caulker, Adekola Adedapo, Karen McCarthy Brown, Gina Ulysse, LeGrace Benson, Nancy Mikelsons, Babette Wainwright, Rubi Rosas, Keila Guimaraes, for hoisting me up when I was "low," and for their love always. A filial nod to the "female" deities is necessary: Gran Brijit, Ezili Danto, Ezili Freda, Lasirenn, Ayida Wedo, were my constant companions, mothers and wives. Ayibobo.

Some brothers shouldered me at crucial junctions. My thanks go to David J. Cusick, Zeev Gorin, Fritz Duroseau, Jr and Jean-Bernard Duroseau, Gib Caldwell, Douglas H. Daniels, Bamidele Agbasegbe Demerson, Gregory Henschel, Jeffrey Sommers, Patrick D.M. Taylor, Richard W. Schulte, Kevin Kreger, Pat A. Robinson, Kareem A.O.W. Ferguson, Franck Daphnis, Hebert Perez Concepcíon, Raul Campos, Jorge Herrera Ochoa, and my mentors, Roger Savain and Guérin

Montilus—*mes chers maîtres*. Thanks to the "male" deities Danbala, Ogou Feray, Ogou Badagri, Shango, Bawon Samdi, Gede Nibo, Gran Bwa—teachers, lovers, father, and brothers. Ayibobo.

With all that love one would expect perfection from me, but they do not. Far from it. They only ask that I try. This is a small contribution to the Haitian construction site on the eve of Haiti's bicentennial. May it please someone.

P.B.-S.

Introduction

THE CITADELLE LAFERRIÈRE IN HAITI IS THE LARGEST FORTRESS EVER BUILT in the Western Hemisphere. Built in the early 1800s in anticipation of a French military invasion, the fortress was never used, but it is still Haiti's most revered national symbol, a monument to the lives sacrificed in the nation's struggle for freedom. The United Nations included the citadel in its list of world cultural treasures, along with the Acropolis, the pyramids of Egypt, the Chartres cathedral, and the temple of Borobudur in Indonesia. Haiti's tropical climate, however, has taken its toll on the fortress.

The international climate has been equally unkind to Haiti, and the effects of this inclement international milieu have been continually aggravated by related domestic upheavals that have left the nation in a shambles. The last episode was the most severe. On February 7, 1986, the twenty-nine-year Duvalier regime was overthrown and replaced by a military dictatorship. The uprisings that led to the fall of Duvalier began in November 1985 and found resonance in the massive demonstrations of 1986 and 1987. Haiti founded the second republic in the Americas, after the United States, yet as in other countries in Central America and the Caribbean, deteriorating economic conditions have caused difficult political problems, and the increasing gap between extremes of wealth and deprivation has created social turmoil and widespread societal dislocation.

The citadel's former glory and current crumbling reflect Haiti's noble past and wretched present. The fall of the Duvalier regime created both a crisis and new opportunities. Popular frustration with the meager results of a cosmetic change in the head of state and the lack of systemic change, however, will lead to more frequent and increasingly severe crises.

Today Haiti is the poorest country in the Western Hemisphere. In the second half of the eighteenth century, however, it created more wealth than any other colony in the world. At that time, 50 percent of France's transatlantic commerce involved Haiti, and nearly 20 percent of the French population depended on trade with Haiti for its livelihood. Almost none of that wealth was left in Haiti, or Saint-Domingue as it was then called. African slaves composed nearly 90 percent of the population of the country. Overall investments in the Haitian economic infrastructure were meager compared to the enormous profits and trade advantage gained by France. Economically, Saint-Domingue was the world's most profitable colony. It soon became known as "the pearl of the Antilles" and was the standard by which the profitability of other colonies was judged. Socially, however, Saint-Domingue may have been the most repressive colony in the eighteenth century because of its disproportionate slave-to-master ratio and the exceedingly exploitative economic structure the French had devised. Terror and coercion were used to keep the Africans in line, and the French systematically exported the resources and profits of Saint-Domingue to France itself.

Haitian scholars generally argue that Haitian poverty and French economic growth and subsequent industrialization were inextricably linked. The enormous wealth generated in and expropriated from Saint-Domingue resulted in a poverty-stricken Haiti. In Haiti, only the plantation owners, who composed about 5 percent of the Haitian population, benefited financially from French domination, and France gained not only enormous profits but a primitive form of capital accumulation that gave it an advantage in the race for economic development and status as a world power.

Haitian scholarship reflects Haiti's evolution and a national perspective that is rooted in the country's collective experience, an experience that gives validity to the Haitian scholar's perspective. Although the evolution of Haiti is in many ways similar to that of other colonized nations, in some respects the Haitian experience is clearly unique. Haiti is the only state to have emerged from slave uprisings, and it was the first country to achieve independence in Latin America. Haiti gained independence through one of the few "real" revolutions in history, in which swift, violent, and radical change occurs in the political, economic, social, and cultural conditions of a country. It was the first state of African origin to be modeled on European political forms and the first modern mini-state, preceding both Belgium and Liberia. Although not French-speaking, it is the only state in Latin America to use French as one of its official languages. Haiti has experimented, albeit unsuccessfully, with the full range of governmental forms, including two empires, one kingdom, and numerous republics. Nine of the republics had lifetime presidencies, a pattern lauded by Simón Bolívar and by other people in the Third World in this century. The country's forty-odd chiefs of state, strong or weak, were continually challenged by a population that was skeptical of their legitimacy.

The wide range of governmental forms in Haitian history reflects Haiti's present as well as its past. Beaubrun Ardouin, a prominent nineteenth-century Haitian thinker, describes the continuing influence of the past on both the present and the future. Thus the task of scholars is to separate lasting truths from transitional situations and to delineate constraints and possibilities. In brief, scholars must work to understand Haiti, predict its future, and assess its potential.

Haitian reality is complex and often perplexing to the casual observer. Haitian scholars often take issue with Western analyses that see Haitians as solely responsible for their nation's plight and that perceive foreign intervention and colonialism as constructive and mismanagement, economic downturns, government corruption, and class and color antagonisms as part of Haitian reality. These dimensions of Haitian society must be viewed, however, within the context of a worldwide structure and an international economic system, which no state can entirely transcend, in conjunction with external, international situations. Global implications of power and powerlessness are significant in terms of their outcomes; they are symbiotic sides of a single coin. Indeed, if those international relationships are studied in terms of the pattern and terms of trade over time and with an understanding of Western racism over time, the evolution of the Haitian social structure and the country's lack of economic growth and political development become comprehensible.

Haiti is populated almost entirely by people of African descent, including 93 percent black and 7 percent of mixed ancestry. This factor militated against objective Western scholarship on Haiti until the 1940s. Haiti is still somewhat inaccessible today because of its economic insignificance and its Kreyol language. Today, however, contemporary events and the potential for social revolution in the Caribbean basin have caused non-Haitians to study Haiti more closely. By declaring Haiti important for U.S. strategic interests in 1986, Secretary of State George Schultz may have accelerated that process.

The best studies on Haiti have traditionally been those produced by Haitian scholars, and their detachment and objectivity were particularly poignant and commendable in the nineteenth century. In terms of actual production, the U.S. critic Edmund Wilson remarked that until the mid-1950s Haiti printed more books per capita than any other Latin American country, despite a chronic illiteracy rate and a lack of publishing houses. Insofar as they help to explain contemporary Haiti, the analyses and conclusions of Haitian scholars are of primary importance to this book. Written in French and little known outside Haiti, the works of Haitian scholars provide a useful and needed contrast to the information that is generally available in the West.

A true picture of Haitian society cannot be realized, however, without a special effort to consider the role, status, and concerns of Haitian women in all major areas of national life. To examine the inclusion or exclusion of women in Haitian national life not only improves the balance and accuracy of a study but changes the story itself. Like many women elsewhere in the world, Haitian women are poorer, less literate, and less powerful than their male counterparts. The condition of Haitian women ironically reflects the condition of Haiti itself; it provides insight into the process of marginalization and patterns of domestic-power (pun intended) relationships.

This book analyzes the nature of Haitian society in six chapters. Chapter 1 presents an overview of the country's people, social structure, culture, and geography, with special emphasis on the human and natural resources, the influence of the Vodou (Voodoo) religion on Haitian culture, and the role and status of women in Haitian national life. Chapter 2 examines the context of Haitian economic development and underdevelopment, Haiti's international relations and foreign policies, and the ideological thought and literature that sustained elite control of the country's governments. Chapter 3 analyzes the modern and contemporary conditions that create or re-create the Haitian "phenomenon," particularly the U.S. occupation and the Haitian national resistance movement in response to it and the series of dictatorships before, during, and after the occupation, leading to perhaps the most severe, the Duvalier dictatorship.

Chapter 4 discusses Haiti's economic situation and the conditions that relegate the country to the very bottom of everyone's and every agency's list. This chapter studies the impact of foreign assistance and investments and increasing poverty, the national security state, and the existence of state terrorism to maintain control, migration, and exile, and the issues of civil as well as human rights in the context of wealth disparity and further decreases in the standard of living. Chapter 5 analyzes the situation since the fall of the Duvalier regime and assesses the possibilities for a meaningful transformation of the society in the social, political, cultural, and economic spheres; whether the changes instituted are profound or cosmetic; and the role of the dominant regional power, the United States, in the kinds of changes it may allow. Finally, Chapter 6 assesses the political developments that transpired during several military-sponsored governments, the events surrounding the election and rule of Presidents Jean-Bertrand Aristide and René G. Préval, and attempts to prognosticate what comes next.

The particular concern for Haitian scholarship and the discussion of the role of women in Haitian society breaks new ground. So does, in a sense, the careful review and analysis of the historical conditions that created contemporary Haiti. Much of social science is ahistorical, and the result is faulty analysis. To understand the last 50 years of Jewish history, one needs to have a grasp of the last 500, 2,000, or 5,000 years of Jewish history. Similarly, Haiti is the product of the African diaspora, and though I do not specifically address this issue, one may need to have a sense of the last millennium in West Africa to do that history justice.

I have tried to keep notes to a minimum. Because the Bibliographical Essay addresses the recent scholarship published in English, many of the notes cite Haitian and French works; hence the dual system used—references to the Bibliographical Essay and notes.

P.B.-S.

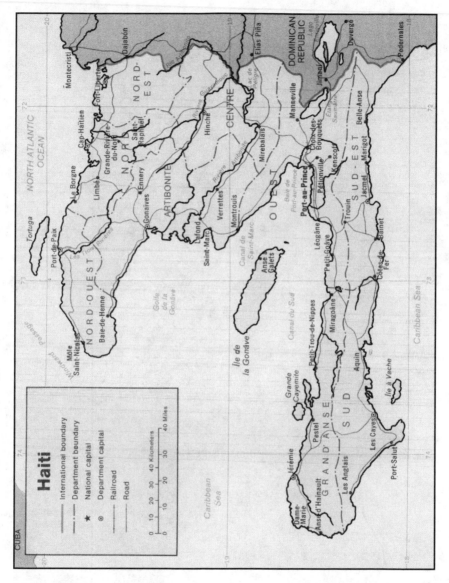

Map 1. Haiti

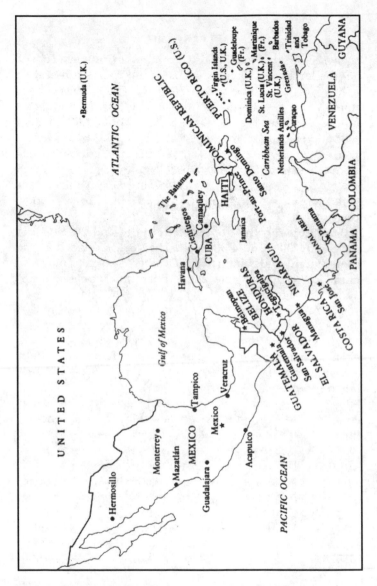

Map 2. Central and Middle America and the Caribbean

Chapter 1

The Nature of Haiti:
Land and Society

Deyè mon, gin mon.
("Beyond mountains are more mountains.")
— Haitian proverb

A NATION'S GEOGRAPHY DETERMINES MANY OF THE COUNTRY'S OPTIONS. The wealth or poverty of its soil and the pattern of its international and domestic relations over time are factors that determine both the potential and the limitations of a nation's development. History, culture, demography, the political economy, the international system, and science and technology overlap and combine to make a country unique or similar to other nations. All these dimensions form the framework from which people develop informed judgments about a nation.

Human and natural resources are marshaled within cultural, ideological, and technological dimensions in the context of the international system to determine the course of a nation's development. The limitations and potential of such development are largely issues of power and power relationships. Statistics tell a story, but the interpretation of statistics is the key to understanding.

THE LAND, THE PEOPLE, AND NATURAL RESOURCES

The land area of Haiti consists of 27,749 square kilometers (10,714 square miles) (Map 1). In 1972 Haiti claimed a territorial coastline of 12 nautical miles and an additional 3 for fishing rights. The Republic of Haiti shares the island of Hispaniola with the Dominican Republic to the east, which has a territory almost twice the size of Haiti (Map 2). A border of 310 kilometers (193 miles) separates the two nations on a north-south axis and cuts across mountain ranges and waterways that run on an east-west axis. The Haitian-Dominican border was finally agreed to by treaty in 1929, and a protocol was signed in 1936, ninety-two years after the Dominican Republic broke away from Haiti.

-(Haiti means "mountainous land" in the Arawak language of the original Taino inhabitants, and mountains cover 80 percent of the nation's territory.) Twenty percent of Haiti lies from sea level to about 180 meters (600 feet), and 40 percent is at elevations more than 450 meters (1,500 feet) above sea level. Small plains between mountains constitute 20 percent of the land mass. Five major mountain chains run east and west and are shared with the Dominican Republic. The highest peak in Haiti is the Morne la Selle in the Massif de la Selle, which extends west into the Massif de la Hotte. The Morne la Selle is about 3,000 meters (9,800 feet) in elevation and is surrounded by some of the last remaining forest in Haiti, mostly Caribbean pine. The sedimentary, limestone, magmatic, and plutonic rocks that form the rather complex geology of the country, together with its mountain ranges, waterways, and farmland, give Haiti a variegated terrain ranging from lush rain forests to semiarid regions where cacti thrive.

Haiti is located in the tropics between 18° and 20° north latitudes and meridians 71°30' and 74°30' west. The year is divided between dry (November–March) and rainy (April–October) seasons, but rainfall and temperatures correlate with elevation. With little variation year-round, temperatures average between 24° and 27°C (76° and 81°F) depending on elevation. Annual precipitation averages from 500 to more than 2,500 millimeters (20–100 inches) depending on whether the locale is on a leeward or a windward mountain slope. Because the rain-bearing winds on Hispaniola come from the northeast, the northern and eastern slopes receive the most rainfall. Thus the Dominican Republic receives more rainfall than Haiti.

More than a hundred rivers and streams in Haiti flow toward the Atlantic Ocean and to the Caribbean Sea (Map 1). The longest river is the Artibonite, which has ten times the flow of any other river in the

Citadelle Laferrière (1990). Photo: Douglas H. Daniels.

country. The Artibonite originates in the Dominican Republic, runs 320 kilometers (199 miles), and drains 6,400 square kilometers (2,470 square miles or 1.58 million acres) in Haiti. Its hydroelectric potential was harnessed in the 1970s, primarily to provide energy for U.S.-owned factories that were then being constructed around the capital city of Port-au-Prince. No river in Haiti is navigable except by canoe, so the river system cannot be used for heavy transportation. However there is a network of sailboats, or cabotage, that have plied between the coastal ports of Haiti since the early nineteenth century.

Haiti is an agricultural country in which arable land is estimated at 17 percent and cultivable land at 29 percent of the total land area. Actually, approximately 43 percent of the land is cultivated, and 75 percent of the population was engaged in agriculture in the mid-1980s. Current estimates are that 66 percent of the population is engaged in agriculture, compared to 17 percent in the Dominican Republic and 25 percent in Cuba.

Haiti is one of the most densely populated countries in the world. The population, estimated at 7.5 million, subsists on the western third of the island, with approximately 250 inhabitants per square kilometer (about 640 per square mile). A direct correlation between territorial size, resources, and population cannot be made, but Haiti is clearly overpopulated. This is especially true when existing economic and political conditions are considered. Although not irreversible, all the demographic factors have a far-reaching impact upon the standard of living, level of science and technology, public health, economic development, and overall future of Haiti.

The birth rate is estimated at 34 per 1,000, and the death rate is about 13 per 1,000. In addition, Haiti has experienced substantial emigration of its population to other countries (migration and exile are discussed in Chapter 4).

Over 40 percent of the Haitian population is under fourteen years of age. The population pyramid reveals a quasi-permanent "baby boom," and the participation of women and children in economic life is unusually high. Sociologist Robert Rotberg has noted that "between 7 and 15 percent of all Haitian children die during the first eight weeks of life from umbilical tetanus [alone]; about 50 percent of all children die before they are five years old" (Rotberg, 1971: 11). In 1985, infant mortality was estimated at 110 per 1,000 for the entire country, but in Port-au-Prince, the one large urban center with a near monopoly of medical services, it is much lower—about 20 per 1,000. In contrast, the infant mortality rate is 13 per 1,000 in the United States and 14 per 1,000 in Cuba.

Fishermen, sailboats, and dugout canoes in southern Haiti (circa 1980).
Photo: Howard Goldbaum.

Particularly significant is the ratio between males and females in the Haitian population. Statistics of the United Nations International Labour Organisation tend to show a predominance of Haitian males through the age of twenty-nine and a smaller predominance of males through age fifty-four, which suggests a high maternal mortality rate. Women outnumber men in all urban centers, especially Port-au-Prince, and infant mortality rates are higher in slum areas. These findings may well indicate that women in Haiti have less access to resources, medical care, and nutrition and suggest class- and gender-based inequities in Haitian social organization in the distribution of goods and services.

After emphasizing Haiti's strategic location for U.S. interests, William MacCorkle commented in 1915 that the island had "within its shores more natural wealth than any other territory of similar size in the world" (MacCorkle, 1915: 25), the same idea that had led to the European partitioning of Africa less than twenty years earlier.

MacCorkle's book, *The Monroe Doctrine in Its Relation to the Republic of Haiti*, reveals the connection between ideology, U.S. domination of the Caribbean region, and Haitian economic conditions.

Mineral resources on the Haitian side of the island are relatively scarce but include sulfur, coal, lignite, marble, porphyry, and gypsum. Metallic ores include nickel, bauxite, copper, manganese, iron, antimony, lead, zinc, and some gold and silver. Bauxite and copper were mined until the 1960s and 1970s, but none of Haiti's mineral resources is currently being exploited.

— The first occupiers of the island, the Spanish, ultimately abandoned the western part of Hispaniola because of its lack of gold; the French who replaced them found "gold" in the form of slaves and sugar. Slaves and sugar were in fact the major resources of Haiti throughout the colonial era. U.S. corporations have also found "gold" in the Haitian labor force, which is the lowest paid in the Caribbean basin. Indeed, cheap labor power is modern Haiti's primary resource, and in the industrial sector, it is largely female. Haiti's cheap labor and geographic proximity to the U.S. market are great advantages for U.S. firms. For Haiti itself, however, the combination of cheap labor, changing land uses, and increased importation of foodstuffs may prove debilitating.

Thus in both the colonial and the modern periods of Haitian history the lack of exploitable natural resources in the western third of the island has meant that the population is the country's most profitable resource. This situation has influenced the thrust of Haiti's history and its economic underdevelopment, including the impact of French colonial policies, the specific population Haiti acquired after the genocide of the Amerindians, Haiti's role in the international system, its present-day relationship with the United States, and contemporary Haitian politics (these overlapping dimensions are analyzed in greater depth in other chapters).

— Haitians are the descendants of former slaves and freed people, the *affranchis*, who fought and defeated the French army in the late eighteenth century. The race and color breakdown of the population is approximately 93 percent black and 7 percent mulatto. Included in these figures are hundreds of Syrio-Lebanese and Palestinians (known locally as *Syrien*) who arrived at the turn of the century; Polish descendants of Napoléon's army that occupied Haiti in the early 1800s; descendants of some German, French, and Scandinavian males; and a few other Caucasians. These people intermarried with Haitian-born citizens and are generally well integrated into the social, political, and economic life of the nation. Ethnicity is not a divisive factor in Haiti, the labels "black" or "mulatto" apply to nearly the entire population, and the few whites who are citizens of the "black republic" in no way dilute the country's Afro-Haitian culture.

It is difficult to become a Haitian citizen. Since the time of Haiti's independence in 1804, all Haitians have been declared to be *noirs* ("blacks") by constitutional fiat in order to reinforce national unity; the legal designation even applied to the few hundred whites who had survived the wars of independence. A law of return allowed foreign-born blacks to claim Haitian citizenship, but until 1918, when the law was rescinded by the U.S. Marine Corps occupying Haiti, whites were not allowed to own property. As a result, European entrepreneurs tended to marry black and mulatto women of the Haitian upper class. Haitian law traditionally required a ten-year residency and an edict from the president of the republic for a foreign-born person to become a Haitian citizen. Children born of a foreign father and a Haitian mother or children born in Haiti of foreign parents are not Haitian citizens. "Black pride" was a major factor in the wars of independence, and "race" remains one of the most important criteria in the overall definition of Haitian nationality. In the context of Haitian history and demography, national pride and racial pride have been almost synonymous.

In a study of time and space, the Haitian geographer Georges Anglade analyzed Haitian development from a succinct theoretical framework and argued that the formation of state and nation occurs in relation to territorial space. Indeed, much can be understood from looking at geographical relationships, including regionalism, settlement patterns, and natural features and resources, all of which influence evolving economic relationships and sociopolitical development. Anglade identified two processes that form the basis of these relationships: (1) the stages of building a national market (which is impossible under colonization and mercantilism) and (2) the evolution of processes for the exercise of power. According to Anglade, "at each period, the *dominant spatial structure* makes way for specific organizational forms."[1] Anglade's formulation, together with those of Haitian historians, economists, and sociologists, forms the basis for this book. When appropriate, this formulation will be contrasted with the mounting and useful works written by non-Haitian experts.

— Coffee and sugar are not native to the Caribbean, yet these crops help to define many significant aspects of Haitian society. The cultivation of these nonfood cash crops was originally based on decisions made in one country (France) and imposed on another (Haiti). Making coffee and sugar the major crops of Haitian agriculture profoundly affected the course of Haitian development, including the continuing relevance of these crops in the Haitian economy, the increased supremacy of regional port cities, the early emergence of the plantation as the primary unit of Haitian social organization, and Haiti's reliance on one or a few trade partners. These results of colonial agricultural policy provide important historical lessons and have helped to formulate the "law of comparative advantage" that has become the national destiny of Haiti and many other underdeveloped nations. The impact of colonial agricultural policies and the plantation economic system continues to affect human and natural resources in Haiti even today.

The Haitian economy is expected to remain agricultural far into the twenty-first century unless major political changes occur internally or the U.S. private sector transfers more of its manufacturing capacity to Haiti. Very different conditions would result depending on whether the first or the second of these options transpires. Based on the understanding provided by the past, however, my prediction is that Haitian society will probably remain divided into two broad classes: a small upper class and a large class of peasants who, in time, may become factory workers. Over the course of a changing world environment, some of the functions of these groups and the terms used to identify them changed, and an insecure middle class developed. Nevertheless, Haitian society continues to be divided into a small elite and a large working class.

VODOU COSMOLOGY: WORLD VIEW AT THE CROSSROADS

The significance of the Vodou (Voodoo) religion[2] in Haitian history is profound and undebatable. The blue and red halves of the national flag represent Ogou, the Vodou spirit of fire and war and the cosmos; the red and black emblem of the Duvalier dictatorship symbolized the Gede, the Vodou spirits of death. In this section, I attempt to define and discuss some of the more important aspects of Vodou. Because of its significance, other factors are discussed in other chapters: the role of Vodou in fomenting the numerous slave revolts and the wars of independence in the nineteenth century (Chapter 2); its role in the Haitian resistance against the U.S. invasion and occupation and in the overthrow of Duvalier in 1986 (Chapter 3); and Vodou institutions, the profound presence of Vodou in Haiti's social organization, and the role that it might play in a democratic Haiti (Chapter 5).

Vodou is the national religion of Haiti and a vital force in Haitian politics and culture. A struggle for the minds and souls of the Haitian people continues, however, between Vodou and organized Christianity, the latter led by the Roman Catholic church and U.S. Protestant missions. Because the forces involved in this struggle are international, the outcome remains uncertain. Beyond a continuation of the precarious equilibrium of the status quo, there can be but two outcomes. The first would be an indigenous Haitian solution involving a democratization of Haiti and the validation of Vodou as the national ethos. Alternatively, a victory for Western Christianity would involve a loss of Haitian self-identity and cultural heritage and make the people spiritually and politically paralyzed and dependent, a form of zombification.

Religion and language are major symbols in all cultures and the embodiment of nationality and personal identity derives from a collective identity, especially in communal societies. Thus an indigenous language and belief system, the parts of a culture no longer combine and interact to form an integrated, meaningful cultural fabric. Judaism helps to define Jewishness, and the French language and Roman Catholicism, under Anglo-Saxon domination, help to define the culture of Quebec. Similarly, Vodou and the Kreyol language are essential parts of the Haitian culture and nationality. The legitimacy of both Kreyol and Vodou was officially recognized by the Haitian Constitution of 1987, but earlier, the practice of Vodou was officially illegal and often persecuted.

My introduction to my ancestral religion came from an upper-class Haitian woman, a psychologist, who described the cosmic implications of the faith. Since that time, I have attended many Vodou ceremonies in which the ritual called forth a kind of racial memory that the Africologist Winston Van Horne, in conversation with the author, has called "transgenerational memory." I have come to realize that Vodou is a central part of the "closed culture" by which Haitian society defines itself and by which even upper-class Haitians, despite their Western trappings, are profoundly influenced. In this closed culture, the cosmos, medicine, psychology, dance, music, visual arts, and social organization constitute an ideological matrix in which everything can be logically explained. The fact that the Afro-Haitian world view clashes with Western cultures is irrelevant to the integrity of the Haitian culture, but the religious, economic, political, and social areas of Haitian life continue to be manipulated by foreign interests.

Most foreigners view Vodou as a pagan, primitive form of "black" magic rather than as a legitimate religion, and even some Haitians adhere to that view. Unfortunately, practitioners of Vodou have written few works to counter Western misconceptions. Most books about Christianity are written by Christians, and few objections about their authors' credibility are ever raised. If Vodouists wrote books about Vodou, however, Western readers would probably challenge their authors' objectivity. Indeed, Western definitions and perceptions of Vodou typically reflect ignorance, misunderstanding, racism, or a willful desire to obfuscate. *Webster's New World Dictionary* (1964) defined Voodoo (Vodou) as "a body of primitive rites and practices, based on a belief in sorcery and the power of charms, fetishes, etc., found among natives of the West Indies and in the southern United States, and ultimately of African origin." Twenty years later, in 1986, one finds an improvement. The *Webster's Ninth Collegiate Dictionary* defined Vodou as "a religion derived from African ancestor worship, practiced chiefly

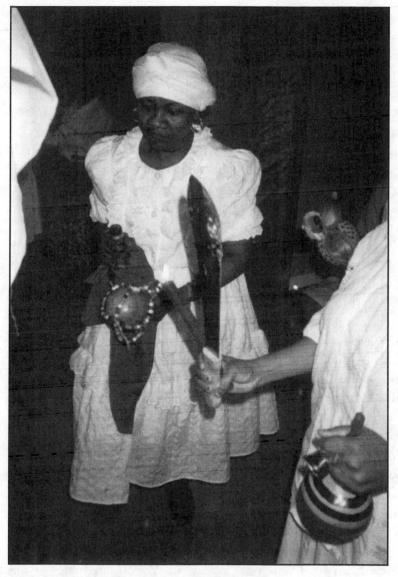

A Haitian *manbo* (2003). Photo: Author's collection

by Negroes [sic] of Haiti, and characterized by propitiatory rites and communication by trance with animistic deities."

Because dictionaries are assumed to be objective, the definitions they present can profoundly influence and distort people's understanding and thereby engender distorted constructions of social reality. Thus the pejorative connotation of Western definitions of Vodou cannot be easily transcended. The message of Western definitions cannot be clearer: cults are not really religions, vernaculars are not really languages, and tribes are not really nations but groups of disaggregated individuals. Columbus's conclusions about the Taino/ Arawaks he stumbled upon in Ayiti in 1492 presaged the colonialist mentality that has characterized Western policy in Latin America generally for 400 years. Because Columbus could not understand their words and saw that they had no cathedrals, Columbus concluded that the Taino/Arawaks had neither language nor religion and hence could be enslaved and colonized.

To understand a people, however, one must empathize with them and comprehend their imagery, myths, beliefs, and history as parts of an internally coherent world view—an unbreached citadel. As a contrast to the distorted and pejorative definitions of Vodou that are popular in the West, I propose a more accurate definition based on my knowledge of the religion. Vodou is a coherent and comprehensive belief system and world view in which every person and every thing is sacred and must be treated accordingly. In Vodou, everything in the world—be it plant, animal, or mineral—shares basically similar chemical, physical, and/or genetic properties. This unity of all things translates into an overarching belief in the sanctity of life, not so much for the *thing* as for the *spirit* of the thing. The cosmological unity of Vodou further translates into a vaunted African humanism in which social institutions are elaborated and in which the living, the dead, and the unborn play equally significant roles in an unbroken historical chain. Thus all action, speech, and behavior achieve paramount significance for the individual and the community of which the individual is a part. (Additional aspects of Vodou cited later in this text will augment or refine this definition.)

I do not mean to imply that Vodou has not borrowed elements from other religions or spiritual disciplines. Christianity, Islam, Freemasonry, and even the aboriginal Taino/Arawak religion have contributed to Vodou and its historical development. Far more significant, however, is the comprehensive compendium of religious ideas that Vodou has borrowed from the Dahomean, Yoruba, Igbo,

Congolese, and other African cultures. But the fact of foremost importance is that the synthesis of Vodou was developed by the Haitians themselves in an exercise of free will and with some degree of social and political independence. The same process occurred in Cuban and Puerto Rican Santería; Brazilian Condomblé, Macumba, and Umbanda; Trinidadian Shango; Jamaican Kumina and Pocomania; and all other variants of African religion in the Americas.

In his compelling work on zombies, the U.S. scholar Wade Davis defined Vodou as

> a complex mystical world view, a system of beliefs concerning the relationship between man, nature, and the supernatural forces of the universe. Vodoun [another spelling] cannot be abstracted from the day-to-day lives of the believers. In Haiti, as in Africa, there is no separation between the sacred and the secular, between the holy and the profane, between the material and the spiritual. Every dance, every song, every action is but a particle of the whole, each gesture a prayer .... Vodoun not only embodies a set of spiritual concepts, it prescribes a way of life, a philosophy and a code of ethics that regulate social behavior. As sure as one refers to Christian or Buddhist society, one may speak of Vodoun society. [Davis, 1985: 72–73]

In Vodou cosmology, distinctions between divine and mortal beings are blurred; one can become the other through ritual possession that recognizes no gender differences. In this sense, Vodou resembles the Gandharva Tantra: "One who has not become a divinity should not worship. Anyone worshiping a divinity without first becoming one will not reap the fruits of that worship." A Zulu teaching picks up that idea, grounding it in the humanism that characterizes all African religious thought: "The challenge of being human is forever to explore myself. I challenge the universe to show me a being higher than myself." The word *Vodou* is said to come from two words *Vo du*, which mean "introspection into the unknown."

Through death, the spirit is transformed into a divine principle in a cycle that moves from the person to the persona to the principle to the personification. One serves, admonishes, and bargains with this divine principle in a web of quintessential relationships that unite both the *sevitès* ("those who serve") and the *lwas* ("spirits"). That interdependence is a daily reality.

Sex and gender matter little in Vodou philosophy, and women and homosexuals are not discriminated against in Vodou hierarchies and ceremonies. In fact, as in the rest of the Afro-world, notably in Brazil and Cuba, many priests and priestesses are homosexual. The Vodou faith is exceptionally democratic; both women and men are priests in decentralized structures that abide no national or regional hierarchies. This decentralized structure of Vodou contrasts sharply with the rigid, complex hierarchies of the Roman Catholic church and the structures of most other denominations of Western Christianity. Although a very formal hierarchy exists *within* each Vodou community (temple), humans have instantaneous access to the gods and the gods to humans, whose bodies they intermittently invade (possess). In a country where the dead are not dead and where most of the living must eke out an existence to survive physically, the metaphysical plane is but a layer that penetrates the physical world, and the body, mind, and psyche are inseparable alloys of a very complex and complete reality. Although Vodou provides rules of behavior that are enforced by social pressure and secret societies, it is a metaphysical rather than a moral or dogmatic belief system.

Vodou is a remarkably fluid religion, partly because its liturgies and theology are not written down and partly because it developed from a synthesis of the religious ideas of diverse African ethnic groups. Transgressions are committed not against the gods but against one's fellow beings, who suffer the brunt of one's actions. The concept of sin does not exist in Vodou; instead, social and moral behavior is regulated by *taboos* that are linked to ancestral values and traditions. The Haitian anthropologist Michel Laguerre has argued that because its development is a continuous process, Vodou is a living rather than a preserved religion such as Christianity (Laguerre, 1980: 22).

In Vodou, nature is sacred insofar as minerals, plants, and animals can become repositories for the spirits, who in a sense are the multiple faces of the divine. One anthropologist has explained and illustrated

Artist Rigaud Benoit's "The Recall of the Dead" (1973). Milwaukee Art Museum, Flagg Tanning Corporation Collection. Published by permission.

the implications of such interrelationships: In Haiti, "there is a marked preference for using generic names .... Names are not lightly invoked, and references to people in the third person are often by pronoun, title, or general term such as 'the man' or 'the other person.' The quality of indirection is a reluctance to name names in public, for naming has magical or political overtones" (Smucker, in Foster and Valdman, 1984: 40).

In Vodou, all beings can take spiritual or physical form at will, and such transformations are under the control of human beings. Thus all appearances can be deceiving (Foster and Valdman, 1984: 40–41). The connections among relationships, social behavior, and social organization are secure, and the belief system is at the core of all behavior (further discussed in Chapter 5). In an extraordinary book on Vodou, Maya Deren questioned the very notion of Western "objectivity":

> Is it not worth considering that reverence for "detachment"—whether scientific or scholarly—might be primarily a projection of a notion of a dualism between spirit and matter? ... Is it valid to use this means to truth [Western objectivity] in examining Oriental or African cultures that are not based on such dualism and that are, on the contrary, predicated on the notion that truth can be apprehended only when every cell of brain and body ... is engaged in that pursuit? [Deren, 1983: 9]

The human body is animated by a *Gro-bon-ange*, which is the psychic spirit or metaphysical soul, and the *Ti-bon-ange*, which is the changeless, impersonal cosmic consciousness. Both are cosmic energy, experienced as radiation. Upon death, the *Gro-bon-ange* passes through stages and may, as a glorified ancestor, reach the status of a *lwa*, the repersonified archetype of some moral principle. The *Ti-bon-ange* rejoins the cosmic forces and is reusable. But no hierarchical rankings exist between the physical body and the metaphysical soul. To the extent that a supreme being (*Gran-Mèt*) is even recognized in Vodou, the *Ti-bon-ange* is as detached as the supreme being. The *Gro-bon-ange* is as immediate as the *lwas*, who interfere daily and who themselves may have passed through human stages in the distant past. Possession, which is a common feature of all black religions, illustrates the dictum of the Gandharva Tantra cited earlier: One should worship a divinity by becoming a divinity.

As in much of African religious thought, the distinct concept of a supreme being or God (*Gran-Mèt* or *Bondieu*) may not truly exist in Vodou. The human being seeks to become his or her *own* God through initiation rituals and arduous personal development and by mastering the antagonistic forces of the universe. When one researcher asked practicing Vodouists the question, "Do you believe in God?" they all replied, "Yes, I believe in chance." The concept of chance plays a crucial role in Vodou as a cosmic force of positive waves, undulations, vibrations, and relativity and represents the *lwas* of Danbala Wedo, the cosmic serpent, and his consort Ayida Wedo, the rainbow.

In the Haitian context, miracles are normal events. In fact, the absence of miracles would indicate imbalance, disharmony, and dislocation. In binding reciprocity, the *lwas* serve humans as much as the living humans serve them. In this regard, Deren wrote the following. "The entire chain of interlocking links—life, death, deification, transfiguration, resurrection—churns without rest through the hands of the devout. None of it is ever forgotten: that the god was once human, that he [she] was made god by humans, that he [she] is sustained by humans" (Deren, 1983: 33). Gods without worshipers are a sad lot indeed! For their part, the ancestors enforce reasonable laws, and the entire Vodou belief system is designed to provide a collective morality.

The way in which Haitians achieve this fusion of the physical and metaphysical planes rather than their dualism, which dominates Western thought, is to visualize the two planes as part of an interpenetrating continuum. Instead of perceiving them as irreconcilable parallels, Haitians conceive of the world as a relationship between the physical and the metaphysical that is represented by the geometric figure of crosscutting right angles called "crossroads." At the crossroads stands the *lwa* Legba, who controls access from the vertical to the horizontal planes and grants permission for other *lwas* to descend through the *potomitan*, the wooden post at the center of the temple (*houmfo*). Deren explained the crossroads best when she described the world of Vodou as a world within a cosmic mirror, peopled by the immortal reflections of all those who have ever confronted it. The mirror is the metaphor for the cosmography of Haitian myth. The metaphor for the mirror's depth is the crossroads; the symbol is the cross. For the Haitian, this figure is not only symbolic of the totality of the earth's surface as comprehended in the extension of the cardinal points on a horizontal plane. It is, above all, a figure for the intersection of the horizontal plane, which is this mortal world, by the vertical plane, the metaphysical axis, which plunges into the mirror. The crossroads, then, is the point of access to the world of *les invisibles* [the *lwas*], which is the soul of the cosmos, the source of the life force, the cosmic memory, and the cosmic wisdom. [Deren, 1983: 34–35]

In this way, the substance of matter and the substance of the spirit are mutually and eternally bound in a symbiotic relationship. Intelligence, wisdom, energy, and power are born of the flesh of their origin, and the divine continues to inhabit the flesh. Morality, too, is born of matter. The spirits released after the death of matter are enticed to work for the good of the community, and they receive desirable gifts in return.

This process occurs through elaborate ceremonies that are performed according to a cyclical ritual calendar of many years' duration. The ritual itself consists largely of splendid songs and dances. According to Laguerre, "In their poetic forms, these songs are easy to memorize. They abound in repetitive sentences, either to make ideas clearer or to show where emphasis is placed. They are concise, compact, and full of imagery, parables, and proverbs. Alluding to past events and behavior, they carry symbolic meaning .... These Voodoo songs, full of religious formulas, esoteric knowledge, metaphors, and allusions, can be fully understood only by initiates" (Laguerre, 1980: 31–32).

The way in which Haitians understand their world has significant ramifications for all aspects of Haitian life, including medicine, pharmacology, and psychiatry. In a fairly closed cultural system, which is rendered even more effective precisely because it is closed, the traditional healing arts take into account the total sociocultural system. In a country that has perhaps 600 physicians for more than 6 million inhabitants, the Haitian people's knowledge of the medicinal properties of the local flora and fauna is awesome. In this sense, Vodou is both metaphysics and philosophy of science. Western science is only now beginning to unravel these wonders.

Vodou influences the visual and performing arts in Haiti, and the unique vibrance and quality of Haitian painting is recognized throughout the world. Haitian dance and music are almost viscerally connected to Vodou. Vodou also plays a crucial role in the political and social organization of Haiti. The "traditional" system of justice is administered by the Vodou secret societies outside the purview of the central government. The Zobop, Shanpwel, Bizango, Vlinbindingue, and other societies have effectively maintained the moral code of the Vodou communities, without undue coercion and with guarantees for the rights of the accused. These secret societies constitute a sort of *govenman lannuit* ("nighttime government") that governs while the official government is asleep.

Thus the peasantry and the elite of Haitian society adhere to different and parallel forms of medicine, art, political, and social organization and other major areas of life. These parallel forms are most obvious in the dichotomies between the French and the Kreyol languages and between Roman Catholicism and the national religion of Vodou. The fact that these forms coexist and penetrate each other at various intervals does not invalidate either form, but neither does that fact create a true synthesis. What it does indicate, however, is that Haiti has achieved a precarious balance in its way of life that may not successfully survive the infusion of many new elements, such as Protestantism. Haiti is a nation whose indigenous culture and paramount symbols are disputed and repudiated by the national state apparatus; such conditions necessarily undermine and drain the nation's unity and social health. If Vodou were to unravel, its demise would bring unforeseen disruptions to every area of Haitian life. Vodou is ultimately a religion based on the anthropomorphization of energetic forces and psychological archetypes that have individual identity and intelligence. Its efforts to look at the universe in rational—and

Gérard Valcin's "Loge Bleue" (1967). Milwaukee Art Museum. Flagg Tanning Corporation Collection. Published by permission.

ultimately, scientific—terms sets it apart from "world" religions in which a de-articulation occurs among religion, science, and philosophy. And because Vodou represents the collective psyche of a nation it helped create, it represents individual and national identity.

The international system and the conditions that arise from it are most intrusive, and little can be done to insulate Haiti from their impact. The ostracism Haiti suffered at the hands of the Western powers in the early nineteenth century cannot be realistically replaced by an isolationism in the first years of the twenty-first century of the kind adopted by Japan in the sixteenth and seventeenth centuries. The issue is not a choice between ostracism versus isolationism but a question of whether or not Haiti can control its destiny and, as part of that process, control the ideological superstructure that gives a nation a fair degree of independence. If in previous eras one result of converting the people of Haiti to Christianity was to make the people compliant slaves, the objectives of contemporary Western policies and Christian missions might lead the Haitian people to develop a measure of self-hatred and repudiate their indigenous culture and way of life.

Western colonial policy in Haiti is perfectly illustrated in the following extraordinary exchange in December 1921 between the French Roman Catholic bishop of Cap-Haitien (Haiti's second-largest city) and a member of a U.S. Senate commission chaired by Senator Medill McCormick that investigated the U.S. occupation of Haiti:

Senator: Your comments on the U.S. occupation of Haiti?

Bishop: The occupation was an act of kindness ....

Senator: The [guerrilla] war against the Americans—how do you explain it?

Bishop: The [Haitian] people was pushed to desperation by [American] arbitrariness, injustice, and mistreatments. It proclaimed its right to self-defense. Does the United States want to impose Protestantism [on the Haitian people] by force?

Senator: The Washington government will never attack Haiti's [Catholic] faith. Can you provide information on Vodun, its practices, and status? Has it diminished since the occupation?

> *Bishop:*   It has increased .... The greatest cause for this is that the *Bokos* ["priests" or "magicians"] were the soul of the [anti-American] insurrection.[3]

Having identified the "problem" in Haiti as the existence of Vodou, the commission then sought to determine an effective means of eradicating Vodou and neutralizing the popular opposition to the U.S. occupation that Vodou was orchestrating among the Haitian people. In reply to the senator's question about the best means to combat Vodou, the Bishop replied, "religion and education."

> *Senator:*   Education is missing [in Haiti]. What if we [Americans] gave it to the Church?
>
> *Bishop:*   The day [the Haitian people] find out that we received schools from you, we would suffer the disfavor attached to the occupation .... The Church is Haiti's ally .... Under penalty of disloyalty, we are to refuse to collaborate with anyone who would jeopardize Haiti's freedom. But, I repeat, we cannot go as fast as we would like because of the lack of funds.
>
> *Senator:*   We could help you.
>
> *Bishop:*   Soon we expect to receive from France stronger contingents of [Catholic] brothers and nuns. Furthermore, we are training local teachers. We won't succeed tomorrow, but we will [in time civilize Haiti].
>
> *Senator:*   These young people [being trained as teachers] ... they do not make the grade. Couldn't we send you inspectors from the United States? ... The American government can give you a sum of money .... The [American] Church can give you its support as well.
>
> *Bishop:*   We will receive with profound gratitude whatever the American Church can give us .... I would be more cautious about accepting [U.S.] government aid.

In the battle of French versus U.S. imperialism in Haiti, the French bishop expressed fear that U.S. Protestant missionaries would weaken the traditional advantage of French interests in Haiti. Addressing this same issue, U.S. Under-Secretary of the Navy Edwin Denby wrote the following to E.O. Watson, director of the U.S. Council of Churches: Missionaries' "good offices would have the beneficial outcome of exciting feelings of friendship between the [Haitian] people and the United States. Haiti is within the sphere of the United States, ... and the churches and missionary societies can be of very real help .... The Navy Department will be happy to facilitate your work in any way possible."[4]

The on-again, off-again persecution of Vodou was on again. Later, when François Duvalier sought to establish a counterforce to the conservative but pro-upper class Roman Catholic church, he facilitated the work of U.S. Pentecostal missionaries, and Christian missionaries from the United States continue their campaign against Vodou and Haiti's indigenous culture even today. In 1987, a U.S. missionary in Haiti gave a visiting physician the following response to a question about AIDS: "It is Voodoo that is the devil here. It is a demonic religion, a cancer on Haiti. Voodoo is worse than AIDS. And it is one of the reasons for the epidemic. Did you know that in order for a man to become a *houngan* ['Vodou male priest'] he must perform anal sodomy on another man? No, of course you didn't! So what can you expect from these people?"[5]

Little has changed since 1921, and today Vodou is persecuted more than previously. The rigidity and dogmatism of this missionary contrast sharply with Vodou's fluidity and acceptance of religious diversity. Whether homosexuality is a ritual in the Vodou priesthood is quite irrelevant. What the missionary does is to cloak Vodou with negative Western perceptions of homosexuality and the false notion that AIDS is an exclusively homosexual and/or Haitian disease, which are views that are neither shared by all cultures nor substantiated by medical science. To complete his mission of discrediting Vodou, the missionary might have accused Vodouists of being Communists, another damning epithet in the eyes of some Westerners.

Western colonial and neocolonial policy in Haiti has generally assumed that what is Haitian is not worth keeping, and this mentality has characterized Western policy throughout the Caribbean and Third World nations in general. Key questions remain: Can Haiti survive

Western manipulations of its culture, religion, economy, agriculture, and political institutions? Can there be a collective Haitian nation without the Haitian language or religion? Can personal identity exist in the absence of national identity? Another issue is illustrated throughout this book: if political structures and the government apparatus are at odds with a nation's cultural heritage and institutions, the legitimacy and stability of those structures, cultural values, and the nation in general are undermined and destabilized. This argument, in fact, was made by peasant groups who hoped to have an impact on the new constitution of 1987 as it was being written.

This analysis of Vodou has avoided the obligatory recitation of the various Vodou *lwas* and their designated religious functions. Although such a recitation would be useful in certain contexts, it would add little to an overall interpretation of Vodou and could actually hamper it. For the purposes of this book, the names and roles of the various *lwas* are best expressed in a table (see Appendix). The Vodou *lwas* are archetypes: they represent the cosmic forces that are integral to the Haitian experience and yet transcend it. They represent power—theirs and humans'—as individuals and as a community. To the extent that the Haitian people are converted en masse away from their national religion of Vodou to Christianity or other foreign religions, their power and self-identity are forfeited. The result is powerlessness—the powerlessness that comes from one's lack of control over one's own destiny. What lies beyond the grave, if anything does, is similar for all, indeed, the interpretations themselves may be the same—everything else is culture-specific. And this is what makes so-called universal religions so pernicious. They rob the world of its richness and imply cultural and racial hierarchies by establishing bad and good religions. Alienation follows the erosion of one's spiritual and cultural heritage. Now more than ever, Haiti needs all its *lwas*—and then some.

WOMEN AND SOCIETY

Haitian women are oppressed by the same patterns of sex discrimination that oppress women in other parts of the world, and the oppression has intensified since Haiti has been dominated by the Western world. The oppression of women in Haiti is somewhat alleviated, however, by two factors. First, Haitian culture has incorporated the sometimes matriarchal heritage of its African origins. Second, in contrast to the theological and political patriarchy of much of the Judeo-Christian world, the ideological superstructure of Vodou assigns women a central and important position in all aspects of life. — In January 1987, a rumor had it that a woman would be named minister of justice in the provisional military government that had replaced the toppled Duvalier dictatorship. A mayor of Port-au-Prince under the Duvalier regime, the woman under consideration would have had to relinquish her seat as minister of education to become minister of justice. This particular woman was not appointed, but the provisional government did name women to two key posts in the Justice Ministry (director general and chief prosecutor).

The Duvaliers appointed a few women to government posts, such as Rosalie Adolphe, the chief officer of the secret state police, the Tontons Macoutes (Volunteers for National Security). Lydia O. Jeanty was named undersecretary of labor in 1957, and Lucienne Heurtelou, the widow of the former president Dumarsais Estimé, was Haiti's first female ambassador. A few women also held seats in the regime's rubber-stamp legislature. In January 1988, Mme. Myrlande Hyppolite Manigat, the president's wife, was selected to serve in the Senate.

Traditionally, however, most Haitian women in positions of political power have acquired those positions through their associations or relationships with powerful males. Examples of such women include Joute Lachennais, the mistress of Haitian presidents Alexandre Pétion and Jean-Pierre Boyer, and Claire-Heureuse Bonheur, whose beneficent intercession as the wife of Emperor Jean-Jacques Dessalines saved the lives of some whites during the wars of independence. Louise Coidavid, the wife of King Henry Christophe, exerted influence over him until his death and the dissolution of his kingdom in 1820. Suzanne Simon married Governor-General Toussaint Louverture and similarly influenced his decisions and policies. In the twentieth-century, examples include Simone Ovide and Michèle Bennett, the wives of François and Jean-Claude Duvalier, respectively, and Marie-Denise Duvalier, François Duvalier's daughter and private secretary.

On April 3, 1986, two days after the creation of several national women's organizations, 30,000 women demonstrated in Port-au-Prince to memorialize the thousands of female victims of the Duvalier dictatorship. Chanting, "Justice! Justice! Justice!" they declined the requests of well-intentioned males to join their march. In October 1986, several women were named to the constitutional assembly that drafted the first post-Duvalier Haitian constitution. But token reforms often lead oppressed groups to demand greater reforms once they have realized that actual power is not being equitably shared. Derived power, that is, the personal power that women acquire through their associations with powerful men, is exercised within an overall institutional framework that sustains male control despite ingeniously small reforms designed to create the illusion of social change. In this sense, women become a "support group" for a social reality that is defined and controlled by men. Marie-Denise Duvalier nearly succeeded her father François as president of Haiti upon his death in 1971, but the accession of a female president would probably have had as little impact on social and political conditions in Haiti at that time as it thus far has had in Argentina, Bolivia, and Dominica, where female heads of state have left repressive institutions and policies intact.

It could be argued that Haitian women are often less restricted than women in Western societies, but traditional sex roles are not easily transcended, and women must break through barriers to their full participation in society as a *collective* class before their individual abilities and contributions are acknowledged and rewarded. Like racism, sex discrimination must be recognized and repudiated before it can be alleviated.

A fledgling Haitian women's movement of the 1930s and 1940s coincided with a severe economic depression that forced many middle- and upper-class Haitian women to work outside the home for the first time, unlike peasant women, who have always worked. As more elite women began to seek secondary and postsecondary education in the mid-1930s, the University of Haiti opened its doors to women, and the first woman to pursue a high school education in Haiti received her diploma in 1933.

The first feminist organization in Haiti, the Feminine League for Social Action (Ligue Féminine d'Action Sociale) was launched in March

The Ligue Féminine d'Action Sociale, the founding mothers of the Haitian women's movement (c. early 1930s). Photo: Author's collection.

1934 but was banned by the government two months later. Its leadership included Madeleine Sylvain, Alice Garoute, Fernande Bellegarde, Thérèse Hudicourt, Alice Mathon, Marie-Thérèse Colimon, Marie-Thérèse Poitevien, and other leading women of the Haitian elite. The league sought to establish more schools for girls, equality for women in family law, equal pay for equal work, voting rights for women, free labor unions, and a labor ministry with a women's bureau. The political left supported these goals, but leftist support only increased the government's opposition to the league and its activities. When the league agreed not to pursue its objectives but merely to study them in small committees for two years, the government reauthorized its existence. Despite government restrictions on its activities, the league was able to effect changes in Haitian laws over the next twenty years, a process that culminated in the extension of voting rights to women in 1957. The original league was followed by a more middle-class organization, the Feminine Sheaf (Faisceau féminin), which consisted primarily of pro-Duvalier women.

The history of the changes in the legal rights of Haitian women forms an important part of the work of Madeleine Sylvain-Bouchereau and, more recently, of Ertha Pascal-Trouillot. In an analysis of the Haitian women's movement, the Haitian scholar Régine Latortue concluded that educated women had helped urban and rural working-class women but had "not yet succeeded in altering the social structure of Haiti in any significant way" (Chioma Steady, 1981: 540). Because the Haitian women's movement was led by elite women, it never intended to change the nation's economic and social structures.

Haitian women have been active in literary movements since the nation's founding, and Virginie Sampeur, Ida Faubert, and Luce Archin-Lay were noted poets and essayists in Haitian Romanticism and the Génération de La Ronde, one of Haiti's most important literary periods. Women have made their greatest contributions to Haitian literature, however, primarily during the past twenty to thirty years. The untimely death of the novelist Marie Chauvet in 1973 deprived Haitian letters of a major voice.

The first school for women in Haiti, the Pensionnat des Demoiselles, was established simultaneously with one for males in 1816. Generally, however, female education has lagged far behind that of males, and today this fact is reflected in the higher literacy rate for men within the nation's overall literacy rate of 20 percent. Under President Lysius-Félicité Salomon, the Pensionnat was directed by Argentine Bellegarde (1842–1901), one of Haiti's most noted educators.

In the 1820s, the acclaimed Haitian educator and journalist Juliette Bussières Laforest Courtois opened a private school for girls to provide educational opportunities that the public sector had failed to establish, and in the 1840s and 1850s, two fashionable schools for young women were opened by Madame Isidore Boisrond and Madame Belmour Lépine. These private schools taught upper-class women only the basic rudiments of Western education, and both funding and government support for women's education were extremely low. Other milestones in women's education were reached with the establishment of French Catholic schools after the signing of a Haitian concordat with the Vatican in 1860 and the founding of the Elie Dubois school in 1907.

Whereas the role of Haitian elite women has been largely peripheral and derivative, peasant women have traditionally played crucial roles in many areas of Haitian life, especially in the Vodou religious structure. By Latin American standards, the participation of Haitian women in commerce and agriculture—and now in industry—has been very high.

A *manbo* ("female Vodou priest"), Cécile Fatiman, whose name has been lost, officiated with the male Vodou leader Boukman Dutty at a ceremony at Bois-Caiman that launched the Haitian Revolution, which began on August 22, 1791. Marie-Jeanne Lamartinière, who is popularly known as Haiti's Joan of Arc, fought in the Haitian wars of independence, most notably at the Battle of La Crête-à-Pierrot of 1802. Other female revolutionaries such as Suzanne Sanite Bélair and Henriette Saint-Marc demonstrated formidable military prowess until they were captured and executed by the French. Although many women served as soldiers, quartermasters, nurses, and spies during the revolution, the status of women improved little after independence was achieved. Louise Nicolas was an energetic leader of the "suffering army" in the massive peasant Piquet Revolt of 1844. During the U.S. occupation of Haiti, 1915–1934, peasant women gathered intelligence on troop movements and actively participated in anti-U.S. guerrilla warfare. As a result, they suffered greatly during the U.S. reprisals.

Manbos and *houngans* play equal roles in the Vodou religion, and Vodou has never differentiated between the roles and contributions of the male priest over the female. The decentralized, nonhierarchical structure of the Vodou pantheon is reflected in the ease with which both male and female spirits (*lwas*) perform miracles regardless of their gender. The sexual equality inherent in the Haitian religion has significant implications for the inclusion of women as participants in all aspects of Haitian society. In Vodou, women have a marked degree of prestige and autonomy, and this equal participation of women carries over into other areas of life, precisely because it is rooted in an institution as basic as religion. In sharp contrast to many Christian and traditional Western religions, in which women are either totally excluded from the priesthood or play only subordinate roles, in Vodou men and women are believed to have equal access to the metaphysical plane.

The sexual equity inherent to Vodou may partly explain the power sharing among men and women in the Haitian countryside and the relative powerlessness of Haitian elite women in the cities, where Christian and other Western influences are stronger. One anthropologist has stated that the sexual equality of Vodou "is congruent with the relative equality of the sexes and the autonomy of women in other areas of Haitian life," in contrast with Protestant and other Western belief systems in which women are ideologically and hierarchically subordinate.[6]

If what is called "modernization" means the Westernization of Haitian culture, it may have negative implications for the status of women in Haitian society, a possibility that is clearly demonstrated by the impact of Haiti's adoption of the Napoléonic Code in 1826, which reduced the legal status of Haitian women to "minors" under the control of their husbands. Some improvements in the legal status of women were enacted in the 1940s, and the Haitian Constitution of 1950 extended women's rights according to a graduated timetable. The erosion of women's rights in the wake of Westernization has stood in sharp contrast to the equal participation of women found in the Vodou religion, Haitian peasant mores, and the West African cultures from which those mores developed.

Because the Haitian legal system is based on Western models imposed by colonial invaders, it lacks the centrality of Haiti's African heritage as attenuated by centuries of slavery; the position and status of women were more elevated in the Afro-Haitian peasantry than in the Franco-Haitian elite. The vision of androgynous gods and the mere existence of female gods in the Vodou belief system presented opportunities for the advancement and empowerment of women and homosexuals that might otherwise not have existed. In addition, the harsh impact of slavery upon marital relations, the rigors of warfare against the whites, and the daily struggles for survival in rural agrarian poverty enhanced and bolstered the role of women in Haitian society.

Despite horrible conditions arising from extreme poverty, contemporary Haitian peasant women appear to have a greater independence and more incipient power than their Haitian elite and U.S. or European counterparts. Scholars disagree as to whether the African traditions of Haitian culture or the impact of slavery has had greater influence on Haitian life. Anthropologist Sidney W. Mintz has observed the following:

It may have been partly in the experience of slavery itself that Jamaican and Haitian males found the capacity to tolerate female autonomy, while Jamaican and Haitian females were finding the capacity to exercise that autonomy—eventually in ways remarkably consistent with those of their West African

Rural market where women predominate (circa late 1980s). Photo: CIDIHCA.

sisters. Such a view is not intended to slight the force of the African past in the lives of Caribbean peoples of African origins, but it does raise a question about assertions of uninterrupted continuities [of African traditions in Haitian culture]. [Cited in Chioma-Steady, 1981: 530]

The sexual division of labor in Haiti is somewhat inverted from African patterns: Women work primarily in marketing, and men work primarily in agriculture; in Africa, 60–80 percent of the agriculturalists are women. The Haitian pattern may have developed in the nineteenth century, when males did not venture into town in order to avoid being drafted into service by the central government and roving armies.

Haitian peasant women have always assumed enormous burdens and responsibilities. Writing in 1869, Reverend M.B. Bird described women in some districts who were responsible for cultivating coffee, the country's major export crop, while they monopolized retail trade in the villages and accumulated resources independently from their mates: "One can truly say that the Haitian woman has an aptitude for commerce, a fact that has more to do with the particularities of Haitian civilization than would otherwise be the case."[7] Madeleine Sylvain-Bouchereau argued that Haitian women inherited this talent from their African ancestors.

In Haiti today, agriculture is a primarily male occupation. But although food production is a male role, the marketing of that produce is still in the female domain, and women are responsible for household expenditures. One anthropologist has argued that "the potential independence in the economic sphere significantly shapes both male and female conceptions of womanhood in rural Haiti .... The economic value of women's domestic labor is formally recognized and codified in customary local principles of conjugal property rights" (Foster and Valdman, 1984: 19–20). Haitian women also keep the proceeds of their own economic activities. The autonomy and economic importance of Haitian peasant women contrast sharply with the status of women in Haiti's Western legal system, which did not allow married women to control their own earnings until the passage of a reform law in 1944. Even that "reform" law stipulated that a married woman must spend one-third of her earnings on her household.[8]

In the peasant's struggle to survive, male-female roles in politics and economics intersect more vividly than among Haiti's Westernized elite. According to Ira P. Lowenthal, "Gender complementarity ensures that labor cooperation between men and women is not strictly limited to the conjugal pair. Similar arrangements may exist between brother and sister, mother and son, and even father and daughter." Citing the Haitian proverb *Chak fanm fèt ak yon kawo tè lan mitan janm ni* ("Each woman is born with an acre of land between her legs"), Lowenthal concluded that "female sexuality is here revealed to be a woman's most important economic resource" (Foster and Valdman, 1984: 20, 22).

The issue of women's political rights was hotly debated by all-male legislatures and constitutional assemblies in Haiti in 1946 and 1950. To some extent, these males were forced to grant women the right to vote in response to the growth of women's political rights in the international climate, and Haitian women were finally granted the right to vote in 1957. Following the overthrow of the Duvalier regime in February 1986, peasant groups lobbied the constitutional assembly in 1987 to incorporate certain rural traditions and practices into the nation's legal system in order to make the nation's laws more accurately reflect Haitian society and evolving social realities.

Chapter 2

The Context of Haitian Development and Underdevelopment

Bourik swe pou chwal dekore ak dentel.
("The donkey works so that the horse may be decorated with lace.")

— Haitian proverb

WHAT TRANSPIRED BEFORE COLUMBUS ARRIVED IN HISPANIOLA ON December 6, 1492, is of little significance to modern Haiti. Greatly significant, however, is the pattern of power relations established when the Taino Indians encountered the Spaniards. This pattern was replicated under French rule and persists even today.

SAINT-DOMINGUE: WEALTH AMID POVERTY

At the time of Columbus's first voyage, the island called Ayiti, Boyio, or Kiskeya in the Marcorix language of the Taino/Arawak inhabitants was divided into five *caciquats* ("kingdoms"). These five states, called Marien, Magua, Xaragua, Maguana, and Higuey, were ruled by a *cacique* and a council of elders called the Nytaino.

The Spaniards described the Tainos as peaceful, gentle, and healthy. In his memoirs, Columbus wrote that "they were all very well built with fine bodies and handsome faces .... They do not carry weapons, nor do they know about them .... They should be good servants, and very intelligent .... I believe that they could be made Christians easily, for they appeared to me to have no religion .... I will bring half a dozen back to their Majesties so that they can learn to speak" (Knight, 1978: 10–11). Estimates of the Taino population at the time Columbus landed in Hispaniola range from 300,000 to 1 million. Soon after arrival, the Spaniards instituted the *repartimentos* and *encomienda* systems, which amounted to slavery of the Indian aborigines. The Spanish also introduced diseases such as smallpox and tuberculosis against which the Tainos had no natural immunity.

The Spanish encountered massive resistance from the inhabitants, which set a pattern for later encounters in Haiti between Europeans and Africans. The Haitian historian Emile Nau (1812–1860) justified his interest in Amerindian history by the fact that Haitians lived in the country Amerindians had inhabited. The historical record is still inadequate, but the names of some of the leaders of the Taino resistance are known: Caonabo, Garionex, Marnikatex, Mayobanex, and Anacaona, the queen of Xaragua, in what is now southern Haiti. Anacaona, a famous poet turned warrior, was burned at the stake by the Spanish. The famous Battle of Santo Cerro was fought in 1495, three years after the Spanish invasion.

The last gasp of Amerindian resistance was led by Anacaona's son Henry, a *cacique* who fled to the Bahoruco Mountains with newly arrived black African slaves after he had been enslaved and his wife raped and forced to convert to Christianity. Their guerrilla camps were called *balenques*. At the end of their struggle barely 500 of the resisters had survived, but Spain was forced to recognize their "independence" by treaty in 1533. The price for the treaty was the mutilation and death of many of the Maroons, the runaway African slaves who had joined the resistance movement (although the Bahoruco mountain chain remained a bastion for the surviving Maroons until the 1790s). It had taken Spain less than fifty years to decimate the population of Hispaniola.

The first European establishment in the Western Hemisphere was the Nativity Fort (La Navidad), which had been built from the Christmas Day wreckage of Columbus's lead ship the *Santa Maria* near the Haitian town of Fort Liberté, founded by the Spanish as Bayaja. The Spanish brought the first blacks to Haiti in 1501, and by 1520, African slaves were used throughout the island. The introduction of the African slaves was based on the premise that Africans were agriculturalists and hence more able than the Amerindians to withstand the rigors of slavery.

The Africans came from relatively well-organized states that had succeeded the great African empires such as Mali, Songhay, Bornu-Kanem, Ghana, and Kongo that collectively formed what has been called the Golden Age of African civilization. Some evidence even indicates that the Malians explored what is now Latin America in the 1300s. The eighteenth- and nineteenth-century West African states whose people were enslaved and abducted to Haiti, including Asante, Oyo, Ibadan, Dahomey, and Benin, were relatively wealthy. Their inhabitants were town dwellers who had developed textile and metalworking cottage industries and created great works of art that would revolutionize Western art in the twentieth century. In this sense Haitians are the descendants of Africans whose cultures, social and political institutions, and economic structures were long established and complex. This heritage has served the people of Haiti well.[1]

The high level of civilization in these African cultures is significant because at the time of Haiti's independence in 1804, more than half the population was African-born. Because of the high mortality rate among slaves and the constant importation of more black slaves, that statistic indicates that black slaves in Haiti had been able to maintain much of their African culture. Although the slaves recognized their common origin by referring to each other as *nanchon* ("nation"), they had lost much of their tribal or national identity because the slave owners intentionally put individuals of different tribal origins together in order to minimize the unity of the slaves and to forestall uprisings. The Haitian historian Dantès Bellegarde (1877–1966) noted that the slaves developed a community and common ideas and customs in a remarkably short span of time. The Haitian ethnic group emerged from the diverse elements that melded in the colonial melting pot of the black population. A national language, Kreyol, also soon emerged (the issue of black community and solidarity is analyzed in greater detail later in this chapter).

In contrast to the Africans and the French, the Amerindians and Spanish contributed little that survives in contemporary Haiti except for a pattern of power relations. The Spanish soon abandoned the western part of Hispaniola and then minimized operations in the east to exploit the more lucrative Latin American mainland.

France gained possession of Saint-Domingue almost by default through the Treaty of Ryswick (1697), which legalized the fait accompli of the French dominance. There had been early settlements by French pirates and buccaneers on the island of La Tortue (Tortuga Island), and thirty-three years before the Treaty of Ryswick, La Tortue had come under the control of the French corporation, the Compagnie des Indes Occidentales (French West Indies Company). In 1670, Louis XIV had authorized the French slave trade in Haiti. After the Treaty of Ryswick, two French corporations subsequently replaced the first: the Compagnie de Saint-Domingue ruling from 1698 until 1718 and the Compagnie des Indes from 1718 to 1724. Thereafter the colony was administered directly by the French crown for the next eighty years; when Haiti became independent, French colonization had lasted about two centuries.

Colonies were supposed to produce an economic surplus to create great wealth for the metropolitan power, which gave that power economic clout and political prestige in the international arena. The slave trade alone created profits of 300–2,000 percent, and, in Saint-Domingue, the colony's currency was deliberately undervalued to ensure that the colony would sell cheap and buy dear. By law, industries could not be built in the colony. Haitian sugar and cocoa, for example, were refined in France itself, and France in turn sold these commodities to half of Europe at a sizable profit. Indeed, two-thirds of Haitian exports were redirected from France with greater profits from units of added value, and despite protectionism, the French controlled the worldwide sugar market with a 40 percent market share.

Saint-Domingue exported twice as much as it imported. Mercantilism, which had been used less successfully by Spain and Portugal, ensured that the French trade patterns with the colony would be "exclusive" at the rate of 95 percent. On the eve of the American Revolution, however, the Thirteen Colonies and Saint-Domingue had already developed a thriving commercial trade (Logan, 1941:7). On the eve of the French Revolution, Saint-Domingue was contributing

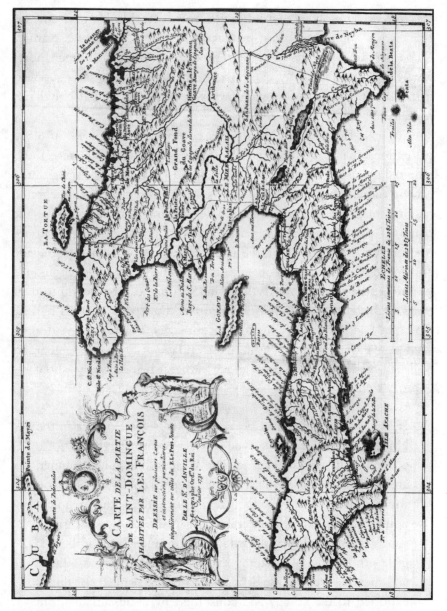

Map 3: Carte de la partie de Saint-Domingue habitée par les François (Janvier 1731).

40 percent of the value of French foreign trade. As mentioned in the Introduction, almost 20 percent of the French population of 27 million

was directly involved in trade with the lucrative Haitian colony. Normandy spun the cotton produced in Haiti; Bordeaux, Nantes, Marseilles, Dieppe, and Orléans refined its raw sugar. French ports were bustling with activity, and dozens of other French cities supplied Saint-Domingue with the manufactured products that it could not produce by law.

— Sugar, coffee, cotton, indigo, and cocoa were produced on 8,500 plantations that covered some 500,000 hectares (203,000 acres) and required the use of 700 ships. In 1789, some 4,100 ships were registered leaving and entering the colony's ports. In the absence of an integrated national plan for Haitian economic development, many more of the country's ports were then open to international commerce than are open in the last quarter of the twentieth century. Georges Anglade concluded that "the spatial organization [of Haiti] is made of thousands of independent small streams that connect units of production to their ports of embarkation .... This atomization, the space [created by] the Colonial Pact, is the production of enclaves, the representation of each plantation as an individualized appendage of France."[2] John Stuart Mill had made the same point much earlier when he wrote about his country's colonies:

> If Manchester, instead of being where it is, were a rock in the North Sea ... it would still be but a town in England, not a country trading with England. The West Indies, in like manner, are the place where England finds it convenient to carry on the production of sugar, coffee, and a few other tropical commodities. All the capital employed is English capital; almost all the industry is carried on for English uses; there is little production of anything except the staple commodities, and these are sent to England, not to be exchanged for things exported to the colony and consumed by its inhabitants, but to be sold in England for the benefit of the proprietors there.[3]

Haitian social and political institutions were clearly devised to benefit the economic growth of the colony, but not its development. Saint-Domingue alone accounted for two-thirds of all French colonial revenues, a sum estimated at 400 million francs in the late 1780s. In this regard, the French banker and minister of finance Jacques Necker stated in 1789, "It is only by selling abroad the merchandise that it has gotten from its colonies for 270 million that France obtains a positive [trade] balance of 70 million."[4] These facts of the colony's political economy were clearly understood at the time. Echoing Necker, Jean-Siffrein Cardinal Maury, a member of the French National Assembly, declared the following in 1791: "If you were to lose each year more than 200 million pounds that you now get from your colonies; if you had not the exclusive trade with your colonies to feed your manufactures, to maintain your navy, to keep your agriculture going, to repay for your imports, to provide for your luxury needs, to advantageously balance your trade with Europe and Asia, then I say it clearly: the kingdom would be irretrievably lost."[5]

During the French colonization of Haiti, there were about 30,000 whites and over half a million slaves on the island. To maintain thriving production and control the slaves responsible for that production, a complex militaristic system was superimposed upon an already corrupt and authoritarian government administration. The French maintained a relatively large standing army of about 3,000 men, and all white males were required to serve in the territorial militia. This military apparatus was the genesis of what later became known by the Spanish term *caudillism*—a network of military chieftains with nearly unbridled power and little countervailing authority from legally constituted bodies. Caudillism became a central feature of the country's political culture, and it has had a lasting impact upon contemporary Haitian politics. (The role and impact of caudillism on Haitian political and social development will be explored in Chapter 3.)

THE HAITIAN REVOLUTION (1791–1806): ECONOMIC AND SOCIAL DYNAMICS

The social structure of colonial Haiti reflected the colony's economic purpose. Because the plantation (*habitation*) economy was established to serve external markets and not to satisfy local demands for foodstuffs or manufactures, the locus of financial and political power was outside Haiti. Thus the plantation economy largely determined the acceptable manner of interaction between the dominant Western culture and the subjugated African cultures.

Inherent contradictions between the requirements of the plantation economy and a kind of quest for cultural assimilation, combined with the widespread survival of African cultural traits, made the plantation system the vector of what evolved into a Caribbean-wide Creole culture. Many scholars agree that real cultural differences between France, England, Spain, Portugal, and other West European nations were of little importance in comparison to the unifying Creole culture that developed in the Caribbean on the basis of economic imperatives. The Afro-American plantation culture encompasses northern Brazil and the southern United States as well as the West Indies archipelago, and similar circumstances elicited similar responses in the development of language, political culture, religion, and popular resistance movements. The insurrections of Plymouth and François Makandal in Haiti; the Maroons in Jamaica, Dominica, and St. Vincent; the Djuka "Bush Negroes" in Suriname; Morales in Cuba; Cuffy in Guyana; the proto-African Palmares state in Brazil; and Vesey and Nat Turner in the United States all arose from the impulse to resist the Europeans.

— At the apex of the Haitian social pyramid were the whites, who were themselves subdivided into *grands blancs*, *petits blancs*, and *blancs manants* ("serfs"). The *grands blancs* included the most powerful planters, merchants, and functionaries and were often of noble birth. Although they constituted only one-sixth of the white population and less than 1 percent of the total population, the *grands blancs* reaped enormous profits in Saint-Domingue. Summarizing the social class ascription of the whites in the French West Indies, people referred to *les seigneurs de Saint-Domingue, ces messieurs de la Martinique, et les bonnes gens de la Guadeloupe* ("the lords of Saint-Domingue, the sirs of Martinique, and the plain folks of Guadeloupe"). The sympathies of the *grands blancs* were with the ancien régime in France, but when the French monarchy collapsed, they favored British control, local autonomy, and free trade to insulate Haiti from the revolutionary contagion. They called themselves "patriots."

The *petits blancs* included lesser functionaries, plantation overseers, and skilled artisans, and in the colonial context, this group constituted a sort of middle and lower-middle class. The *petits blancs* were despised by their wealthier compatriots and in turn despised the mulattoes and blacks, some of whom were wealthier and better educated than many of the whites. The *petits blancs* hated yet emulated the *grands blancs*. As Dantès Bellegarde wrote, "The Europeans upon arrival ... [sought] to acquire luxurious clothing and black servants."[6] This group was extremely racist yet sympathetic to the French Revolution and its slogan of *Liberté, Égalité, Fraternité*.

The *blancs manants* were the poorest whites and formed a sort of rebellious urban proletariat whose status was almost indistinguishable from that of the slaves. The slaves despised the *blancs manants* for their poverty and would say the *Blan mannan kase kod blan batiman, manje kasav, pwason ak pimen, bwè tafia konkou nèg* ("The *blancs manants* are ill-mannered, rustic white stowaways and escapees from white ships who eat cassava and dried fish with hot peppers and drink cheap rum like slaves"). *Blan mannan* is still an insult in Haiti today.

Throughout Europe, the Haitian plantocracy enjoyed a reputation for extraordinary wealth and ostentation. An important cultural life developed around the *grands blancs*, even though their absenteeism from Haiti was chronic. In contrast to the previous Spanish colonists, the French whites in Saint-Domingue generally kept abreast of metropolitan developments and benefited from the intensity of the French Enlightenment. The contemporary Haitian historian Jean Fouchard described the theatrical arts in Saint-Domingue as being for those people who had vast leisure time and little to do. Three thousand plays were produced between 1764 and 1791 in the major towns, and according to one scholar, "at one time fifty substantial weekly newspapers or reviews were regularly published in the colony" (Rotberg, 1971: 31).

Whites in Saint-Domingue were also divided between those who had been born in France, and therefore by law monopolized the highest bureaucratic positions, and the Creoles, 20 percent of the white population, who had been born in the colony. The distinction between these two groups led to great difficulties throughout Latin America.

⸺ Most significant in the social dynamics of the colony was the relative scarcity of white women. As late as 1789, the ratio of white men to white women was two to one, and the sexual ratio varied significantly among the three classes of whites. The numbers of men and women were about equal among the *grands blancs*, but among the *petits blancs* the ratio was three men to one woman. Interracial unions (miscegenation) were not forbidden in the early colonial period, and the male-oriented buccaneers had established families consisting of two males (*matelotage*) and their indentured servants.[7] Miscegenation became widespread, but when the mulatto population increased, the French authorities feared losing control and adopted restrictive antimiscegenation laws throughout the 1700s that became more severe in the latter half of the eighteenth century. Concubinage remained the prevalent form of such a union and continues in Haiti today.

⸺The *affranchis* ("freed" people) composed an intermediary group of about 28,000 that included mostly mulattoes and a few thousand Blacks. Generically they were known as *gens de couleur* ("people of color"). Not all mulattoes were free—40,000 were in fact slaves—but the vast majority of the slaves were black. The *affranchis* were quite Westernized and often well educated, and they owned about one-fourth of the plantations and slaves, primarily in the south. As the *affranchis* grew in number and economic importance, they suffered increasing discrimination and social opprobrium. A few "passed" for whites, and the worst slur in the white community was to imply that a person was of mixed racial parentage or a *descendant des gens de la côte* ("descendant of the people of the [African] coast").

The Code Noir (Black Code) enacted in France in 1685 was derived from similar Spanish codes and differentiated only between free citizens and slaves. In practice, however, the *affranchis* were severely discriminated against. They had no political rights and were eventually barred from having "white" surnames, wearing certain kinds of dress, being addressed as "sir" or "madame," and using certain public accommodations. Adding injury to insult, they were barred from practicing law, medicine, or pharmacy, and they were not allowed to be members of the priesthood or the teaching profession. A classification of 200 color combinations was established that ranged from "pure white" at one end of the spectrum to "pure black" at the other. Of course, no person of color could ever quite "make it" into the white group. This racial discrimination reinforced the continuous correlation between color and class in Haiti and the rest of the Caribbean and explains the desire of some people to "add more milk to their coffee" when selecting a mate.

Although the *affranchis* were immeasurably better off than the slaves, they were very oppressed by the white ruling class. As discrimination against the *affranchis* in Saint-Domingue became increasingly severe, the events surrounding the French Revolution presented these people with increased opportunities to press their demands. To gain political rights, the preferred approach of most *affranchis* was accommodation with the whites, but since about 1,500 *affranchis* had participated in the American War of Independence under General Jean-Baptiste de Rochambeau, they were mindful of the possibility of a military solution to their problems. Many future leaders of the Haitian Revolution fought in the American Revolution, including Henry Christophe, André Rigaud, Jean-Baptiste Chavannes, Martial Besse, and Mars Belley.

An early leader of the Haitian independence movement was the national hero Vincent Ogé, who led an ill-fated *affranchis* revolt and was drawn and quartered with his comrade Jean-Baptiste Chavannes in 1791. The year before, Ogé had appealed to the white ruling class to grant basic rights to the *affranchis*: "I [have] not included in my demands a change in the fate of the Negroes who live in slavery .... We have only claimed for a class of free men who have been under the yoke of oppression for the past two centuries."—Asking for reconciliation between white and *affranchi* planters, he warned, "Behold the slave who raises the flag of revolt" (Bellegarde-Smith, 1985: 36). Blinded by racism, however, the white plantocracy was unable to make common cause with mulatto and black slave owners to prevent a united front against the "real enemy," the half million slaves.

Each group in Saint-Domingue had its own agenda, but none of those agendas included the other groups. The grand alliance between the *affranchis* and slaves that led to Haitian independence in 1804 was partly a calculated and cynical attempt by the *affranchis* to co-opt the slaves for their own purposes, but it was probably necessary for the revolution to succeed.

⌐ At the bottom of the social pyramid were the slaves, who were continually being imported to make up for the high slave mortality rate and brutal efficiency of the plantation system. Between 1697 and 1791, the slave population of Saint-Domingue grew from 5,000 to about 500,000, a hundredfold increase. The fact that more than half of the slaves at the time of independence had been born in Africa indicates that ill treatment and early death of slaves were very common. From the moment of capture, the life expectancy of a slave was only seven years. Fouchard wrote about "blacks burned at the stake ... stuffed with gunpowder and set ablaze ... blacks ground in sugar mills."[8] The plantocracy was legendary for its brutality. The "best" slaves captured in Africa were reportedly reserved for the wealthy seigneurs of Saint-Domingue. These planters were richer than most, but their slaves were not less poor than others. By definition, slaves owned nothing regardless of the wealth of their masters.

⌐ The slaves were divided between field slaves and house slaves and between those born in the colony, the Creoles, and those born in Africa, the *bosal*. Today the expression *nèg bosal* has the same meaning it had two centuries ago: a savage, uncivilized beast who is not yet housebroken. ⌐

⌐ Slaves were treated no better than farm animals. The infamous overseer with his whip was often a slave himself—an interesting note of colonial psychology. The quality of life for all slaves was extremely harsh, but the lot of women was particularly difficult. The threat of rape and sexual assault was constant, and being powerless, the black woman might submit, knowing that she had no choice and no recourse and hoping to appease her master and render her situation more tolerable. The mortality statistics for mulatto slaves alone reveal that this avenue for self-preservation was usually futile, but the same mentality persists in Haiti today in terms of the relationship between servant and head of household. ⌐

⌐ Pregnant slaves were not exempt from heavy field work until the birth of the baby, and the rates of miscarriage and abortion were astronomical. It was a common feeling among planters that it was cheaper to buy "niggers" than to breed them. Slaves were considered and treated as agricultural commodities. To supplement a diet of imported dried, salted fish, which is a basic staple in Haiti even today, the slaves were expected to cultivate gardens of maize, sweet potatoes, and yams for their own consumption, but they were allowed to work in their gardens only after completing work for the day in the master's fields.

Among the plantocracy's relentless measures concerning the slave population was the conversion of slaves to Christianity, because many planters believed that such conversion made slavery morally justified. Some slaves were swayed. In this regard, one Haitian writer and social critic wrote the following: "The Creole, meaning the black born in the colony, had, according to Moreau de St. Méry, a 25 percent added retail value to that of the *bosal*, the uncivilized newcomer from Africa, *and this superiority the Creole attributed to baptism*, the symbol of his [her] initiation to Christian civilization."[9] Several scholars have agreed that the *bosal* slaves were more likely to be belligerent than their Creole counterparts, but based on what transpired historically, this difference could only have been a matter of degree. In any case, the colonial distinction between Christian and "uncivilized" slaves became the basis for the religious discrimination against Vodou that continues today.

Slaves were seldom docile, instigating constant rebellions and acts of passive resistance. To maintain the wholeness and continuity of the black people that was being destroyed by slavery, the Maroon communities of escaped slaves waged continuous guerrilla warfare. Perhaps the most powerful instrument of resistance, however, was the Vodou religion. The eradication of African religious ideas had been a priority of planters throughout the Americas because the planters understood that the African religion would undermine their colonial power and authority. Today, in the latter part of the twentieth century, the strength of Protestant missionaries in Haiti—and by extension in Central America—is greatly connected to a strengthening of the hegemony of the United States in the first part of the twenty-first century. A rallying force in the Maroons' call to arms, Vodou rapidly became a defining component of Haitian culture.

The Vodou ceremony of Bois-Caiman on August 14, 1791, conducted by Boukman Dutty and a female priest, Cécile Fatiman, was attended by 200 people and led to the general insurrection of

August 22. Like his predecessor Plymouth, Boukman had been born in Jamaica. His message was clear as he spoke to the crowd of insurgents:

> Hidden God in a cloud
> is there, watching us.
> He sees all the whites do;
> the Whitegod demands crimes
> ours wants good things.
> But our God that is so good
> orders vengeance, he will
> ride us, assist us.
> Throw away the thoughts of
> the Whitegod who thirsts
> for our tears, listen to
> freedom that speaks to our hearts.[10]

Boukman led 50,000 insurgents who seized control of the important Plaine du Nord for ten days, massacring 1,000 whites but at the cost of 10,000 insurgents. Uprisings broke out throughout the country, seemingly the result of a resistance network, and women participated in the insurrection along with the men. In the Plaine du Cul-de-Sac, Romaine the prophetess—who was actually a man—was an important resistance leader. After the death of Boukman, his principal lieutenants, Jean-François, Jeannot, Biassou, and Toussaint Louverture, crossed into Spanish-held Santo Domingo to continue the struggle.

The revolt led by Boukman in 1791 and one that had been led by François Makandal in 1757 were directly related, and Makandal's revolt had been similarly inspired by previous revolts in 1691 and 1697. Born in Africa, the son of a chief, Makandal was Moslem with particular skill in the use of medicinal plants. Believed by his followers to be a Vodòu priest or maybe a magician (*houngan* or *bòkò*), his mission had been to rid Saint-Domingue of whites and establish an independent "African" kingdom. His followers were particularly adept at the use of poison, and today, the word *makandal* refers to poisonous charms used against an enemy. After Makandal's death at the stake in 1761, the

Significant leaders from Haiti's history, eighteenth to nineteenth century (undated).

plantocracy passed measure forbidding slaves to "transfer" medicine to each other. Bellegarde wrote that the slaves' belief that Makandal had survived death played an important role in organizing later uprisings. The belief that Makandal had survived cemented "the trust of the slaves who had found in the Vodou cult a particularly strong ferment to exalt their energies, since Vodou—formed from diverse cults imported from Africa—had become less a religion than a political movement, a kind of 'black carbonarism' whose objectives were white extermination and black liberation."[11]

— One month after the Boukman insurrection, the traumatized whites and *affranchis* reached a temporary agreement in the Accord of Damiens, but two French commissions and 14,000 fresh troops proved unable to resolve the political and military conflicts that wracked Saint-Domingue. One-third of the 30,000 whites in Saint-Domingue fled to the United States, where they settled permanently and later worked *against* an independent Haiti. Spain invaded Saint-Domingue in 1792, and in 1793 England, at war with revolutionary France, invaded the island after lobbying by the white French colonists, who feared both the slave insurgency and the radicalization of France. —

— In a statement he later retracted, the French commissioner and parliamentary lawyer Léger-Félicité Sonthonax declared that "property in Saint-Domingue must belong to the blacks; they have earned it with the sweat of their brow." Faced with the treason of pro-British whites in Haiti, the Spanish and the English invasions, and widespread slave uprisings, Sonthonax was forced to abolish slavery on August 29, 1793. When he later passed 30,000 rifles to the newly freed slaves, he did so with these words: "This is your freedom; the one who will take this rifle back will want to enslave you anew."[12]

— Pierre-Toussaint Dominique (1743–1803), principal lieutenant of Boukman who was later known as Toussaint Louverture, abandoned the Spanish at this juncture and by 1795 had reconquered for France the towns occupied by Spain. Spain recognized French authority over eastern Hispaniola as well that same year in the Treaty of Basel. Toussaint defeated the English in 1797 and crushed a mulatto insurgency in the south, led by General André Rigaud, in which 15,000 mulattoes were massacred.

Toussaint had been a slave for forty years, had taught himself to read, and was universally recognized as a military and administrative genius. His political acumen led to six years in power as governor-general for life—the first of nine heads of state in Haitian history to be given a lifetime tenure. He signed the first diplomatic accords between Haiti and foreign powers in agreements reached with England and the United States. Toussaint also re-established civil order and some semblance of economic prosperity and opened Saint-Domingue to foreign commerce. Although his regime was highly militaristic and authoritarian, all segments of Haitian society seemed pleased with his administration. Toussaint was the first Latin American caudillo.

Under Toussaint's leadership, Saint-Domingue was only nominally a French colony, a situation that became particularly odious to Napoléon Bonaparte after Toussaint promulgated the constitution of 1801. In 1797, Saint-Domingue had had an integrated army of 51,000 men, 48,000 blacks and mulattoes and 3,000 whites. In 1802, incensed that France had lost control of Saint-Domingue, Napoléon sent his brother-in-law Charles Leclerc at the head of an expeditionary force of eighty-six ships and 22,000 veterans of French campaigns in Europe to unseat Toussaint and restore French control. Alarmed at the "danger" of blacks in power, England, Holland, Spain, and the United States gave tacit support to Napoléon's reconquest of the island, although Francophile Thomas Jefferson broke from that position when it became clear that French control of Saint-Domingue would secure the Louisiana territory for the French and facilitate their designs in North America. Toward the end of his life, Napoléon admitted that French interests would have been better served if he had been content to rule Saint-Domingue through Toussaint.

Napoléon's secret instructions were to imprison black and mulatto army officers, disarm the former slaves, and re-establish slavery. Despite heavy resistance during which Cap Français, Port-de-Paix, Saint-Marc, and Gonaïves were torched by their defenders, the Haitian effort collapsed. History records remarkable battles at Ravine-à-Couleuvres and Vertières as well as the militarily memorable retreat from the fort Crête-à-Pierrot, where the Haitian resistance fighter Marie-Jeanne Lamartinière distinguished herself.

Toussaint was arrested through treachery and deported to France. Upon embarking he declared, "With my overthrow, one has merely cut down the trunk of the tree of black freedom. But it will grow from its roots that are numerous and deep." He died in prison in the Jura Mountains on April 7, 1803.

After Toussaint was overthrown, the resistance movement started anew. Under General Donatien Rochambeau (1725–1807), the French intensified their systematic reign of terror in a vain attempt to eradicate the resistance. Once the black and mulatto officers realized that French racism would not abate, they defected to the bands of slave insurgents and strengthened the resistance movement with French training and military expertise. Soon the insurgents became unified under the command of the brilliant tactician General Jean-Jacques Dessalines (1758–1806).

On May 18, 1803, the present-day Haitian flag was created using the three colors of the French tricolor to symbolize the three classes of Haitian society. The white center of the French flag was torn, and the blue and the red were joined to represent the black and mulatto alliance forged in battle. There were seemingly other flags and an alternative Vodou interpretation for the Haitian flag, which given the Haitian cultural context was more sensible. Blue and red—the colors of the Vodou spirit Ogou-Feray, the cosmos, and Ezili Dantò— represent fire, war, and motherly love.

Aided by a yellow fever epidemic in the French ranks and England's renewed war with France, the insurgents achieved military victories that astounded European military experts, but the cost was great. As many as 100,000 Haitians may have been killed before the thirteen-year conflict finally came to an end in December 1803.

The document that was drafted as Haiti's declaration of independence was a radical version of the U.S. one, which the Haitians considered too timid, juridical, and moderate for a republic whose people had emerged from slavery. Dessalines's secretary, Félix Boisrond-Tonnerre, drafted a more belligerent act of independence, exclaiming, "To write [this act], we need a white man's skin for parchment, his skull for an inkwell, his blood for ink, and a bayonet for a pen."—

French colonialism and racism had generated a "race war" and had unified two antagonistic classes in the colony that otherwise would not have been allied. French intransigence had helped give birth to an independent "black" republic. In response to provocations from the French who still occupied Hispanic "eastern Haiti," as known by recently freed Haitians, the remaining 2,000–3,000 whites were murdered, except for physicians, priests, some artisans, and hundreds of Poles who chose to remain. Slavery and the terror that had been unleashed by Leclerc and Rochambeau against the insurgents ensured that the reprisals against the whites were violent and unrelenting.

 — Dessalines was named governor-general for life and made himself emperor of Haiti as Emperor Jean-Jacques I, after Napoléon had proclaimed himself emperor of France. Dessalines's empire was nonhereditary, and there was no aristocracy. Because the Haitians assumed that the French would try to regain control, the state was militarized, dozens of forts were erected (including the symbol of Haitian nationhood, the Citadelle Laferrière), and the capital was moved inland to the village of Marchand (now the town of Dessalines). Article 28 of the 1805 constitution declared: "At the first cannon shot, cities are destroyed, and the nation rises, as one."

 — The Haitian Constitution of 1805 summarized the new thrust and national policy of Dessalines's administration:

1. Article 12. No white, irrespective of his country, can land in this territory as a master and property owner and will not in the future be permitted to acquire any property.
2. Article 14. Any concept of color among children of an only and same family whose head of state is the father, having to necessarily cease, Haitians will be known henceforth by the generic name of blacks.
3. General Dispositions, Article 12. All property having belonged to a white Frenchman is by incontestable right confiscated to the benefit of the state.[13]

Beyond these measures, the constitution established freedom of worship, abolished any distinction between "legitimate" and "illegitimate" births, forbade the creation of a nobility (or class structure), and confiscated all land owned by the French, which was virtually three-fourths of the national territory. —

The assessment of Haitian philosopher Louis-Joseph Janvier (1855–1911) is particularly useful. Commenting indirectly about the authoritarian regime instituted by Dessalines, Janvier declared that "political freedom is an inferior good [compared to] national independence. Nations will sacrifice easily the former for the latter. They rightly prefer a national dictatorship ... to foreign domination, even if [that domination] proves to be liberal, the mildest in the world, promising wealth."[14] This perspective may explain Haitian patriotism and national pride even under subsequent dictatorships and the U.S. occupation.

Haiti was the first nation in the world to argue the case of universal freedom for all humankind, revealing the limited definition of freedom adopted by the French and American revolutions. In this respect, the Dessalines regime aided other revolutionary movements in the Western Hemisphere, but the policy adversely affected Haiti's early relations with Spain and the United States. When the Venezuelan revolutionary Francisco Miranda visited Haiti in 1805, Dessalines advised carnage and a scorched earth policy: "Behead heads, burn the cities." But if Haiti was seen abroad as radical, at home the former *affranchis* were unwilling to relinquish the privileges of their birth. Dessalines hoped to nullify their continuing demands for privileges, exclaiming, "And the poor blacks whose fathers are in Africa, won't they inherit anything?"

The alliance of slaves and *affranchis* that had led to independence was wrecked by unresolved class-based conflicts between a Franco-Haitian group of mostly mulatto property owners and an Afro-Haitian group of former slaves, three-quarters of whom had been born in Africa. These conflicts had their genesis in colonialism and have not been transcended; they continue to affect the course of social, economic, and political development in Haiti even today.

The founder Jean-Jacques Dessalines was assassinated on October 17, 1806, by former *affranchis* who felt that he had taken the side of the masses. His death brought to a close Haiti's revolutionary period; and a territorial split ensued between a northern kingdom, with Christophe, and a southern republic with Pétion, between 1807–1820.

POSTINDEPENDENCE CRISES: STRUCTURES, INSTITUTIONS, AND DEVELOPMENT

Two concerns immediately came to the fore at independence: the organization of a new government and the provision for national defense. Both were necessary for the new nation to stabilize and survive. At great cost, fortifications were erected throughout the country in anticipation of a French reinvasion. These forts, and the earlier colonial regime, were the precursors of the militarism that dominated the Haitian government until 1913; the government apparatus and the military were almost interchangeable for a century after independence. Intense competition between provincial power centers and the new capital, Port-au-Prince, for political and economic hegemony aggravated regional conflicts, and caudillism was a central feature of the Haitian system until the U.S. invasion in 1915.

In every phase of Haitian history, the authorities in power have had compelling reasons for devising an authoritarian structure, and since the colonial powers did not want to train slaves for self-government, they sought to keep control through terror. Because one of the prime reasons for having colonies is economic exploitation, colonialism is antidemocratic by definition.

In the postindependence phase, the requirements for securing freedom were subordinated to measures that established the control of the ex-*affranchis* over the former slaves. But controlling the political and economic life of the country necessitated "strong," authoritarian governments and repressive, authoritarian governments fueled popular discontent, which in turn generated further repressive measures.

The limits of the authoritarian government at any given time depended on financial resources, technology and economic infrastructure, and the viability of competing power centers. A repressive regime usually indicates not a strong but a weak government that is threatened by its own people and destabilized by challenges to its political legitimacy. Stable political institutions and government legitimacy appear to be closely related.

Following the precedent set up by Toussaint Louverture, the imperial constitution of 1805 established a military government.

Military generals made up the Conseil d'État (Council of State) and exercised legislative functions in a political system with a strong executive branch. These generals and their subordinates also exercised total judicial power within their districts.

One powerful and perhaps unintended result of the rampant militarism was the exclusion of women from participation in the evolving political system. Notwithstanding the significant contributions of mostly anonymous women, such as Marie-Jeanne Lamartinière, who had fought in the wars of independence and those before them who had helped to create the bands of Maroons, female participation in the political life of independent Haiti was largely thwarted by discriminatory institutions. The political role of women was generally confined to whatever personal power wives exercised over their husbands. The *bonté* of women—their kindness and strength of character—tempered the actions of often "intemperate" men. It is in this sense that history recorded the beneficent acts of Empress Claire-Heureuse, Queen Marie-Louise, and Joute Lachennais, the mistress of Haitian presidents Pétion and Boyer. The impact of women was and continues to be more significant in commerce, religion, and literature than in the political life of Haitian society.

An important task facing the new government was an economic reorganization that would provide for the interests of the emerging peasantry. The arduous process of assessing land titles started on the second day of national independence, January 2, 1804, and all property belonging to whites was nationalized, which made the state a huge landowner. Meanwhile, stringent vagrancy laws divided the population into urban artisans with skills in the mechanical arts and country dwellers who were to remain on the land. The only other alternative was soldiering.

Between 1809 and 1814, President Alexandre Pétion (1770–1818) and the Haitian Senate inaugurated the first comprehensive land reform program in Latin America. The net effect of the agrarian reform was to establish a system of small landholdings (*minifundia*) in southern Haiti for subsistence agriculture. In the northern state/kingdom of Henry Christophe (1763–1820; king 1811–1820), the latifundia pattern (large landed estates) persisted a while longer.

Using differing methods, the governments of Toussaint, Dessalines, Pétion, and Christophe re-established agricultural production, although not at colonial levels. The noted economist Celso Furtado observed that the Haitian peasantry had the highest standard of living of any country in nineteenth-century Latin America,[15] and a partial explanation for this prosperity is found in Haiti's isolation and the ostracism it suffered after independence. Haiti was not being plundered by outside interests. Rotberg observed that "as peasants more concerned to consume than to sell hard-won crops on a declining [Euro-American] market, Haitians—beholden to no one—began to grow maize, millet, and beans where they had once been compelled to tend sugar or other plantation crops. On the plantations that remained, too, there was a serious shortage of labor ... there was no shortage of land" (Rotberg, 1971: 68).

Like slavery in a previous period, the latifundia had become uneconomic under changing conditions and was fast becoming inoperable. A different economic base had to be found because the peasants began farming the hillsides and were exacerbating the soil erosion already begun by the cultivation of sugar under French rule. As a result, Haiti's main agricultural commodities shifted from sugar to coffee and to foodstuffs that were unfortunately mislabeled "subsistence" agriculture. The enduring popularity of President "Papa" Pétion was based on the land reform he enacted and his relatively mild rule.

The Haitian Revolution had briefly deflected the course of the economy. After the assassination of Dessalines in 1806, the leadership sought to restore the power of the *affranchis* and their control of the economy as landowners and merchants. Thus, the year 1806 marks, in my mind, the effective end of the mass-based Haitian Revolution. This fact is made very clear in the constitution the former *affranchis* wrote in December of that year.

Until the U.S. takeover in 1915, all Haitian constitutions forbade foreign ownership of land. This policy was obviously intended to restrict *whites* from owning land; a "law of the return" allowed any person of African descent to claim Haitian citizenship after arriving in Haiti. As products of the Enlightenment and capitalism, the new rulers inscribed the cardinal principles for their actions in the 1806 constitution: "Property, inviolate and sacred, is the right to enjoy and to dispose of one's belongings, of one's income, and the fruits of one's work and industriousness."

— At the dawn of the industrial age, the Haitian upper class, like that class throughout Latin America, hoped to promote both national economic growth and their private wealth through various schemes and control of the nation's government and apparatus. It is in this light that Dantès Bellegarde relates the establishment of a textile mill and weapons and munitions factories under government control in the first decade of the nineteenth century.[16] These efforts were short-lived and could not be sustained because of domestic factors and competition from more technologically advanced countries that wished to impose free trade. Here, the concise definition of development introduced by the scholar Walter Rodney is clearly relevant: "Development implies an increasing capacity to regulate both internal and external relationships."[17] In his effort to determine a nonethnocentric definition of development, Rodney emphasized the importance of a nation's ability to control its environment in terms of science and technology. Although this definition has great merit, a more complete and useful definition must include a concern for the *international* environment and specify the limits imposed by the policies of a developing nation's leadership.

EARLY FOREIGN POLICY: DIPLOMATIC AND TRADE RELATIONS

— Haiti's first diplomatic "victories" were accords signed in 1798 between Toussaint and England and the United States, which would in time open Haiti to these two powers. In return for British "protection," the British demanded complete control of the Haitian economy, as related by the West Indies' foremost historian, C.L.R. James: General Thomas Maitland "assured [Toussaint] of British protection, 'a strong squadron of British frigates would always be in his harbours or on his coasts to protect them,' and asked in return for the exclusive trade with the island" (James, 1963: 211). Having defeated the British on the battlefield as he had the Spanish, and applying the threat of Haitian pressure against British Jamaica, Toussaint outmaneuvered Maitland and received what he wanted, the abandonment of English demands. Toussaint realized that a trade monopoly would lead to economic dependence and possible territorial conquest.

Shortsightedly, the French colonists had argued against mercantilism and for free trade. In reality, neither mercantilism nor free trade could benefit a dependent colonial outpost whose export economy was not directed at meeting internal needs, and economic control eluded the French despite their best-laid plans. Ten years before the Haitian accord with the British, more than 2,500 of the 4,100 ships that visited Haitian ports were American (Rotberg, 1971: 32). In 1803, France sold the Louisiana Territory to the United States, largely as the result of instability in French North America caused by the Haitian Revolution (Logan, 1941: 142).

But the emergence of the Haitian state was not "business as usual" for Western governments. Haitian independence challenged the foundation of the existing international system in which enormous profits were made through colonization and slavery. The demonstrative effect of the Haitian Revolution in destabilizing other European colonies and the slave-holding southern United States created highly exaggerated fears among the metropolitan powers. In reality, slave revolts and native American uprisings had erupted continually since the Europeans first arrived in the hemisphere and occurred before Haitian independence as well as after it.

The United Kingdom, Holland, and the Scandinavian countries engaged in commercial trade with Haiti without the benefit of diplomatic recognition. Under Thomas Jefferson, the United States adopted a complex policy that took into account its own relatively weak international position and the desire of its slave owners to isolate Haiti and its revolutionary germ. Calling for Western solidarity, the French foreign minister Prince Charles Talleyrand wrote to U.S. Secretary of State James Madison in 1805, "The existence of a Negro people in arms, occupying a country it has soiled by the most criminal acts, is a horrible spectacle for all white nations."[18] The United States banned trade with Haiti in 1806 and renewed its embargo in 1807 and 1809.

— The fear that the Haitian Revolution would spread existed until the U.S. Civil War. A senator from Massachusetts, Edward Everett, declared: "I would cede the whole continent to whoever wants it: to England, France, or Spain. I would wish that it drowns to the bottom of the ocean before I see a part of white America converted into a continental Haiti by this horrible process of bloodletting and of desolation by which such a catastrophe could be realized."[19] In Everett's mind, the Haitian Revolution proved the existence of a "black menace," and slaves, and not slave owners, were responsible for the mayhem. This particular view of Haiti was also widespread among contemporary scholars, as one can see in the works of T. Lothrop Stoddard, John Fortescue, Edward Long, Bryan Edwards, Pierre Victor de Malouet, Moreau de Saint-Méry, and others.

Such an anti-Haitian view was extended to Latin America as a whole by a senator from South Carolina, Robert Y. Hayne: "You find men of color at the head of their armies, in their Legislative Halls, and in their Executive Departments .... There is not a nation on the globe with which I would consult on that subject [Haiti], least of all, the new Republics."[20] The anti-Haitian hysteria created serious misgivings in the United States about its participation in the first inter-American conclave, the Panama Congress of 1826, until Haiti's invitation to attend was withdrawn under U.S. pressure despite the assistance Haiti had given to Latin American independence movements. Haiti was also excluded from the "protection" afforded by the Monroe Doctrine, which was established by the U.S. government in 1823.

— Dessalines had received Francisco Miranda, an early leader of the northern Latin American independence movement, in 1805 and had allowed him to leave Haiti with a contingent of Haitian volunteers. In both 1815 and 1816, President Pétion welcomed Simón Bolívar, and Bolívar was influenced by the Haitian constitutional provision for a lifetime presidency. The historian Paul Verna related that in March 1816 Bolívar also left Haiti with men, money, munitions, weapons, and a small press for printing South American revolutionary literature and the proclamation abolishing slaves. Bolívar began by freeing his own 1,500 slaves, Haiti's only demand. A Haitian naval officer, Sévère Courtois, became a Colombian admiral, and supposedly, the design of both Venezuelan and the Colombian flags was based on the Haitian flag.

Despite assisting South American revolutionaries, Haiti was officially "neutral." It sought primarily to placate the United Kingdom and the United States, but its policy toward Spain was less accommodating, because Haiti did aid white Creoles, Spaniards born in the Americas, not Latin American slaves or Indians. In his independence day address, Dessalines stated:

> We must guard ourselves that the spirit of proselytism does not destroy our work. Let us allow our neighbors to breathe in peace, to live peacefully under the law *which they have made.* And let us not, firebrand revolutionaries, erect ourselves as the legislators for the Caribbean—and to give consistency to our glory—disturb the tranquillity of the islands that surround us. *They have not been, as the one we inhabit, washed by the innocent blood of their populations;* they have no vengeance to extract against the authority that protects them.[21]

The irony and sarcasm of Dessalines's remarks are clear, but so was the need for the fledgling Haitian nation to compromise in order to survive. Moreover, the Haitian leadership had interests that coincided with the interests of other Latin American leaders. Slave revolts in British, French, and Danish colonies could have had outcomes similar to Haiti's if other conditions had been met, but Haiti was not in a position to help meet those conditions.

The foundations of Haiti's foreign policy were laid in Article 9 of the Haitian Constitution of 1807: "The Government of Haiti declares to those powers that have colonies in its neighborhood its firm determination to give no disturbance to their governments. The Haitian people make no conquest outside their own islands, and Haiti confines itself to the preservation of its own territory." The Haitian leadership generally adhered to this pledge of non-interference, but the policy did distinguish between conquests and assistance. In this spirit, Haiti supported resistance movements in South America and the Dominican Republic and the Greek struggle against Turkish domination. Haiti's shrewd non-interventionist policy was necessitated by its assessment of conditions existing in the international system itself.

In a letter to the English abolitionist Thomas Clarkson, King Henry Christophe wrote: "For a long time past, my ships of war have been used only along the coasts and have never traveled any distance from our shores .... How can anyone [i.e., the plantocracy] do us the injury of suggesting that we should ever seek to upset the regime of the British colonies? Is it because these same colonies have experienced troubles and internal commotions?" (Griggs and Prator, 1968: 99). — Although formal British recognition of Haitian independence was slow in coming, the wording of a treaty in 1839 indicated diplomatic recognition. Once again, England tried to gain special commercial privileges with Haiti, but Haiti accepted only the resettlement in its territory of Africans seized in the illegal slave trade in the Caribbean Sea. —

— Because Haiti's independence had cost France its most lucrative colony, Haiti's efforts to gain recognition from that country proved difficult. In 1825, the French king Charles X granted a form of recognition that hinged upon Haiti's paying an indemnity of 150 million francs to former slave owners for the loss of their "property." King Louis-Phillippe and President Jean-Pierre Boyer of Haiti negotiated a treaty in 1838 for outright recognition and reduction of the indemnity to 60 million francs, the final payment of which was made in 1922.

Recognition of Haiti by Britain and France did not, however, induce the United States to grant recognition, despite the fact that even in 1820–1821 Haitian-U.S. trade amounted to $4.5 million. U.S. Secretaries of State John Quincy Adams and Henry Clay remained staunchly opposed to U.S. recognition of Haitian independence. —

In 1822, Haitian Secretary of State Joseph-Balthazar Inginac had addressed the following to Adams: "The United States government is the first to which Haiti feels compelled to report on its political situation, soliciting that an act of Congress ... recognize its independence."[22] Inginac's plea, and many more after it, went unanswered. The United States maintained that based on the terms of King Charles X's ordinance and the Treaty of 1838, Haiti's independence was illegitimate. The issue remained so delicate that, as mentioned earlier,

Haiti was not considered to be part of the Monroe Doctrine. Haiti and Liberia, the first and second modern states of African origin, had to await Abraham Lincoln and the 1862 emancipation of the slaves in the United States to receive formal diplomatic recognition from that country.

Meanwhile, negotiations between the Vatican and the Haitian government of Fabre-Nicolas Geffrard resulted in the concordat of 1860. This agreement consolidated the Roman Catholic church in Haiti, bolstered the prestige and international recognition of the Haitian upper class, promoted Western education, and intensified the persecution of Vodou.

A most significant domestic as well as international issue was "Spanish Haiti." Having passed into French control as a result of the Treaty of Basel in 1795, Santo Domingo had been declared independent in 1804 alongside Saint-Domingue. However, there was little enthusiasm for independence in Santo Domingo, whose population— one-fifth that of Haiti—comprised 50,000 whites, 50,000 mulattoes, and 25,000 blacks. That end of the island reverted to the Spanish crown in 1814 and presented a threat to the new country. The French authorities, then in control, had given carte blanche for enslaving Haitians along the border, which had led to an invasion of 25,000 Haitian troops in 1805; the sacking and razing of Puerto Plata, Isabela, Monte Christi, San Pedro de Macoris, and Santiago; and the death of numerous white Dominicans. Much of this destruction was repeated in 1821 when Santo Domingo came under Haitian domination for twenty-three difficult years. In 1844, Santo Domingo became the only territory—with the later exception of Panama in 1903—to win its independence from another American state.

The Dominican question was clearly tied to Haiti's national security. The substitution of European control by Haiti or, alternatively, the maintenance of an independent state in the eastern sector were the favored Haitian solutions. Haiti invaded the Dominican Republic several times after it was created, primarily as the result of national security imperatives and, less importantly, because of endogenous conditions such as land pressure. These repeated Haitian invasions created a legacy of hostility between the two nations, which helped lead to the 1937 massacre of as many as 30,000 Haitians during the rule of Dominican President Rafael Leonidas Trujillo.

When Spain suddenly reannexed Santo Domingo in 1861, Haitian President Geffrard issued the following blunt statement:

> None will contest that Haiti has a major interest that no foreign power establishes itself in the eastern part [of Hispaniola]. When two people inhabit the same island, their destinies in terms of foreign initiatives are necessarily interdependent. The survival of one is intricately linked to the survival of the other; each is duty-bound to guarantee security of the other .... These are the powerful motives why our constitutions, from our political beginnings, have declared continuously that the entire island should form a single state. And it was not an ambitious conquest that dictated such a declaration, but a profound commitment to our security. [Price-Mars, 1953: 2: 210–211]

Price-Mars and Logan both relate that the Haitian cabinet drafted a message to the queen of Spain that Colonel Ernest Roumain presented to the Dominican insurgents for a speedy resolution of the conflict. Faced with great difficulties at home and the determination of the Dominican resistance movement, Spain gave Santo Domingo its independence back in 1865.

These events had transpired during the Civil War in the United States. After that war, the United States initiated its expansionism in the Caribbean, and toward this end, U.S. Secretary of State William H. Seward visited the Danish Virgin Islands, the Dominican Republic, and Haiti. President Ulysses S. Grant even proposed to the U.S. Senate that the United States annex both Haiti and the Dominican Republic (Logan, 1968: 46).

In a report to the U.S. Navy Department in 1870, a vice admiral wrote the following:

> I said to His Excellency [the President of Haiti] that ... I would take advantage of my visit to inform him of the reason of my arrival in Port-au-Prince. I then told him that the instructions

I had received from my government consisted of this: that
negotiations were pending between the United States and the
Dominican Republic, and that during the duration of the
negotiations, the Washington government was determined to
use all its powers to prevent an intervention .... The President
and the Secretary of State [of Haiti] expressed the hope that
the friendly relations that now exist between the Haitian and
American governments would not be interrupted. They added
that, although they were conscious of their weakness, they
knew their rights and would maintain these as well as their
dignity, and that one should expect them to be the only judges
of the policy to follow.[23]

Grant's annexation initiative was defeated in the U.S. Senate in the
same year, but Grant continued his efforts to annex the whole island
until 1874. In the 1880s, the United States sought to gain control of
the island by other methods including an unsuccessful bid to establish
a naval base at Môle Saint-Nicolas and using Lebanese, Syrian, and
Palestinian petty merchants to pressure French and German
commercial interests on Hispaniola. Between 1857 and 1900, the U.S.
Navy intervened nineteen times on behalf of U.S. business interests
(Schmidt, 1971: 31).
— The conflicting interests of France, Germany, and the United States
in Haiti created an interesting division of neocolonial power. France
received about half of Haiti's exports and made massive loans to the
Haitian government to pay the indemnities to former slave owners. By
1903, the United States controlled 60 percent of Haiti's imports, but
in the words of U.S. Ambassador Mercer Cook, wanted to "control the
resources of the little country."[24] German interests controlled the
wholesale trade and made onerous short-term loans to insurgents
competing for Haiti's lucrative presidency. Germany was also involved
in the Haitian bank. Great Britain had largely abandoned Haiti to exploit
its interests in Central America. —
During the second half of the nineteenth century, Germany
developed an intriguing relationship with Haiti and other nations in
Central and South America. German commercial expansions occurred

largely through the intermarriage of German men with elite women, because these marriages effectively skirted protectionist business and real estate laws intended to ensure native control of capitalist development. The German language and that country's culture were influential in Haiti in the late nineteenth century, and even today several black upper-class Haitian families are of German descent.

The German government repeatedly intervened in Haiti on behalf of German-Haitian businessmen, and these interventions were facilitated by Haiti's open support for France during the Franco-Prussian War and World War I. In 1872 and again in 1897, German warships forced the Haitian government to pay large claims to German businessmen. The Haitian government requested that the United States invoke the Monroe Doctrine and prevent German intervention, but significantly, the United States refused to intervene.

Following the 1897 incident, the Haitian Foreign Affairs Ministry sought resolution of these crises through international arbitration and collective security arrangements, new international organizations, and even through invocation of the Monroe Doctrine and what Foreign Minister Solon Ménos called a new policy of *bon voisinage* ("good-neighbor policy"). Ménos's arguments for inter-American solidarity and collective security continued to infuse Haitian foreign policy for many decades. As a small, increasingly weak nation unable to keep pace in an increasingly technological world of industrial capitalism, Haiti had a vested interest in the development of strong international institutions that could preserve its independence. In keeping with this objective, Haiti participated actively in the League of Nations and, unlike most Latin American countries, paid all its foreign obligations to forestall foreign intervention (Schmidt, 1971: 43).

HAITIAN SOCIAL THOUGHT AND LITERATURE

Haitian social thought and literature, like those of Latin America in general, have sought to facilitate the process of nation building. In the Caribbean context, Haitian intellectuals were pioneers in the fields of social development, national integration, and foreign policy related to race relations. The seminal international relations and small-state leadership of Haitian intellectuals in the development of Caribbean social thought were largely a result of Haiti's early independence. In the words of author Pétion Gérome in 1890, Haitian literature tended to avoid the "coquettish affectation" of older European literatures (Bellegarde-Smith, 1985: 89). Haitian literature has generally been militant and politically conscious of the racism that Haiti has confronted in the international arena.

The earliest Haitian intellectuals expressed their grievances in economic terms similar to those expressed by the North American colonists against the British. White, mulatto, and black slave owners protested their exploitation by France, and some had been willing to ally themselves with England. After Haitian independence in 1804, the mulatto and black property owners defended their control of Haiti by arguments that were partly designed to placate the Western powers. In 1817, the prolific Haitian writer Valentin de Vastey advocated French and English colonization of Africa before it even occurred on the grounds that Africa "could be civilized only by conquest." Vastey is nonetheless considered a founder of Pan-Africanism because he believed that "one day, Africa will occupy the preeminent position in the world while Europe, jaded by centuries of civilization, will return to barbarism." In 1819, Juste Chanlatte commended England as being the first nation to concern "itself with developing African civilization" (Bellegarde-Smith, 1985: 196, 40).

After the Piquet Revolt in 1844, a plethora of skillful Haitian historians arose to defend elite control. A new Haitian bourgeoisie was emerging that was similar to those established by the Creole elites of Central and South America, and disparities in wealth and power between this bourgeois elite and the Haitian peasantry led to the social tensions and rural uprisings of the Caco Wars.

In an eleven-volume opus published in 1843, Beaubrun Ardouin argued in favor of mulatto hegemony over the entire Caribbean region. Ardouin perceived the struggle between the dominant Franco-Haitian group and the Afro-Haitian majority as a struggle between "superior" and "inferior" classes and maintained that the Haitian lower classes would have to submit to elite control in order to ensure their own development and Haiti's emergence as a powerful nation. In five volumes published between 1847 and 1904, the Haitian historian Thomas Madiou wrote that civilization was the result of the amalgamation of races and cultures. These Haitian historians, and others such as Joseph Saint-Rémy and Beauvais Lespinasse, argued against white racial supremacy but recognized European cultural superiority. They therefore favored rapid cultural assimilation to Western norms and advocated class harmony under elite tutelage.

Toward the turn of the century, the positivism popularized by French sociologist Auguste Comte and the British social thinker Herbert Spencer held sway in the regions of the globe that were in contact with Europe. This theory proposed that all knowledge was based on natural phenomena, and thus could be acquired empirically. The Haitian elite accepted positivism in much the same way that it had taken to liberalism and conservatism, partly as the "latest Paris fashion."

Demesvar Delorme made the connections seen by some as apish mimicry, when he stated in 1867 that "this civilization we want to introduce in the country will penetrate through public education. These are lights that ... will spread throughout the Republic healthy notions of order, law, and progress" (Bellegarde-Smith, 1985: 48). In a reprise of this theme, Jean Price-Mars, the great figure of the negritude movement, wrote in 1930 that "Haitian education has had but one objective ... which consists of producing highly educated men so that by their very existence and great culture they can refute the thesis upheld by others that the Negro is inferior."[25] The aim was not, however, to educate the population at large. Even today the curriculum in Haitian public and private education is "classical" in the tradition of nineteenth-century France, and little effort or money have been expended to develop public education in Haiti during the past 200 years. In 1988, approximately 80 percent of the Haitian population was illiterate. Significantly, much of the Haitian educational system is controlled by the Roman Catholic church and U.S. Protestant groups, but their influence has not enhanced the quality of education.

Racism and the impact of racism upon Haitian development reached its zenith at the turn of twentieth century. Racial prejudice and the belief in the innate inferiority of blacks had actually increased since the eighteenth century and were used to justify colonial expansion and Western industrialization. The Haitian intelligentsia responded to Western racism with articulate works on racial equality and calls for racial justice, but their works had little impact. In 1884 Louis-Joseph Janvier published *L'Egalité des races* [The equality of the races]. One year later, Anténor Firmin published his massive *De l'égalité des races humaines*, in which he argued that "Haiti must serve the rehabilitation of Africa." In *Monsieur Roosevelt* (1905), Firmin wrote that "the idea of race fatally dominates the issue of Haitian destiny. Insofar as blacks continue to be the subject of disdain for other men ... Haitians will never be taken seriously." Other Haitian scholars such as Hannibal Price and Justin Dévot also published compelling criticisms of Western racism and commented on the devastating impact of racial discrimination on Haitian social development. Most Haitian intellectuals, however, ascribed to the school of thought led by Bénito Sylvain, who argued against racism but for colonization.

The procolonial philosophy of most Haitian intellectuals in the early twentieth century was a radical departure from the revolutionary fervor of the "black Jacobins" who had led Haiti to independence in 1804. A counterrevolution in Haitian political thought had clearly occurred. Some of the fervor of the early Haitian revolutionaries would be reignited among the Haitian intelligentsia and peasant insurgents during the U.S. occupation.

In the wake of Haiti's political reconciliation with France in the 1820s, the pseudo-classicism of early Haitian literature gave way to Romanticism. This period saw the emergence of Haitian poetry and theater in the works of artists such as Ignace and Eugene Nau, Pierre Faubert, Liautaud Ethéart, and Coriolan Ardouin. Haitian Romanticism reached full bloom in the mid-nineteenth century with the works of the major poets Oswald Durand, Massillon Coicou, and Tertullien Guilbaud. Virginie Sampeur (1838–1919) emerged as Haiti's first important woman poet and also published essays on poetics, and the Haitian theater continued to develop with the plays of Henri Chauvet. *Stella*, the first Haitian novel, was written by Emeric Bergeaud several years before it was posthumously published in 1859. That novel and the several hundred Haitian novels produced since its publication are patriotic in theme, and Haitian theater has also been dominated by nationalism. Haitian poetry, however, has generally tended to be more universal.

A major Haitian literary circle called the Génération de La Ronde developed around a magazine of the same name and dominated Haitian literature. The novels of Frédéric Marcelin, Fernand Hibbert, and Justin Lhérisson, who wrote the words to the Haitian national anthem, *La Dessalinienne*, were social satires that contained biting criticisms of Haitian society. Antoine Innocent's epoch-making *Mimola* (1906) was a sympathetic depiction of Vodou culture and a precursor to the "peasant" or proletarian novels that later emerged as an important dimension of Haitian literature.

The best-known thinker and historian of La Ronde was Dantès Bellegarde. With almost no originality but great clarity, Bellegarde synthesized the ideology that had animated the Haitian elite throughout the nineteenth century. Pro-Western and pro-French, he was nonetheless a nationalist who continually warned Haitians about the possible loss of their nation's independence. With foreboding humor and foresighted alarm, Bellegarde warned his countrymen in 1907 that "God is too far, and the United States too close" (Bellegarde-Smith, 1985: 62). Eight years later the United States seized Haiti, and the military occupation lasted nineteen years. The U.S. occupation was supposed to ensure elite control of the Haitian peasantry and foreign control of the Haitian elite. Ironically, however, the occupation revived both the peasant resistance movement and the nationalistic passions of the Haitian intelligentsia.

In the broad sweep of U.S. history and foreign affairs, the frequent U.S. interventions and eventual occupation of Haiti were minor episodes of fleeting significance. In Haiti, however, these invasions and the occupation were watershed events. The occupation realigned Haiti with the United States but also changed the way in which many intellectuals defined themselves. Facing a racist invader, the Haitian intelligentsia developed profound racial pride. This change in Haitian racial attitudes was especially visible in literature and scholarship and in the reassessment of the Vodou religion, the Kreyol language, and the African heritage generally.

Led by a group of writers known as the *génération de l'occupation*, these intellectuals emphasized the development of a distinct Haitian national identity and advocated control of the national economy. The *génération de l'occupation* quickly expanded into an intellectual and political movement called indigenism, which greatly stimulated the growth of negritude, or the international black cultural movement. The movement's "uncle" was Price-Mars, Haiti's major twentieth-century thinker. In his celebrated *Ainsi parla l'oncle* [So spoke the uncle], published in 1928, Price-Mars delineated the basis for a new cultural order in which race was seen as a social construct evolving in a historical context in accord with more recent scientific studies of racial groupings. Most Haitian intellectuals became "Marsists" and adopted Price-Mars's vision. Influenced by the French philosopher Henri Bergson, Price-Mars did not take the more extreme positions of some of his disciples, such as Presidents François Duvalier of Haiti and Léopold Sédar Senghor of Senegal.

The major Haitian historian to chronicle the U.S. occupation was Roger Gaillard. His seven-volume *Les Blancs débarquent* [The whites land], published in 1974, set the standard for subsequent research on the U.S. occupation. Suzy Castor, another Haitian historian, set the precedent for exacting scholarship. The leading literary critics included Ghislain Gouraige, who admirably captured the psychological climate of Haiti over 200 years in his 1974 *Diaspora d'Haiti et l'Afrique* [The Haitian diaspora and Africa]; Pradel Pompilus, author of the main text on literature; and Jean Fouchard, who wrote major works on language and the arts.

These and many other publications represented a significant increase in the analytical sophistication of Haitian scholarship. Even earlier scholarship has been noted for its objectivity in comparison to similar European and American works on Haiti over the course of time. Until 1951, Haiti had produced more books per capita than any other Latin American nation. The U.S. critic Edmund Wilson observed "that the literature of Haiti ... is highly sophisticated and has a long and sound tradition."[26]

One novel Wilson did not like was Jacques Roumain's *Gouverneurs de la rosée* (1944), translated by Langston Hughes and Mercer Cook as

Masters of the Dew (1947). Wilson considered *Masters of the Dew* to be the predictable proletarian novel. Roumain, a wealthy aristocrat whose grandfather had been president of Haiti, was a gifted poet, novelist, and ethnologist who cofounded the Haitian Communist party with Max L. Hudicourt, another aristocrat. Although few Haitian novels have been translated from the original French, *Masters of the Dew* has been translated into seventeen languages and is generally considered the best novel yet produced by a Haitian author.

During the occupation era, few novels were published as compared with the postoccupation era. Among the major novelists one may cite Jacques Stephen Alexis, who published three well-received works, and Edris Saint-Amant, the author of the remarkable *Bondieu rit* [God laughs]. Few of these Haitian novels have been translated into English, but among those that have been translated are the works of Pierre and Philippe Thoby-Marcelin. Other major figures include Jean-Baptiste Cinéas, Roger Dorsinville, Anthony Phelps, Jean Métellus, Anthony Lespès, Lyonel Trouillot, Pierre Clitandre, Danny Laferrière, and Emile Ollivier. Some, such as Frankétienne, now write in Kreyol, and there is also an excellent production of poetry in that language, such as that of Félix Morisseau-Leroy and Georges Sylvain. Poetry has always been the strongest element in Haiti's written literature, and it is worth mentioning a few of the major names, such as Léon Laleau, Jean F. Brierre, and René Depestre. In the field of Kreyol studies and linguistics, one must cite a pioneer, Yves Déjean, and the contemporary work done by Michel de Graff, and Hughes St-Fort.

Major women writers in Haitian literature include poets, novelists, and playwrights such as Marie Chauvet, Paulette Poujol-Oriol, Mona Guérin, Marie-Thérèse Colimon, Nadine Magloire, Adeline Moravia, Jan Dominique, Yanick Lahens, Edwidge Danticat (the major voice in Haitian-American literature), and Liliane Dévieux-Dehoux. The emergence of these women writers is finally bringing recognition of the role of upper- and middle-class women in Haitian literature and society, and their numbers have increased dramatically since the 1930s, years that saw an expansion of the educational facilities for women.

La Ronde, indigenism, and negritude were efforts to go from the particular to the universal. Despite the many works of real value, however, the enormous body of Haitian literature and scholarship remains largely unknown outside Haiti—or outside the small literary group inside Haiti. The international obscurity of Haitian literature stands in contrast to the worldwide attention that Latin American writers have received in recent years.

Haiti's insularity and lack of power have made it an island in a literal as well as a geographical sense. Jean-Paul Sartre defined the radical self-acceptance and celebration of Blackness in Haitian literature as "antiracist racism." Nevertheless, recent Haitian literacy movements have fostered the development of a Haitian national identity, and its evolution has paralleled the development of other Black literature in similarly oppressed situations, such as the Harlem renaissance in the United States, Afro-Cuban literature, and the indigenist movements in Mexico and Puerto Rico. This development has also been related to political movements, such as the Pan-Africanism of W.E.B. DuBois and Kwame Nkrumah, and the Marcus Garvey movement in an Antillean-American-African cultural stream that has flowed through Europe since the seventeenth century. Haitian intellectuals also anticipated the Martinican Frantz Fanon, the Black Liberation movement, and the African and West Indian independence movements.

From their antislavery and pro-emancipation stance and thwarted efforts to prove human equality regardless of race, Haitian intellectuals rediscovered their own worth through a collective search for African civilization. This reaffirmation of Black consciousness was largely the result of Haitian adaptation to new forms of cultural oppression and economic exploitation. Haitian intellectuals thus came to reject the "whitening" process inherent in cultural assimilation, as in this extract of a poem by Léon Laleau:

> Borrowed customs, borrowed sentiments
> From Europe. Do you not feel the sufferance,
> The Despair, of taming with words from France
> This heart that comes to me from Senegal?

The same theme resounds in the following stanza about international solidarity by Jean F. Brierre:

When you bleed, Harlem, my handkerchief is crimson.
When you hurt, your lament is prolonged in my song.
With the same fervor, in the same black evening,
Black brother, we both dream of dreaming.[27]

The not-so-perceptible change from engagé to militant literature was equally pronounced among Haitian social scientists. Thus virtually all Haitian intellectual production, as described by Gouraige, has been a "literature of tendencies," that is, a literature that shows slight rather than extreme differences from one epoch to the next. This observation is further supported by the upper- and middle-class origins of most Haitian intellectuals and by the steady deterioration of Haiti's position in the international system over time.

Haitian writers are continuing to produce a wealth of scholarship. On Vodou, one notes the works of J.C. Dorsainvil, Louis Mars, Milo Rigaud, Michel S. Laguerre, Claudine Michel, Réginald D. Crossley, Leslie Desmangles, Patrick Bellegarde-Smith, and Laennec Hurbon. Lorimer Denis, François Duvalier, Colbert Bonhomme, Emmanuel C. Paul, and other new writers with a primarily Marxist perspective have produced important studies on color and class. A very significant author who uses Vodou, but extends its scope to include the significant area of mythology and national culture, is Maximilien Laroche. Madeleine Sylvain-Bouchereau, Ertha Pascal-Trouillot, Mireille Neptune Anglade, Régine Latortue, Carolle Charles, Kathleen Balutansky, and Ghislaine Rey Charlier have written important works on the role of Haitian women. The study of Haitian history and socio-economic development has been led by writers such as Rémy Bastien, Patrick Bellegarde-Smith, Alex Dupuy, Gérard M. Laurent, Leslie F. Manigat, Hubert de Ronceray, Gérard Latortue, Cary Hector, Jean-Jacques Honorat, Claude Moise, Leslie Péan, Michel-Rolph Trouillot, Frantz Voltaire, Robert Fatton, Jr., and the geographer Georges Anglade. Many of these Haitian scholars were in exile because of their opposition to the dictatorship and some decided to return to Haiti and help rebuild the nation's intellectual community together with people who chose to stay and fight in Haiti.

Ironically, the new "universalism" found in literature has in part benefited from the exile of Haitian intellectuals because it provided them with access to universities in Africa, Western and Eastern Europe, and North and South America. Speaking of the exiled Haitian poet Roussan Camille, René Piquion observed:

> In cosmopolitan Paris, he sensed the palpitations of the ardent souls of the Afro and Native American masses. Admire these brown bohemians, his friends: the black Brazilian da Silva, the Cuban Eduardo Aviles Ramirez, the Panamanian Jorge Tulio Royo, the Peruvian Guillermo Benavides, the Honduran Rosando Martinez .... In the lavish City of Lights, he saw the bourgeoisie on the eve of its demise, dancing on a volcano. Then, in the lower-class sections of cities, he heard with anguish the wail of the oppressed.[28]

The international solidarity of Third World intellectuals is not new. The history of the "first black republic" spanned colonialism and neocolonialism, and it is not surprising that the Haitian intelligentsia became radicalized in the process. The internationalism that marked Haiti in the early nineteenth century, as seen in its Pan-American foreign policy and its support of Greek independence against Turkey in 1821, later reemerged in the Pan-Caribbeanism of Anténor Firmin, the Pan-Africanism of Bénito Sylvain and Alfred Nemours, and the negritude movement inspired by Jean Price-Mars.

The development of a true left wing in the Haitian body politic was long thwarted by elite hegemonic control but finally emerged, partly in response to U.S. interventions. Haitian nationalism was also strengthened by U.S. domination, and Haitian intellectuals have used racism to transcend race. As the French critic Auguste Viatte observed, these new writers "do not really claim to belong to any particular continent, nor race, except to intensify their revolutionary action."[29] Commenting on the apparent paradox between Haitian nationalism and internationalism, the Afro-American historian Rayford W. Logan has said that "a nationalist understands ... that his aims cannot be achieved solely within his own country."[30]

The importance of the Haitian diaspora, particularly in the United States and Canada, is of increasing significance to Haiti. Two scholars, in particular, have written works on this, Léon Pamphile and Flore Zyphir.

In this section, I have not attempted to analyze the oral literature or the popular culture of the Haitian peasantry. The overthrow of the long-standing Duvalier dictatorship in February 1986 through a provincial and rural uprising indicated that an alliance between the Haitian peasantry and the Haitian intelligentsia was developing for the first time in 200 years. Such an alliance failed to materialize even during the U.S. occupation, however, and some of the same foreign and domestic influences that prevented or tried to prevent the formation of Haitian national unity in 1791, 1915, and 1986 are still powerful forces in Haitian national life.

Chapter 3

Modernization and Dependence:
Twentieth-Century Haiti

Makak pa jam kwè pitit-li lèd.
("A monkey never thinks her baby's ugly.")

—Haitian proverb

CAUDILLISM REFERS TO A SYSTEM OF PERSONAL AND MILITARY POWER exercised by a single individual who commands the loyalty of a network of people in a specific region or country. Caudillism inherently involves elements of regionalism and a quasi-feudal relationship between a local elite and other groups within a homogeneous regional population. These elements are anchored in deep-rooted historical traditions and are bolstered by significant economic and political grievances among regional groups against centralizing forces that are often viewed as "modern."

A problem for social analysts lies in the evaluation of the social origins of caudillism to determine whether it is a social system based on feudal class relations or a social structure that defines the leadership of an essentially popular movement, because the distinction between the two conceptions of caudillism will influence the analysis. In the first instance, caudillism is a primitive historical stage to be transcended by modernization; in the second instance, it is a quasi-permanent, ill-defined struggle for social justice.

CAUDILLISM AND MODERNIZATION

In the Haitian case, caudillism occurs both as a feudalistic class system and as a structure for popular movements, with some overlap. This dualism renders the task of the social historian horrendously complex. Traditional elite historians, for example, saw the 1913 election of Michel Oreste as the first civilian president of Haiti as a victory for a modernizing elite over more-traditional nationalist generals. But the same event could have been interpreted as a struggle between nationalists, populists, and protectionists on the one hand and liberals and free traders on the other.

The existence of caudillism in Haiti in the nineteenth century meant that all was not well in the body politic. And because all was not well, the on-again and off-again uprisings in the countryside probably indicated dissatisfaction with the status quo rather than support for it, which would have indicated "true" caudillism. The fact that many caudillos seemed to be natural leaders who had garnered the respect of their constituency, or were Vodou priests, would seem to reinforce the argument. This fact was never clearer than during the guerrilla war that accompanied the U.S. occupation of Haiti when, despite their best efforts, the Americans could never prove that Haitian peasants were coerced into joining the ranks of the rebellion.

The increase in the level of Haiti's incorporation into the worldwide economic system of capitalism seemed to be accomplished with stronger social dislocation and stronger expressions of discontent as the years went by. After the 1880s, Haiti became more tightly integrated into the international economic vortex, and major domestic developments such as the advent of banking, cable and postal communications, and the award of fifty or more contracts to foreign enterprises occurred during the presidencies of Lysius-Félicité Salomon (1879–1888) and Florvil Hypolite (1889–1896). These developments inaugurated massive foreign influence in education, the economy, and all other areas of Haitian life. As will be seen, this period was crucial in Haiti's national development (or lack thereof) and culminated in the military takeover of Haiti by the United States in 1915. Meanwhile France, Germany, and the United States vied for control of Haitian trade and resources. A large influx of Palestinian, Lebanese, and Syrian merchants altered retail trade patterns and also introduced a permanent Caucasian element in the population, but this influx had little effect on Haitian culture and mores. The three major Western powers quickly gained control of Haiti's commerce.

The members of the Haitian elite were acquiring more education at home and abroad. By the late 1800s, public education was free and, by law, universal. The emergence of the Liberal and the National parties brought organized parties to Haitian politics for the first time. The bloody battles between these two parties hid the fact that they represented two factions of the elite whose platforms actually differed very little.

The Brazilian economist Celso Furtado has implied that during the period between independence in 1804 and foreign penetration of the Haitian economy in the 1830s, the standard of living of the peasants was higher in Haiti than anywhere else in Latin America. Before foreign penetration, the Haitian economy was characterized by little foreign commerce, the production of foodstuffs, and a *de facto* land distribution pattern that provided many peasants with sufficient arable land to raise enough food for their extended families. After foreign penetration, however, Haitian agriculture gradually moved away from food production to the cultivation of commercial cash crops such as coffee, sugarcane, and tobacco. Foreign interests in Haiti also led to land consolidation schemes to form cash-crop plantations, concentrating the growing population into smaller land areas. These combined factors led to a fall in the peasants' standard of living and an increase in rural unrest. Thus the decline in the Haitian standard of living appears to have been related to foreign penetration of the Haitian economy.

Economic statistics for the period reflect the failure of the native Haitian elite to develop as an autonomous capitalist class, despite its best efforts and the protectionist legal system it devised. Between 1891 and 1908, Haitian businesses lost considerable influence in the Haitian economy. In 1891, 68 percent of the leading merchants were Haitian; seventeen years later, 50 percent were non-Haitian, with the highest concentrations in banking, the export trade, and shipping (Plummer, 1984: 128–130). Virtually all non-Haitian merchants were allegedly involved in contraband, which deprived the state of revenue. As their role in Haitian business and commerce continued to diminish, increasing numbers of Haitians entered the lucrative field of politics. Chased out of business, the elite concentrated on politics and found that corrupt practices were necessary if they were to make a living. It is significant that the same behavior in business would have been considered legitimate.

Internationally, the link between politics and commerce was strong. The social scientist Brenda Plummer has observed:

> Therefore the buildup on Haiti was part of a global struggle for markets and political influence among the great powers .... France utilized the ties of language and culture .... Its liberal lending policy encouraged dependence on the part of needy nations. Germany's self-promotion relied greatly on the efficiency of its enterprises and the high quality of its manufactures. Britain linked its Caribbean trade to traditional textile exports .... The United States, while preserving commercial preponderance in the area, employed the Monroe Doctrine to reduce European challenges to its power. [Plummer, 1984: 130–131]

These states intervened militarily on the advice of their business people, and the interventions by Great Britain, Germany, and the United States were particularly severe. As mentioned in the previous chapter, the United States intervened in Haiti nineteen times between 1857 and 1900 (Schmidt, 1971: 31).

The Haitian poet laureate Oswald Durand (1840–1906) addressed these lines to the Haitian people:

> Listen,
> and hear the homicidal
> bronze!
> children
> of eighteen-o-four
> is he back to trample

our orange-scented soils
to flex again liberticidal arms?
Then, rise, firebrand
now as then: towns burn
but the nation stand!
Stand! and their vile troops
will admire you then.[1]

General Smedley D. Butler's personal testimony regarding the events described above adds to the assessments of the poet and the political scientists:

> I spent thirty-three years and four months as a member of ... the Marine Corps. And during that period, I spent most of my time being a high-class muscleman for Big Business, for Wall Street, and for the bankers .... Thus, I helped make Mexico ... safe for American oil interests in 1914. I helped make Haiti and Cuba a decent place for the National City Bank to collect revenues .... I helped purify Nicaragua for the international banking house of Brown Brothers in 1909–1912. I brought light to the Dominican Republic for American sugar interests in 1916: I helped make Honduras "right" for American fruit companies in 1903.[2]

In the rapidly declining situation, Haitian women played an unwittingly negative role, a role assigned to them by the prejudices of their society. The desire to "Haitianize" business and commerce was at odds with the prowhite bias inherited from colonialism. Haitian women married Europeans for prestige; the Europeans married them largely to achieve legal access to the Haitian economy. Despite the protectionist laws to enact and sustain Haitian control—honored in the breach—the Haitian economy was being increasingly dominated by foreign or quasi-foreign groups whose allegiance to Haitian interests was suspect. As a result, Haitian laws on nationality are among the most stringent in the world. For a time, Haitians who married foreigners—who hoped to thus circumvent Haitian laws on land

Late nineteenth- and early twentieth-century example of Haitian architecture.
An upper-class mansion being used as U.S. headquarters during the occupation.
Photo: United States National Archives.

ownership—lost their Haitian citizenship and could thus become stateless persons. Conversely, in the first decade of this century, 10,000 individuals claimed foreign citizenship, and that number included Haitians who had managed to acquire dual or triple citizenship for additional protection in their business dealings.

The Germans married women of the upper class, but sensitive to race, Americans did not seek the same remedy. They penetrated the Haitian market by working through the *Syriens* (the Haitian term for all Middle-Easterners) and Afro-Americans in Haiti. The net results of these cross-national marriages and the foreign penetration of the Haitian economy included a more cosmopolitan elite with less power, an aggravation of the "color question," increased wealth inequality between the elite and the peasantry, and the growing dominance of Port-au-Prince over provincial centers. In view of the pernicious impacts of foreign penetration, perhaps Haitian caudillism, if it had been allowed to continue, might have led to a more equitable sharing of power among Port-au-Prince and regional elites and their clients.

THE U.S. OCCUPATION, 1915–1934

Conflicts between the privileged elite and the impoverished masses in Haiti never ended. The grand alliance between slaves and *affranchis* had succeeded in overthrowing the French and establishing Haitian independence in 1804, but the old class antagonisms quickly reemerged after the French had been thrown out. The nation's founder, Jean-Jacques Dessalines, remained loyal to the egalitarian spirit of the Haitian Revolution and sided with the former slaves. His assassination in 1806 signaled the advent of a counterrevolution that would continue and consolidate throughout the nineteenth century.

Political instability and perpetual turmoil in Haiti were the results of crosscutting cleavages and dichotomies that divided the Haitian people and undermined national unity. Class antagonisms were reflected in the divisions between French-speaking and Kreyol-speaking populations, black and mulatto color distinctions, Roman Catholic and Vodou religious groups, and African and Western cultural influences as well as in regional conflicts and power struggles. In a sense, these conflicts and divisions still constitute the sum total of the nation's domestic problems and as such are analyzed throughout this book. Here it suffices to say that Haiti's process of developing a national identity may have lagged behind the fact of its statehood: Haiti became an independent nation in 1804, but the formation of its national identity may have taken the better part of the nineteenth century.

The development of a Haitian national unity was chronically thwarted by periods of extreme political instability followed by periods of severe dictatorial repression. In the two years 1844–1846, four different presidents took office; in 1849 President Faustin Soulouque established a dictatorship and ruled as Emperor Faustin I until 1859. During the first part of the twentieth century, Haiti had seven presidents in seven years; this crisis culminated in the dictatorial occupation of Haiti by the U.S. Marine Corps between 1915 and 1934 and saw the inception of "Haitian fascism." Martial law was enforced throughout the U.S. occupation, and the Haitian legislature was dissolved in 1917, not to reconvene until 1930. In a six-month period in 1956–1957, five Haitian governments followed one another in rapid succession until the United States helped to install the dynastic Duvalier dictatorship, which ruled Haiti with an iron fist until its overthrow in 1986. The demand for more democracy in Haiti has always resulted in more rather than less repression as a ruling regime answers challenges to its control with even more repressive measures to maintain the status quo.

— The first major peasant revolt occurred in southern Haiti forty years after independence. The historian J.-C. Dorsainvil wrote that "the peasants in the south tired of waiting for reforms and happiness."[3] A woman, Louise Nicolas, is credited with organizing the movement in 1844. The members of the movement soon became known as the "suffering army" (due to an acute lack of provisions and material), and *Piquets* (they carried picks as weapons). The Piquet Revolt had two overarching objectives: first, to suppress the politically dominant mulattoes and place a black in the presidency; second, to dispossess the rich and distribute their landholdings and the large state lands to the peasants. Jean-Jacques Acaau, Dugué Zamor, Jean Claude, Jeannot Moline, Antoine Pierre, Augustin Cyprien, Louise Nicolas, and other peasant leaders led the *Piquets* in defeating government troops in major battles at Les Cayes, Jérémie, and l'Anse-à-Veau. The revolt was soon quelled, however, by the mulatto general Fabre-Nicolas Geffrard and the black general Jean-Baptiste Riché, both of whom later became presidents of the republic. —

— The Piquet Revolt had two major outcomes, neither of which advanced the peasants' interests. First, the *Piquets* unwittingly stimulated an extraordinary outpouring of reactionary literary justifications for elite control, and the Haitian literature on history and social thought was the first in the entire Afro-world. —

— Second, the revolt engendered a political policy in Haiti called *la politique de doublure*, according to which controllable, preferably elderly and illiterate black generals were made president of the republic to create the illusion that the government was in fact reflective of the Haitian people and in league with their interests.[4] The aged black generals who became presidents of Haiti were usually heroes of the wars of independence and were popularly perceived as heads of state. In reality, however, they were usually installed as the pliant puppets or stage-managed stooges of the elite. *La politique de doublure* was thus highly effective as a system of political psychology that mollified the overwhelmingly black population while perpetuating elite control, an example of the fact that the history of Haitian politics is largely a study of smoke and mirrors.

The breakdown of the Haitian political system began either in 1844 with the outbreak of the Piquet Revolt or in 1859 with the overthrow of Soulouque. Dantès Bellegarde stated that the period between Soulouque's fall in 1859 and the final defeat of peasant insurgents by the United States in 1929 was one long "caco war" that lasted seventy years. Cacos were northern peasant insurgents whose loose organization and presumably ill-defined goals caused them to be easily labeled as "bandits" by the U.S. military and State Department. In this book, *cacoism* is used to mean the entire range of peasant resistance, particularly armed resistance, against that group's perceived foes. Viewed in this context, Haitian political instability was perhaps not so much the result of stagnation as the result of a dynamic interaction between antagonistic social classes, the political system, and the economy.

The steady erosion of the peasants' standard of living throughout the nineteenth century, the simultaneous and rapid decline of the commercial power of the Haitian elite, and the concurrent increase in government corruption made any restructuring of the political system even more impracticable. The struggle for economic hegemony among the United States, France, Germany, and Great Britain into Haitian national life had shifted the major problem in Haiti away from questions of the distribution of wealth and power among the elite and peasants to a situation in which there was little wealth and power to distribute. The problem of class poverty was eclipsed by the problem of national poverty.

The same spirit that had animated the revolutionary slaves in 1791–1804 may have animated the insurrectionary peasants in 1844–1929. The continuous caco uprisings of that period indicated popular dissatisfaction with the status quo, and the instability of the Haitian governments reflected a search for some political solution. The peasantry had not been completely powerless in its struggle to change the status quo, as is indicated by the quasi-permanent turmoil, the introduction of the *politique de doublure*, and the ferocity of the later effort on the part of the United States to wipe out the peasant rebel movement through military occupation. Between the end of the eighteenth and the beginning of the twentieth centuries, however, Haiti's position in the international arena had changed significantly. Feared as a bastion of revolutionary black power in 1804, the economic competitive advantage of the industrialized nations by 1900 ensured the demise of Haitian capitalism. Haiti's military capacity against foreign incursions—or to carry out invasions of its own—had also declined. Whereas in the 1800s the Haitians had enjoyed the tactical advantage of retreating into a wooded interior beyond the range of naval firepower, by the early twentieth century the aerial bombing undertaken by the United States had rendered this tactic obsolete.

Following nineteen interventions and earlier attempts to annex Môle Saint-Nicolas as a naval base, the United States launched a full-scale military occupation of Haiti in 1915 that would continue until 1934. The immediate causes of the occupation were two separate disputes. The first was between the Haitian Banque Nationale (National Bank), owned mostly by French investors with some U.S. and German money, and the New York National City Bank. The second dispute was between the Haitian government and the U.S.-owned Haitian National Railroad.

The United States had applied pressure to gain control of Haitian customhouses—as it had previously done in the Dominican Republic and elsewhere—but these provided the Haitian government's sole source of revenue and, until 1915, serviced the foreign debt to the tune of 80 percent, leaving 20 percent of revenues for all other state expenditures. Although under foreign control, the National Bank acted as the state's treasury, and it devised a plan to starve the Haitian government into submission so that it would accede to U.S. demands. One U.S. envoy to Haiti gave a succinct summary of the 1914 crisis in a report to the U.S. Department of State:

The government will find it most difficult to operate. The statement that the government, in the absence of a budget convention, will be without income is based upon the fact that ... the bank is designated as the sole treasury of the government, and as such receives all moneys of the government, and further is empowered to hold such moneys intact until the end of the fiscal year .... It is just this condition that the government, when confronted by such a crisis, would be forced to ask the assistance of the United States in adjusting its financial tangle and that American supervision of the customs would result. [Balch, 1927: 15]

In 1914, the bank impounded all Haitian government revenues. At the bank's request, the USS *Machias* then landed a contingent of marines to seize the country's gold for "safekeeping" in New York.

The U.S.-owned National Railroad had secured a concession to build twenty-one sections of railway between Port-au-Prince and Cap-Haitien, a concession that included extraordinary tax advantages and the acquisition of vast landholdings along the tracks. The railroad built three unconnected segments, then alleged that political unrest was interfering with its work. The Haitian government refused to pay the staggering bill given it. The two main players, the National Bank and the National Railroad, were connected in the person of Roger L. Farnham, vice-president of the National City Bank, the U.S. State Department's main adviser on Haiti, and an associate of Franklin D. Roosevelt, and John McIlhenny of Louisiana, of Tabasco sauce fame.

The documents announcing the occupation were drafted ahead of the invasion; the date had been left blank. The pretext for the invasion was the brutal assassination on July 27, 1915, of President Vilbrun Guillaume Sam, who had ordered the execution of 173 of his closest political enemies. Interestingly, the president was murdered because U.S. warships had been sighted off the Haitian coast. It was known that the United States had helped Sam, and the belief was strong that he would be protected by the imminent invasion. Admiral William Caperton landed his troops on July 28, 1915, "to protect property and preserve order."

President Dartiguenave and his U.S. bodyguards during the occupation (c. 1917).
Photo: United States National Archives.

Several sectors in Haiti supported the U.S. occupation. The mulatto elite hoped that the United States would pacify the country, dismantle *la politique de doublure* and restore the mulattoes to power, and invest heavily in the Haitian economy, as it had in Cuba and Puerto Rico. The French-controlled Roman Catholic hierarchy embraced the U.S. occupation in the hope of realizing the church's dream of eradicating Vodou. Both the French and the Americans appeared to be intent upon imposing their own cultures and conceptions of "civilization" on the Haitian people and society. Foreign merchants in Haiti expected that the occupation authorities would grant them commercial concessions that would increase their business. All were ultimately disappointed: The U.S. occupation brought neither economic investments nor political stabilization at expected levels. The Vodou culture was strengthened rather than weakened when it aligned itself with patriotic resistance against the U.S. occupation, and the occupation forces saw the foreign merchants as native Haitians and granted them no concessions.

The United States installed Philippe-Sudre Dartiguenave as the new president of Haiti two months after the invasion. In *Le Moniteur*, the official government gazette, Dartiguenave declared that the Haitian "land tenure system could not remain as it was, since it discriminated gravely against the well-intentioned and positive action of foreign capital."[5] Louis Borno, the second president installed under U.S. rule in 1922, said that "we had but [two] choices: either total disappearance [as a nation] or redemption with the help of the United States. I preferred that redemption. If I must sacrifice my life for it, I am ready."[6] The third president, Sténio Vincent, a "nationalist" during whose term the U.S. occupation forces withdrew from Haiti, wrote in his memoirs that "the conditions under which the American government intervened in Haiti opened an easy path for its civilizing influence .... The most intransigent patriots ... came to consider it a necessary evil ... faced with the evidence of the results."[7] Although these men were held in contempt by both the Americans and most Haitians, they were maintained in power. A U.S. official in Haiti during the occupation wrote that "there were, of course, a few of this class who were prompted by their conception of patriotism to favor U.S. control as necessary for the good of the country." Some members of the Haitian elite, however, protested the occupation. "In general, the politicians were against the occupation because it deprived them of their former opportunities for power and profit" (Millspaugh, 1931: 86). This attitude was attributed to a lack of patriotism.

Georges Sylvain (1866–1925) and other prominent Haitians founded the Union Patriotique in 1915, and that group took the following position on the U.S. occupation:

> [We shall] reserve judgment in regard to the occupation, since the situation has yet to be defined. If, as is said, it is a temporary experience of loyal cooperation—analogous to that of Cuba—ensuring the Haitian nation the proper and free direction of its destiny, with greater security, we shall [then] discuss the terms objectively. But if, as the methods would seem to indicate, it is a more or less disguised protectorate ... we will know to claim our violated rights.[8]

Despite the moderation of this response, the United States seized Haitian government ministries, dissolved the Haitian parliament, and censored the press and the mails. Haitian journalists were remitted to the jurisdiction of the U.S. military courts, and all prominent Haitian citizens were placed under the surveillance of military intelligence. At gunpoint, the U.S. authorities held a plebiscite to legalize the occupation of Haiti. With only 5 percent of the population voting, the fraudulent results were 98,255 yea, 768 nay.

The United States implemented these repressive measures with the relative acquiescence of successive Haitian governments. In a confidential letter to the Honorable J. Butler Wright in 1916, General Smedley D. Butler wrote: "In the first place, you back as president of Haiti a most unpopular man .... His government is widely despised and distrusted by a vast majority of the people at large."[9] One year later, Butler wrote the following to a prominent U.S. businessman:

> The Haitian National Legislature became so impudent that the Gendarmerie had to dissolve them [sic], which dissolution was effected by genuinely Marine Corps methods. If I ever get to the States, I shall certainly seize the opportunity to ... give you a mouth to ear account of this dissolution. [I] am afraid to write it for fear the Department of State might get a hold of this letter by means of the censors.[10]

The U.S. occupation forces built an infrastructure of roads and bridges, but these were built largely to facilitate military response to peasant insurgency. The marines also carried out sanitation projects, mostly in Port-au-Prince, and created an army that, according to U.S. anthropologist Sidney W. Mintz, "may have ended forever the possibility of an agrarian revolt against the central authority" (Leyburn, 1966: xvii). That, in fact, was the exact purpose of the U.S. occupation.

Elite resistance to the occupation emerged largely in the reaction to U.S. racism. In the first decade of the century, Haitian intellectuals had debated the merit of French versus Anglo-Saxon cultures as models for Haiti and development. The shock and brutality of the U.S. occupation, however, introduced the Haitian elite to the virulence of racism and left them disenchanted with the Anglo-Saxon model, making the French model more attractive once more. Persistent racism provided the impetus for a far-reaching change in Haitian attitudes and values toward a new consciousness of and pride in Haiti's African heritage. In Haiti, this movement toward African and away from Western models was called *indigénisme*; later it became known worldwide as negritude. Despite the emergence of indigenism, however, little alignment or cooperation developed between the elite and the peasant resistance movements.

The racism was rooted in the very fabric of Western thought at the time, that is, in positivism and social Darwinism. Positivism was a conservative retrenchment in Western thought that accompanied industrialization; social Darwinism provided a biologistic support for racism by delineating the innate inferiority of peoples of color, based on European theories of evolution. Imperialism was thus justified by the axiom, "the survival of the fittest."

When U.S. Secretary of State William Jennings Bryan was briefed on the Haitian situation by an officer of the National City Bank, he exclaimed "Dear me, think of it! Niggers speaking French!"[11] Admiral H.S. Knapp wrote the following to the secretary of the navy: "The people of Haiti had no immediate contact with the superior cultivation and intelligence such as the negroes of the United States have had .... I consider that the bad traits are more in evidence in Haiti than in the United States, where they [Blacks] are under better control."[12]

The U.S. high commissioner in Haiti, John H. Russell, thought the average Haitian had the mental development of a seven-year-old child. A U.S. State Department official wrote that Haitians "are not even children in the sense that we use the word, since they have had no ancestry of intelligence as a foundation." General Butler testified before the U.S. Senate that the Marines were "imbued with the fact that we were trustees of a huge estate that belonged to minors" (Plummer, 1981: 485). A U.S. Marine major seeking promotion to the rank of lieutenant colonel wrote the following in 1916:

As far as I am able, this country shall be run as a piece of machinery, with no preference being shown any negro owing for a supposed superiority due to the infusement of white blood in his veins .... There will be a deadline drawn between me and the Haitians, the same as there is in Egypt ... between the British ... and the Egyptians.[13]

After referring to Haitians as "cockroaches," he added: "All of us gendarmes are mighty tired ... and I, for one, am going to ask to be relieved at the first opportunity .... If we had war with Mexico, I had intended to make every effort to join my own white people in the struggle with [against] the Mexicans."

Writing to J. J. Oliver in 1918, U.S. Secretary of State Robert Lansing said that black states could not produce good governments because of their "inherent tendency to revert to savagery," which in his view made "the negro problem unsolvable" (Logan, 1968: 126). President Woodrow Wilson later wrote that "the biological law of the tendency to revert to the lower type as the higher attributes are disused is at work among nations; and nature, in its rough method of uplift, gives sick nations strong neighbors and takes its inexorable course with private enterprise and diplomacy as its instruments."[14]

Roger L. Farnham, director of the National City Bank, wrote to General Butler in 1918: "I have had some opportunity to tell the officials in Washington of what to me is the wonderful work which you have accomplished in two years' time .... To bring the fruit of all this, it remains now for American capital to come along to furnish the sinews of war for development on a considerable scale."[15] U.S. business people had anticipated developing vast plantations in Haiti and bemoaned the lack of a Haitian plantocracy, such as existed in other Caribbean islands under European rule. The reinstitution of vast plantations and a plantocracy in Haiti would have dismantled the foremost achievement of the Haitian Revolution, that is, the creation of a peasantry of small independent farmers, and replaced it with foreign-owned enterprises in which owners would become workers. The intent of U.S. business to dispossess the Haitian peasantry and reinstitute the plantation economy soon generated the massive peasant-guerrilla resistance that erupted as the Caco Wars.

Referring to protests against the U.S. occupation by Haitians and their few allies in Black and liberal newspapers in the United States,

Brigadier General Charles G. Long wrote to Senator Reed Smoot in 1920 that such protests were "but part of a propaganda instituted by the factions who, either because of their Bolshevik tendencies or their own selfish interests, have not the good of the Republic of Haiti at heart, and are consequently opposed to American occupation."[16] In the contorted justifications for continued U.S. intervention in Haiti, the earlier Franco-German threat to U.S. national security had now become the Communist threat.

The Caco Wars

The U.S. occupation appears to have maintained a system that was close to collapse and thwarted efforts within Haiti to redefine the nation's culture and political structure. Martial law was generally enforced throughout the occupation, and the Haitian legislature, dissolved in 1917, did not reconvene until 1930. Resistance to the U.S. occupation might have been more successful if national unity had prevailed, but unresolved structural problems prevented the emergence of a unified national response. Haitian disunity facilitated the occupation and aided the U.S. objective of maintaining some form of elite control of, not mass participation in, the Haitian economy and society. The major opposition to the invasion came from the peasantry.

The ensuing guerrilla war had two immediate causes: the reinstatement of the corvée and the establishment of agribusiness enterprises. The corvée was an old 1864 law that required peasants to provide free labor for road construction. As applied during the occupation, the corvée became forced labor in a pattern similar to French and British colonial practices in Africa. The reinstatement of the corvée led Haitians to believe that the United States was reinstituting slavery in their country. In 1917, General Butler wrote to John McIlhenny, who later became the leading U.S. official in Haiti, a letter from which the following passage aptly describes the methods and policies of the U.S. occupation:

It is not well to describe in a letter the methods used by us to build this road, but it might be interesting to you to know that when this highway is finished, it will have cost the Haitian government only about $500.00 a mile .... Nearly 9,000 men worked on this road from here [Port-au-Prince] to Cap-Haitien. We have over 15,000 at work in the whole of Haiti, a goodly-sized body of intelligent voters for any project the U.S. may wish to put across. We have nearly 50,000 men under our control through various activities, so I wish you would encourage the State Department to "cook up" some schemes to drive the German influence out of this country, now that the "open season" for Germans is upon us, as after the war we should control this island. Don't worry about our ability to "put over" any kind of popular demonstration down here; just tell us what you want done and everybody from the President down will shout for it. I am taking His Excellency and his Cabinet to Cap-Haitien and Ouanaminthe on January 5th [1918] for a big celebration and official opening of the road, during which trip he will justify through his own people any rough stuff we may have employed in the building of the road.[17]

The policies of the U.S. occupation aggravated preexisting land pressure, thus increasing unemployment and accelerating the replacement of subsistence agriculture with commercial agriculture and agribusiness. In her book, *Les Paysans haitiens et l'occupation américaine* [The Haitian peasantry and the American occupation], the Haitian social scientist Kethly Millet has observed that "this new contract [one with J.P. MacDonald, head of the National Railroad] was accompanied by a concession guaranteeing his company exclusive control for fifty years, at the cost of one dollar per cultivable *carreau* [1.2 hectares (3 acres)], on either side of the railroad track, for a distance of 20 kilometers [12 miles]." The peasants soon took up the battlecry of *A bas MacDonald, à bas le chemin de fer!* ("Down with MacDonald, down with the railroad!")[18]

In 1918, a new U.S.-drafted constitution that allowed non-Haitians to own land was approved by plebiscite. This change had long been sought but was achieved only through military occupation. The continuous turmoil that wracked Haiti from 1859 to 1920 reflected the elite's difficulty in controlling the hinterland, and the arrival of the U.S. forces focused and radicalized the caco guerrilla movement. Some caco leaders accepted bribes from U.S. officials to cease their resistance efforts, but many caco leaders were intransigent in resisting the U.S. occupation. One U.S. historian wrote that "those [cacos] who did not come to terms with the Americans were subjected to vigorous pursuit and decimation .... Indeed, Marine hunt-and-kill operations were sustained throughout the period of negotiations [with rebels]" (Schmidt, 1971: 84). U.S. Secretary of the Navy Josephus Daniels later informed Admiral Caperton that he was "strongly impressed with the number of Haitians killed," and he suggested caution.[19]

Guerrilla warfare against the U.S. occupation forces was waged throughout the countryside and at the height of the struggle may have involved between 20,000 and 40,000 fighters, fewer than 5,000 of whom were armed with machetes and old rifles (Map 3). One U.S. writer wrote typically, that "both sides were guilty of atrocities" (Rotberg, 1971: 122), but no one who defends his or her freedom by force of arms is as guilty as those who would initiate violence to deprive a people of its freedom. U.S. reprisals against the insurgents were swift and drastic. Hans Schmidt wrote that the first recorded instance of coordinated air-ground combat in military history occurred in Haiti in March 1919 (Schmidt, 1971: 103). As many as 50,000 Haitians may have died during the struggle, as can be inferred from population statistics for the period, whereas U.S. casualty reports in 1920 claimed 3,250 Haitian and 14 or 16 U.S. casualties.[20] The grossly disproportionate number of Haitian to U.S. casualties was accompanied by the detention of thousands of Haitians in camps set up by the United States.

A U.S. Senate investigation of the Haitian situation in 1922 reported that

> the transformation from peasant to bandit and vice-versa could
> be made at an instant's warning. There was reason to suspect
> almost any male adult of being from time to time engaged in
> active lawlessness and habituated to guerrilla warfare .... It is
> impossible to give the exact number of engagements, but it is

accurate to say that in one place or another armed encounters occurred daily.[21]

Between July and September 1919, 83 military engagements were noted, and 200 were recorded in the first six months of 1920.[22]
—   The first phase of the caco resistance had ended in November 1915 with the U.S. capture of Fort Rivière. The U.S. forces took no prisoners in the battle and annihilated the Haitian forces; for this
                        (smedley D.)
success General Butler was awarded the Congressional Medal of Honor.
— By the second phase of the resistance in 1918–1920, the caco movement had become much more politically radicalized, partly as a result of increased U.S. repression, the development of agribusiness, and the severity of the corvée. The two major caco leaders, Charlemagne Péralte (1885–1919) and Benoît Batraville (1888–1920), vowed to "throw the invaders into the ocean and liberate the country" and "not to lay down our weapons until the Americans are thrown out."[23] Unlike the peasant resistance movements led by Augusto César Sandino in Nicaragua and the Gavilleros in the Dominican Republic, the caco resistance in Haiti received no international support from either Latin America or other parts of the world. The Haitian caco leaders thus realized that a military victory was not feasible and concluded that a political victory through military pressure was their only viable option.

Popular support for the guerrillas is evidenced by the ongoing U.S. reprisals against rural populations and the unpopularity of the regime the U.S. had installed in Port-au-Prince. U.S. Marine Corps Commandant John LeJeune wrote to the U.S. secretary of the navy in 1920 that President "D'Artinav [sic] would not live a day without military protection" (Plummer, 1981: 591–592). The U.S. analysis of the Haitian resistance movement was fraught with contradictions. On the one hand, the authorities argued that peasants were coerced into joining the caco movement; on the other hand, they cited the stability of the movement and its rapid spread throughout the country as evidence of the need to continue military counterinsurgency operations.

One U.S. writer who was sympathetic to the U.S. occupation observed that "regardless of material benefits which might possibly

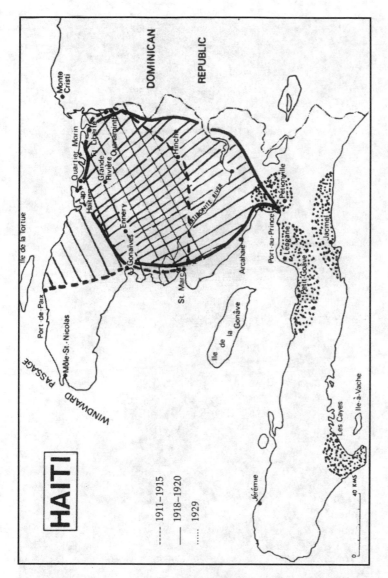

Map 4. Peasant movements against the United States, 1911–1929.

result, the Haitians did not want to be governed by Americans and by a President supported by the armed forces of the United States" and argued that the military operations necessitated by Haitian resistance inevitably resulted in civilian casualties (Davis, 1936: 238, 224). In a

Guerrilla leader and national hero Charlemagne Péralte shortly after he was killed by U.S. troops in 1919. Photo: United States National Archives.

report published in 1927, the Women's International League for Peace and Freedom described innumerable atrocities committed by U.S. occupation forces in Haiti that were never included in official military reports:

> We may cite a signed memorial presented to our party in Haiti which refers to the burning alive of Cazeau Noël, and of Médard Bélony and his wife, the summary execution of the three children of Hergéné, and of the twin sisters Athélia and Cloraine Etienne, the beating and torturing with fire of the widow of Romain Brégarde ... the burning alive of one Vixina in broad daylight in the Gendarmerie at Maïssade, the execution by beating of Dorléan Joseph, the execution by machine gun of the daughters of the widow Célicour Rosier in the yard of their house, when their mother, aged 84, received two bullets in her thigh; daily shooting of cattle, the many burnings of crops, distilleries, mills, and houses. [Balch, 1927: 126–127]

Because the support of peasant populations for guerrilla resistance movements is generally necessary if they are to succeed, women's participation in the movement was probably relatively high, as can be inferred from the women's league report. Under the guise of supplying the towns with produce, Haitian women smuggled ammunition and intelligence on U.S. troop movements to insurgents throughout the countryside (Davis, 1936: 224). Men and women guerrilla fighters were labeled "gooks," "bandits," and "cockroaches" by the occupiers.

Unfavorable public reaction in the United States to published reports of the aerial bombing of Haiti's third-largest city, Les Cayes, and the killing of an unarmed peasant at Marchaterre contributed to the change in U.S. foreign policy from the "big stick" and "dollar diplomacy" policies of the early twentieth century to the good-neighbor policy inaugurated in 1935.

The third and final phase of the insurgency occurred in southern Haiti in 1929 when the United States turned its attention to that region. The *minifundia* system of small property owners came under attack, resulting in new taxation, bankruptcies, massive emigration to Cuba,

U.S. troops protecting the Haitian-American Sugar Company (HASCO) during the occupation (circa 1920). Photo: United States National Archives.

and land consolidation to benefit the Haitian-American Sugar Company (HASCO).

In retrospect, the Haitian resistance movement was a gamble that failed. It was undermined by the lack of national unity, U.S. military superiority, and lack of sympathy abroad. Besides the heavy death toll, 300,000 of Haiti's 2 million people left for Cuba or the Dominican Republic, aggravating antiblack sentiment in those countries as the influx of Haitians depressed wages on U.S.-owned plantations. The movement's failure inaugurated precisely what the peasants had most feared: the establishment of an economic structure that would further reduce their standard of living and restrict their opportunities for full participation in Haitian society. Gérard Pierre-Charles, a leading Haitian economist, effectively assessed Haiti's situation at the end of the U.S. occupation in the following summary:

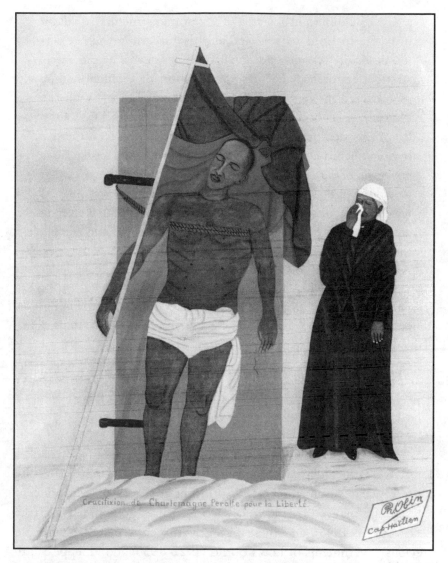

**Internationally known Philomé Obin's rendition, "The Crucifixion of Péralte"
(1970).** Milwaukee Art Museum, Flagg Tanning Corporation Collection. Published by
permission.

Powerful economic forces, thus, do battle behind the scenes
of the political stage. Much pushing and pulling, the shock of
varied, interests, social clashes, [all] translate into a search for

a new equilibrium in the area of economic structure. Would it not be too bold to assert that this violent growth crisis [domestically] would end inevitably in a new realignment: a strong dictatorship and the consolidation of a feudal regime as occurred in Venezuela with the dictatorship of Vincente Gomez, or [as occurred] in Mexico under Porfirio Diaz? Or a bourgeois democratic government as perhaps dreamt about by [nineteenth-century Haitian liberal] Boyer Bazelais? Or a government with a strong popular element where the peasantry would emerge as a sociopolitical force? The historical process was never consummated. The United States had already entered an era of expansionism. Manifest Destiny condemned the countries of the Caribbean basin to suffer the U.S. Marines, American capital, or both.[24]

Paraphrasing the U.S. author Samuel Flagg Bemis on the Dominican Republic, the United States was determined to save Haiti despite the Haitians' best efforts to resist salvation.[25]

THE AFTERMATH OF THE U.S. OCCUPATION: STABILITY AND TURMOIL, 1934–1956

The U.S. Marines departed Haiti in August 1934, leaving behind the conservative government of Sténio Vincent (1930–1941). The Vincent regime was followed by the equally conservative government of Elie Lescot (1941–1946), and these two governments, together with the previous governments of Louis Borno (1922–1930) and Philippe-Sudre Dartiguenave (1915–1922), gave Haiti thirty-one years of relative political stability. The chronic instability of the seven presidents who had succeeded one other in the seven-year period 1908–1915 did not reoccur until 1956–1957.

This relative stability was limited, however, and was maintained only with government repression. The elite controlled the government and stymied the development of democratic participation in the political process. As in other countries where the United States intervened, power was increasingly concentrated in the executive branch and the army. The government utilized its U.S.-sponsored army to stifle all dissent and further centralized political and economic power in Port-au-Prince at the expense of the provinces. Class and color divisions were deepened and intensified.

Thus the political stability of Haiti was based on repressive maintenance of the government apparatus rather than on normalization of democratic political processes. For nearly thirty years the situation in Haiti paralleled the forty-year Somoza dictatorship in Nicaragua and the thirty-one-year Trujillo dictatorship in Dominican Republic. But whereas the U.S. Marines had quelled the caco resistance movement in Haiti, the Dominican Gavilleros and the Nicaraguan insurgents led by Sandino had not been militarily defeated by the United States. This difference partly explains why Nicaragua and the Dominican Republic endured brutal dictatorships in the aftermath of their U.S. occupations, whereas the government repression in Haiti was comparatively less severe; in the absence of an armed rebellion and an organized opposition, the Haitian government was relatively less brutal. Despite a growing middle class, Haitian society remained largely polarized between the elite and the peasantry, and the power of the elite had never been greater. The United States placed elite mulattoes at the helm of the government to promote Western interests, and the political and economic status of the black majority continued to decline.—

As observed earlier, one unintended but significant outcome of the U.S. occupation was the newfound pride among Haitian intellectuals in the nation's African origins. This emergence of black consciousness among Haitian intellectuals, combined with their sharpened understanding of class antagonisms, ensured that the situation would become increasingly volatile. New scholarship by disaffected middle-class intellectuals continued to alienate the Haitian intelligentsia from the status quo.

Although President Borno's government during the U.S. occupation represented the emergence of Haitian fascism, President Lescot's administration was known for its heightened persecution of Vodou and for favoring very light-skinned individuals, particularly in the diplomatic corps. In response to governmental racism, the black consciousness that originated in the literary movement became increasingly political and radicalized. The movement of Haitian intellectuals toward greater militancy was further ensured by the fact that few sources of employment existed outside the political arena.

Intellectuals often dominate government and society, especially when a country's population is predominantly illiterate. The Haitian poet and social thinker René Depestre succinctly summarized the relationship between politics and culture in a neocolonial context when he wrote the following in 1968:

> This concept of negritude had been ... the effective response of the exploited and humiliated black facing the global scorn of the white colonist. For his privileged position in colonial society, the latter used his white skin as proof of his alleged biological superiority. Similarly, the black man was carried to internalize his lamentable historical situation and oppression as a pariah ... a man alienated in his very own skin. Hence negritude ... was a cultural movement that made black intellectuals from Africa and the Americas conscious of the validity of Negro-African cultures, of the aesthetic value of the black race, and of the capacity of their respective peoples to exercise the right to historical initiative that colonialism had completely suppressed.[26]

The Haitian intelligentsia endured a double alienation. In addition to racial and cultural alienation, their political radicalization began to inspire alienation based on social class. Racial and cultural alienation, however, tended to blur the alienation based on social class. At the outset of black consciousness, most dissident Haitian intellectuals were of the upper or middle class. As a result, their analyses and agendas for social change were not primarily focused on class issues. Although they saw themselves as a vanguard for those behind or below them, Haitian intellectuals were unlikely to emphasize class issues in view of their own status as elites. Transformed into black nationalism/ internationalism, political negritude lost some of its "revolutionary" fervor and became increasingly opportunistic. Opportunistic negritude was exemplified later by the right-wing governments of Presidents François Duvalier in Haiti and Léopold Sédar Senghor in Senegal.

The relatively smooth transitions of power between heads of state between 1922 and 1941 ended in 1946. When Lescot tried to extend his term of office for another six years and closed a newspaper supported by young intellectuals, high-school and university students went on strike, and the student strike soon precipitated a general strike. Lescot had been closely aligned with the United States and had received payoffs from Dominican President Rafael Leonidas Trujillo. Now, however, both of these governments abandoned him, and his government fell to a junta headed by Colonel Paul-Eugène Magloire.

The excesses of the Lescot regime and pressure from the black middle class led to a reassessment of the country's government policies. Guided by the army, the National Assembly elected Dumarsais Estimé, a black deputy from the village of Verrettes, as the nation's new president. The Estimé government effectively illustrates the achievements and failures of Haitian governments in general in the context of domestic and international politics.

In retrospect, the Estimé government was perhaps one of the most progressive in Haitian history. The U.S. government had strong reservations about Estimé even before he came to power, and he did not disappoint Washington's suspicions. At the outset of his administration, Estimé increased the minimum daily wage from thirty to seventy cents, promoted the creation of labor organizations, and favored Haitian businesses over U.S. interests. Estimé paid off the Haitian government's debt to the United States, nationalized the central bank, instituted an income tax, and passed laws favoring social security and welfare. He also developed the waterfront slums of Port-au-Prince into a national cultural and diplomatic center and for a time recognized left-wing parties. Later he tried to placate U.S. opposition to his government by banning these socialist parties and establishing tight control over labor unions and the student movement.

The situation in 1946 might have led to revolutionary social change in Haiti if more than the upper and middle classes had been involved in the nation's political life and social movements. These classes either represented the old order or saw themselves as a revolutionary vanguard

Three sisters from the mulatto upper class in their nineteenth-century home (circa 1980). Photo: Howard Goldbaum.

for the peasantry. The upper class claimed the right to rule autocratically because it was "best prepared"; the vanguard intelligentsia claimed the right to power as the "true representative" of the black masses. The defeat of the caco guerrilla movement by the United States had ensured that the lower classes could be easily controlled and excluded from participation in political power. Both the upper and middle classes, black and brown, had inherently elitist conceptions of society, and this elitist philosophy was present in all movements for social change in Haiti, including the fledgling left-wing parties.

Despite Estimé's efforts to promote Haitian interests, the nation's economy continued to be dominated by foreign interests, and his government suffered from a general lack of policy that left Haiti's economic conditions unchanged. Estimé's first cabinet included his political opposition and was dominated by warring factions, because he recognized the three-dimensional reality of Haitian society and shaped his administration within these constraints. First, there was an attempt to reestablish and strengthen the idea of mulatto and black joint rule. Second, the newly constituted army could defend the status quo and become the arbiter in Haitian politics. Third, discontent among the lower classes had to be addressed if only to placate peasant unrest.

The "revolution of 1946" left Haiti's economic and financial structures dependent on foreign interests. As cultural negritude was transformed into political negritude, it developed a nationalist agenda but no economic policy. The political program appears to have been limited to a simple political axiom, *Ôtes-toi que je m'y mette* ("Move over, it's my turn now"). At the time, the connections among domestic misery, government impotence, and worldwide economic conditions that exacerbated the inequality between states were not readily understood. In addition, the elite-class orientation of the movements for social change was sufficient to dictate certain outcomes. Perhaps this fact is best illustrated by Estimé's ineffective reformist policies and by the conservative economic policies of the François and Jean-Claude Duvalier governments later.

The successes and failures of the efforts of this first "middle-class" government to reform Haitian society are crucial for understanding what later transpired during the Duvalier dictatorship. The Estimé presidency represented a sharp break with previous Haitian governments because it did not maintain the elite control the U.S. occupation was supposed to ensure and because it tried to reconcile color and class antagonisms from an earlier age. In the Pan-Caribbean context, however, Estimé ought to have represented an extension of middle-class participation in Haitian society similar to concurrent developments in Jamaica, Trinidad, and Barbados. In those societies, black middle-class intellectuals who had been barred from holding political office during much of colonial rule were organizing labor unions and political parties that would carry them to power as leaders of stable, liberal-conservative governments. This situation was understood intuitively by the Haitian Communist party (PCH), which disbanded in 1946 to help Estimé in his difficult relationship with the United States.

Members of the Haitian mulatto upper class in Paris, France (1952). Photo: Author's collection.

The Estimé presidency was thus revolutionary only in comparison to previous Haitian governments and how it was perceived by the United States. Viewing that period, the Haitian political scientist Leslie F. Manigat concluded that the "revolution of 1946," which brought Estimé to power, "was in reality a social and nationalist explosion. At its root was the accumulated resentment of the urban, black middle class against the misrule of the mulatto oligarchy" (Manigat, 1964: 36). In this regard, the testimony of Afro-American historian Rayford W. Logan is telling:

> Members of the black elite in Port-au-Prince, who believed that I had spent too much time with the mulatto elite, invited me to dinner the night before my departure. Not all of them, particularly their wives, were black. They were as cultured and as sophisticated as the mulatto elite. The last words of Dr. René Salomon, who drove me to my hotel were, "when you next come to Haiti, Dr. Logan, the black elite will be in power." They were, in considerable measure when I returned in 1960. [Logan, 1968: 148–149]

Like other Haitian leaders, Dumarsais Estimé, the "peasant from Verrettes," spoke exquisite French. The literary critic Edmund Wilson wrote the following in this regard: "The President pronounced a *discours* which struck me as exhibiting a brilliance of style and a sweep of historical imagination well beyond the reach of any living white statesman known to me, not excluding Winston Churchill" (Wilson, 1956: 91).

As earlier, government corruption was rampant during 1941–1950. Haitian commerce and high finance had been dominated by foreign interests since the turn of the century, and Haitian elites had had no choice but to make a livelihood in politics. Because business practices that are acceptable in the private sector are not always tolerated in government service, government officials frequently felt that they had to be corrupt in order to survive. The Estimé administration was wracked by financial scandals and the greed of officials who ignored the advice of a nineteenth-century Haitian president: "Pluck the chicken, but don't make it cluck."

Opposed by the traditional elite, the United States, and the Dominican Republic; outflanked on his left and his right; and abandoned by the army at whose pleasure he served, Estimé was deposed in May 1950 by the same military junta that had overthrown Lescot and raised him to power in 1946. Like Lescot, Estimé fled into exile to the United States.

— Paul-Eugène Magloire, the son of an elite black family from the northern city of Cap-Haitien and now a general, was installed as president after the overthrow of Estimé. Magloire held the presidency from 1950 to 1956, and under his regime, the old system quickly reemerged with flair and panache. Supported by the United States and favored by worldwide economic conditions that sustained Haitian economic growth, Magloire's government led to a lull in Haitian society and gave political forces time to regroup. The Magloire government was a hiatus between two middle-class governments, and during its years, the traditional elite sought to regain its control over Haitian politics and the contending middle class prepared for another attempt to take power. Unopposed by the bourgeoisie, Magloire remained the best hope of the middle class that the changes that allowed its participation in politics would not be forsaken. Magloire himself called for a policy of "equal balance" and "social equilibrium" in which the upper and middle classes, blacks and mulattoes, the traditional elite and the nouveaux riches could coexist and re-establish social harmony. Like Lescot, however, Magloire tried to extend his term of office and was deposed by the same army he had led in two *coups d'état* (1946 and 1950). He had lost the crucial support of U.S. Ambassador Roy Tasco Davis and had now become a liability. As mandated by the 1950 constitution drafted under his aegis, Magloire turned power over to the president of the Cassation Court (chief justice of the Haitian Supreme Court). Like his predecessors, he fled into exile to the United States.

PRELUDE TO DICTATORSHIP: THE ELECTIONS OF 1957

Irreconcilable political antagonisms often create periods of great instability that lead to the establishment of authoritarian regimes. This pattern is observed in Haiti in the "victory" of one camp over another, where conciliation is out of the question even for "national unity," and where the very definition of what constitutes the nation is at stake.

Historians will see the three decades of the Duvalier dictatorship as the worst in Haitian history and consider that dictatorship one of the harshest regimes in the Western Hemisphere. The Duvalier regime compares unfavorably with the dictatorships of Trujillo in the Dominican Republic (1930–1961), the Somozas in Nicaragua (1931–1979), and Alfredo Stroessner in Paraguay (1954–1989), but the Duvalier years also represented a form of stability that, when contrasted with uncertainty, always appealed to the region's paramount power, the United States. The United States played a significant role in the events that led to the establishment and the long duration of the dictatorship.

The years of Magloire and the policy of "social equilibrium" had merely postponed the crisis among conflicting groups whose symbols and rhetoric were dissimilar but whose vision, methods, and policies were rather similar in terms of outcome. The prize was control of the Haitian state.

Unable to bring about speedy presidential elections, Chief Justice Joseph Nemours Pierre-Louis transferred power to a minor player, Franck Sylvain. Sylvain was soon replaced by a Government Executive Council comprised of coequal cabinet ministers representing the major presidential candidates. This collegial government was soon replaced by a provisional president, Daniel Fignolé. After nineteen days in office, Fignolé was deposed by a junta headed by General Antonio Kébreau. Haiti had had five governments in six months and no "permanent" administration.

This very rapid succession of governments paralleled an earlier period when seven presidents came to power by "revolutionary" means in four years, between 1911 and 1915, and as in that earlier period of instability, the United States would play a major role in 1956–1957. Twice, in 1946 and 1956, provisional governments had sent Dantès Bellegarde, the country's foremost diplomat, to Washington, DC, to assuage fears there about the direction of Haitian politics and secure U.S. recognition of the Haitian government. Haitian governments have always assumed that they could not retain power or function without the support and approval of the United States, and, indeed, inimical relations between the United States and the Lescot, Estimé, and Magloire regimes in their closing years had sealed the fate of those administrations.

The United States had hoped to stabilize Haiti and strengthen oligarchic control, but the U.S. occupation had failed to change political norms appreciably, having been itself a brutal dictatorship. In a sense, postponed by the U.S. occupation, the crisis of the "traditional" political system and political culture recurred, since none of the underlying causes for mass nonparticipation had been resolved. One U.S. historian wrote, with respect to the instability at the time, that "the failure of any set of norms to win widespread acceptance and the inability of the usual mechanisms to achieve a lasting consensus illumine the character and vagaries of Haitian politics in microcosm" (Rotberg, 1971: 187), but I believe they showed the inability of the system to maintain or reform itself in light of the stress and tensions of the society. But since universal suffrage was to apply to the 1957 election, with women voting for the first time, mass participation even in the absence of politicization could and might alleviate the structural blockage; politicization might have brought about a showdown with the United States, as happened in Santo Domingo in 1965 and Grenada in 1983.

Nineteen candidates hoped to succeed Magloire, but the field was soon reduced to thirteen, and only four of those were serious contenders. (In 1986, approximately 100 men and 1 woman laid claim to the Duvalier succession.) Senator Louis Déjoie (1896–1969) was the first to declare his candidacy, even while Magloire was still trying to renew his term in office. An industrialist, Déjoie represented the Haitian aristocracy at its most obdurate. His ancestors, General Nicolas

Geffrard and President Fabre-Nicolas Geffrard, had played significant roles on the national stage in the eighteenth and nineteenth centuries. And his candidacy, representing *les forces du bien* ("the rightful forces" or "the forces for good"), would re-establish decent government to a nation marred by ten years of "black misrule." He was supported by big business, the upper echelon of the army, the Roman Catholic church, and the "mulatto" south.

⌐ François Duvalier (1907–1971), a mild-mannered physician whose father was said to be a French citizen from Martinique, was a middle-class black who had served as a cabinet minister under Estimé. Duvalier's association with the Estimé presidency, a very progressive government by Haitian standards, endeared him to many people. His scholarly defense of Haiti's African heritage also won him support among the Haitian intelligentsia. His middle-class background and mild manner won him the loyalty of middle- and low-ranking army officers, who chafed under slow promotions and a mulatto General Staff, and his intimate knowledge of popular culture and Vodou won him some powerful alliances in the countryside. There is evidence that he was "the U.S. candidate." He had studied briefly at the University of Michigan and had worked as a country doctor under U.S. auspices. Although he was a "black nationalist," Duvalier seemed less threatening than the Francophile Déjoie. Components of the U.S. embassy distributed charity in Duvalier's name, and Haitian anthropologist Rémy Bastien argued that "in 1957 it was the opinion of the United States Department of State that Haiti needed a middle-class, middle-of-the-road reformer. Of the four candidates for the presidency, only one met the requirements .... Dr. Duvalier seemed the perfect choice" (Courlander and Bastien, 1966: 55).

There is, however, disagreement about how much support Duvalier actually received from the United States, and Haitian political scientist Leslie F. Manigat—an early Duvalier supporter who was later exiled—argued much differently (Manigat, 1964: 43). What was important, however, was that Duvalier was widely perceived to be the U.S. candidate. Colonel Robert D. Heinl, Jr., head of a U.S. Marine training mission to the Duvalier government, wrote that U.S. Ambassador Gerald Drew "had serious reservations but was unable to keep an uncritical USAID (U.S. Agency for International Development) director from ostentatious support of the Duvalier bandwagon, a factor which very likely carried the election."[27] Although the U.S. government was to reveal in 1986 that it had had evidence of massive fraud in the 1957 election and that Déjoie had probably won (according to U.S. government records obtained through the Freedom of Information Act), it did support the Duvalier dictatorship—for "lack of an alternative," in order "not to penalize the Haitian population," and because he "was consistent in his anti-Communism." U.S. policy thus seems to substantiate the belief that Duvalier was largely a U.S. creation and that he would never have survived without the United States.

Except for Fignolé, none of the candidates truly displeased the United States, and Duvalier may have well been the preferred option; indeed, that view is logical, in view of the fact that all other Caribbean countries were led politically by their middle-classes. Furthermore, "black power" in whatever language it occurs, need not be disruptive of the status quo if it has no economic agenda, and U.S. social scientists have traditionally viewed the middle class as a source of stability and a bulwark for democracy—in Latin American sociological analyses, the reverse is often argued. Déjoie had publicly called for French assistance and had castigated the army for unprofessional behavior. His positions might have hurt the pride of the army and the United States.

A successful candidate for president would want to have U.S. support and be able to reassure the public that Haiti would continue to receive U.S. economic aid. Caribbean populations have readily acknowledged this U.S. factor. A similar argument was made by the successful candidate Joaquin Balaguer in his contest against Juan Bosch in the Dominican Republic, and later by "socialist" President Antonio Guzman. In the Virgin Islands, Melvin Evans claimed the goodwill of the Nixon administration to help him win the election, and the Jamaican and Grenadian prime ministers Edward Seaga and Herbert Blaize also utilized the ploy successfully.

The third serious contender in the 1957 election was Clément Jumelle (1915–1959), an economist trained at Fisk University and the University of Chicago, a technocrat, and the minister of finance under Magloire. He had some difficulty in clearing his name from suspicion regarding the financial scandals surrounding that government, as a result of which the president was said to have left office with $12–$28 million. Jumelle gathered support from elements of the upper and middle classes, black and mulatto, and among technicians, professionals, and technocrats. He would have, it seemed, continued the gradual reformism and "social equilibrium" policy under the old system whereby the National Assembly—House and Senate—elected the president. He might have emerged as the compromise candidate.

As part of his program, Jumelle wanted a "revolution," but said that the "revolution—to be different from those of yesteryear that blossomed in bullet smoke—in order to carry its fruits and be inscribed in permanent reality, will have to acquire its life force not just from an integral humanism that, to moral values, adds a concern for method and scientific organization to the fecund alliance of theory and experience."[28] This speech was in French, as were all the major speeches of the candidates, but because 90 percent of the Haitian people speak only Kreyol, few understood the speeches. Significantly, the Francophone 10 percent of the population correlated with the percentage that was defined as belonging to the upper and middle classes.

The last major candidate, or the first minor one, was a high-school mathematics teacher, "Professor" Daniel Fignolé (1913–1986), a former minister in the Estimé cabinet and, of course, a former president that year, albeit briefly. The founder of the Worker-Peasant Movement (MOP), he was a union organizer who managed to be disliked by intellectuals, army officers, the upper and middle classes, the church, business, and the United States. He was called a fascist *and* a Communist, but he was a populist of uncertain ideological bent, à la Ataturk and Argentine *Peronismo*. His celebrated oratory in Kreyol rendered him powerful with the residents of the Port-au-Prince slums, whom he would order into the streets "to flatten" (*rouleau compresseur* ["steamroller"]) all things at their passage. He had accepted the provisional presidency and remained in office for nineteen days before being exiled to Brooklyn, New York. Upon Fignolé's departure, a U.S. journalist reported that on one frightful evening in June 1957, the army apparently massacred 1,000 of his supporters (Diederich and Burt, 1969: 93–94).

The country was at a standstill. By default and by design, power fell to the army, which suffered in a mini-war. Dr. François Duvalier was declared elected to the presidency, for a non-renewable six-year term, on September 22, 1957, with 679,884 votes. According to U.S. State Department records, however (obtained through a request under the Freedom of Information Act), the actual numbers were Duvalier 212,409 and Déjoie, 975,687.

The stakes had been high, and the victorious side would show no mercy. The father of Haitian negritude, Jean Price-Mars, wrote in 1967 about the "true nature" of the conflict in a work banned by his disciple Duvalier. In one sense, it was an epitaph for a movement he had helped create, but he felt betrayed by it at age ninety:

> On one side [one finds] those privileged by wealth and power who formed the ruling class, which was composed of blacks as well as mulattoes .... On the other hand [one finds] the immense majority of "jobbers," nonspecialized workers, unemployed workers, the numberless crowd of peasants. This is, as far as I am concerned, what has constituted the "social question." ... One has denatured it, one has systematically hidden it by dressing it with false claims for so long, that blacks and mulattoes have killed each other to accede to supreme power without that success ... having changed anything in the lives of those more or less black, more or less light, with no wealth.[29]

Although Price-Mars was supposedly writing about the period *before* 1915, his criticism of the Duvalier group was transparent, hence the banning.

DYNASTIC DICTATORSHIP: THE DUVALIER YEARS, 1957–1986

The Duvalier dictatorship, in its two phases, *père* (1957–1971) and *fils* (1971–1986), was easily the most brutal experienced by Haiti in two centuries of national life. Between 20,000 and 50,000 Haitians are said to have been murdered by that government, and about one-fifth of the population now lives abroad in political or economic exile, the second-highest ratio in the Western Hemisphere—Puerto Rico has the highest ratio. By the mid-1960s, 80 percent of Haiti's professionals had already fled, by some estimates.

The efficiency in methods of repression was rendered more likely by the technological means made available through the modernizing efforts of the U.S. occupation and the centralization of power favoring Port-au-Prince at the expense of regional interests. Two specific instances were the road network built largely for pacification of the interior by the Marines and the modern army whose impact is felt from the *départements* (departments) to the small *sections rurales* (rural sections). The only other institution with a national scope was the Roman Catholic church, which was under foreign control and threatened by the decentralized national religion of Vodou. Decentralization is a key concept here.

History will not be kind to the Duvaliers, whose fortune is estimated to be between $400 million and $1 billion. The judgment of one U.S. scholar is not too harsh: "Haitians experienced tyranny, rapacity, and an all-encompassing, disfiguring dictatorship which surpassed all its Third World counterparts in single mindedness of purpose, tenacity and lack of redeeming social and economic features" (Rotberg, 1971: 197–198).

François Duvalier came to power with the blessing of certain segments of the population. To many Haitians he seemed to be a non-threatening man of the people. As a middle-class politician, Duvalier had not enriched himself while serving in the Estimé cabinet and had defended the beliefs and value system of the peasantry. The harrowing brutality of his regime did not begin until six months after he had taken office and took most Haitians by surprise. The repression and terror of Duvalier's government continued unabated until his death by natural causes in April 1971. Duvalier's ability to hold power was largely the result of weak state institutions, his uncanny intelligence, and intimate knowledge of the Haitian culture, and the effectiveness and surprise tactics of his secret police and state apparatus.

Jean-Claude Duvalier succeeded his father as president of Haiti on April 22, 1971, at the age of nineteen. The succession was supported by U.S. Ambassador Clinton Knox and was accomplished within sight of U.S. naval units. This very smooth transition of power from father to son was unique in Haitian history and indicated both foreign and some domestic support for the Duvalier dynasty. Fourteen years of purges under the senior Duvalier had neutralized or decimated all political opposition and institutional resistance to the regime. The foundations of traditional elite rule had been destroyed and replaced by a rapacious group of political hacks and cohorts of diverse class backgrounds whose only unifying ideological feature was their unflagging allegiance to Duvalier and the status quo. Indeed, the duration, brutality, and economic plunder of the Duvalier dictatorship from 1957 until its collapse in 1986 may have permanently altered the norms of Haitian political culture. The eruption of the peasantry onto the national stage during the overthrow of the Duvalier regime signaled that changes are developing in the nation's political power structure. Time will tell whether the growing political participation of the peasantry will continue (see Chapter Six).

Duvalier's government had to withstand armed attacks soon after it came to power. Eleven different invasions, plots, mutinies, and palace intrigues were launched against "Papa Doc" during the years of his reign. Although political and economic conditions in Haiti worsened under Duvalier, none of these revolts succeeded in rallying the population against the regime. Throughout most of the Duvalier era the government's opponents were upper class elites; the rural population was indifferent to resisting the regime because most people believed that another elitist government would be as bad or worse than the Duvaliers. In contrast, the movement that finally overthrew the Duvalier government in 1986 originated in the peasantry and provincial centers with little visible support from other social groups or foreign governments.

Almost from the inception of his regime, Duvalier used prison, torture, murder, and exile to silence his opponents, and the armed forces were neutralized from the outset. In March 1958, Duvalier initiated frequent transfers and dismissals in the officer corps. The high officer turnover and politicized promotions destroyed the army's *esprit de corps* and solidified the president's control. The officers' candidate school, the Ecole Militaire, was closed, and the military chain of command was substantially altered to incorporate new crack units— a presidential guard, the Casernes Dessalines battalion; the infamous Tontons Macoutes (Volunteers for National Security), a secret police; and later the Leopards, a U.S.-trained counterinsurgency unit that reported directly to the president. Armaments were stockpiled in the basement of the presidential palace, which also housed some of the regime's torture chambers. The only requirement for military promotion was loyalty to the president.

Political repression, martial law, dusk-to-dawn curfews, press censorship, and government by presidential decree became quasi-permanent features of the Duvalier rule and continued in various forms for nearly thirty years. In an interview in the late 1950s, François Duvalier claimed that under his leadership, Haiti had achieved political stability, and he boasted that he had the situation well in hand. To demonstrate U.S. support for his regime, Duvalier procured a seventy-man U.S. Marine Corps training mission in December 1958—which he expelled in 1963. These marines promptly became known as the "white Macoutes," and their presence was more than psychologically devastating to Duvalier's opposition, particularly when they were called upon to repel an invasion by anti-Duvalier Haitian exiles.

In May 1959, a U.S. Navy medical team was secretly flown into Haiti from the U.S. naval base in Guantanamo, Cuba, and remained at Duvalier's bedside for thirty days as he recovered from a nearly fatal heart attack complicated by diabetes. Duvalier succeeded in placating the United States until 1963, when he clashed with President John Kennedy regarding human rights in Haiti and Kennedy suspended economic assistance to Haiti until two years later, when Haiti delivered crucial votes at the Organization of American States and the United Nations in support of the U.S. 1965 invasion of the Dominican Republic.

Like all Haitian presidents since the first decade of the twentieth century, Duvalier assumed that his regime would not survive without the support or at least the benign neutrality of the United States. Based on the experience of the previous sixty years, most Haitians also believed that no regime in Haiti could maintain its power without U.S. support. U.S. military missions had trained the Haitian army intermittently since 1939, and William Wieland of the U.S. State Department told the head of the U.S. Marines in Haiti that U.S. policy supported Duvalier and that the marines should strive to maintain the power of the Duvalier regime (Diederich and Burt, 1969: 133).

The United States provided $7 million in economic aid to the Duvalier government between February and September 1959 and another $11 million in 1960. U.S. aid amounted to $13.5 million, almost 50 percent of the Haitian national budget, in 1961 alone, and from 1957 to 1986. U.S. aid to the Duvalier regime may have amounted to as much as $900 million.[30] As late as 1983, 40 percent of the Haitian government's budget and 60 percent of its development funds came from foreign sources. In 1985, the government received $150 million from Western governments, including $54 million from the United States. Thus the Duvalier regime could ill afford to alienate its foreign benefactors in major areas affecting their economic interests.[31] Meanwhile, Haitians were becoming the most highly taxed people in the Western Hemisphere, and Duvalier initiated many schemes, including bond issues, payroll deductions from public employees, compulsory lotteries, special taxes, and tolls on major roads, to collect additional revenue. By the mid-1960s, more than 65 percent of the national budget was allocated to the many security forces (Weil et al., 1973: 117).

The United States may not have intended to support the Duvalier regime per se, but it did feel that it had no other options for establishing a base of influence in the Caribbean after the U.S. invasion of Cuba at the Bay of Pigs in 1961. François Duvalier's excesses and his fraudulent reelection in 1961 and as president for life in 1964 occurred at a time when the United States required Latin American support for its covert war against Cuba and its invasion of the Dominican Republic. Haitian support for U.S. policy in the Caribbean was crucial in these two instances, and Haitian political "stability" rather than social justice dictated U.S. policy toward Haiti. The policymakers failed to realize that the lack of social justice and economic development would be detrimental to political stability in Haiti in the long run.

In the final analysis, international considerations, economic and military aid, and "new contracts with commercial firms from the United States were ... useful in the unremitting psychological wars between a Haitian head of state and those of his citizens who would make or break a regime" (Rotberg, 1971: 209). Although slow to materialize, U.S. private investments in Haiti increased dramatically after 1971, and that approach to economic development was systematized in the Caribbean Basin Initiative (CBI) launched in 1983. Foreign support aside, the dictatorship could not have survived without domestic support in key areas, particularly in the "new" military, the state bureaucracy, and the business sector. In this sense, a major difference in the two phases of the dictatorship, between father and son, revolved around the more personal power of the father being more or less institutionalized under the son. But despite cosmetic changes undertaken to satisfy the United States under the aegis of Haitian technocrats, domestic economic policies, international considerations, and extraordinary corruption remained similar throughout.

Controlled access to information is of critical importance to a dictatorship, and in the 1960s, no Haitian newspaper had a circulation of more than 5,000 copies, reflecting the country's literacy rate at that time of 10 percent. Yet, for 100 years, newspapers had been highly influential in elite politics, in the absence of popular participation. Within months, the printing shops of four major newspapers—*Haiti-Miroir*, *Le Matin*, *Le Patriote*, and *Indépendance*—were bombed or destroyed and their staffs tortured. The arch-conservative *La Phalange* proved more difficult—it was controlled by that other (foreign) elite, the Roman Catholic church—but it too, was finally closed in 1961. *La Phalange*, however, did become significant in the elder Duvalier's effort to control the church.

The press was muzzled, although the small amount of international news came from the *Agence France Presse* and the United States Information Service (USIS). Radio stations fared no better. For "hard news," most Haitians relied on the Voice of America, Radio Havana, the quite accurate *télédiol* ("ear-to-snout," word of mouth), and the New York–based paper, *Haiti-Observateur*.

The situation in Haiti remained essentially unchanged until 1972 when a period of "liberalization" was introduced under younger technocrats who had joined the government. President Jimmy Carter's human rights policy made the Haitian government's repression somewhat more restrained. Spearheaded by *Le Petit Samedi Soir*, Dieudonné Fardin's mimeographed newspaper that reached a circulation of 10,000, and the *Radio Haiti-Inter* led by Jean Dominique and Konpè Filo, Haitian journalists became bolder and more critical of the Duvalier regime, although they distinguished between the president for life and his hapless subordinates and blamed the latter, never the former. The "thaw" lasted the length of the Carter administration; President Ronald Reagan's election was marked by severe repression in Haiti, which most everyone in Haiti agreed was the dictator's gift to the new president. More than 100 leaders were arrested, and some of the most prominent of them were exiled in November 1980.

One difference between the 1958 and 1980 crackdowns was the more liberal use of exile and imprisonment in the latter period while torture and death had been the preferred solutions earlier. The *presse parlée* ("spoken press") acquired great importance in view of an overall illiteracy rate that remained constant, but the switch to Kreyol by journalists was also important. These journalists were turning to the Haitian people—a novel approach; nothing else had worked.

The Roman Catholic church has had a tattered record in Haiti. Declared the official religion by the 1860 concordat, it had become an ideological weapon in the hands of the elite and a force for Haiti's westernization. Intermittent church persecutions of Vodou had become an issue for progressive intellectuals and politicians, and for all people who spoke for Haiti's autonomous cultural development, by the mid-1940s. Inevitably, a clash would come, particularly since most clerics and the entire church hierarchy were foreign.

When the dictatorship was challenged by student groups aided by the church, Duvalier killed two *malfinis* (Haitian birds of prey) with one stone. He accused the arch-conservative Breton archbishop, François Poirier, of financially supporting Communist agitators. This charge was made on the eve of the centenary of the concordat and raised essential questions about the future role of the church in Haiti. Duvalier's persecution of the church lasted from 1959 until 1964 and culminated with the expulsion of the archbishop, two bishops (including Rémy Augustin, the only Haitian bishop at that time), and numerous priests. The Jesuits were also deported in 1964, and the U.S.-born Episcopalian bishop, Alfred Voegeli, was expelled after twenty years of residence. The president and his entire cabinet were excommunicated, but this censure was lifted in 1966 when formal diplomatic relations were renewed with the Vatican. The indigenization of the bishoprics had the blessing of both President Duvalier and Pope Paul VI. The former had weathered a strong challenge to his rule and by meeting that challenge, had ensured years of tranquillity in the process. Duvalier received enormous credit in Haiti for haitianizing the church, and he gave himself yet another title, that of "spiritual leader." The church had taken five years "to fall."

The student strikes were broken, their leaders killed or imprisoned. The church was neutralized. One critic wrote, "The cry of *Communism* had restrained the business community from providing greater help and barred any sympathy or tacit aid from the American Embassy" (Diederich and Burt, 1969: 167).

François Duvalier's accusations were without foundation, but they worked successfully on the United States. But the president had not anticipated that a Haitian church would later prove a mightier opponent because it *was* Haitian. The struggle was about differing conceptions and among various social classes. Despite a century in Haiti, and despite being the most efficient purveyor of education, the church was still alien and an interloper. It had defended the interests of France against those of Haiti, and it had sided unequivocally with the U.S. authorities during the occupation, supporting them in their "civilizing mission."

Throughout the Duvaliers' thirty-year tenure, they gave massive support to U.S. Protestant missions, which strongly backed the status quo while claiming to be apolitical, and active government support for some Vodou priests was a further element of control that also worked against the Roman Catholic church. One anthropologist reports that some fifty U.S. Pentecostal groups active in Haiti have encouraged "social and economic dependence" on the United States. He pursued this analysis in the following words: "Protestant missionaries teach Haitians that they are backward and poor because they are mired in sin. Thus Haiti's poverty vis-à-vis the United States is rationalized on spiritual grounds. A young Haitian convert echoed this when he said to me, 'The American people are the *real* people of God.'"[32]

The one-day visit of Pope John Paul II to Port-au-Prince in March 1983 crystallized opposition to the Duvalier regime that had been developing over several years. The pontiff appealed for social justice for Haiti's poor and declared, "I have come to encourage this awakening, this leap, this movement of the Church for the good of the whole country." Accused of aiding Communists in the early 1960s, the Catholic church now stood accused of being a Communist organization by Duvalier supporters. The Roman Catholic archbishop, François Wolff-Ligondé, had been named by François Duvalier and was a relative of Madame Jean-Claude Duvalier. He was nonetheless obliged to heed the pope's warning that "something in this country must change."

More than 500 "base communities" were established by the Catholic church in the 1980s. This Ti Légliz (Little Church) movement sought to mobilize against the roots of Haitian poverty and provided an organizational framework in which peasants could challenge the system and demand change. The Ti Légliz movement was as concerned about the quality of life on earth as in the afterlife. A similar reassessment of Haitian society was also developing in other community organizations and in the Vodou community, and soon the Duvalier government could not control the flood of opposition. The Sunday mass and the Catholic Radio Soley also became popular sources of information after Duvalier muzzled the press in the 1980 wave of repression, and in July 1985, a seventy-one-year-old Belgian priest was murdered by government agents, and three foreign priests were deported.

— The regime of Jean-Claude Duvalier ("Baby Doc") has claimed that it sought economic revolution in Haiti, whereas Papa Doc had claimed to seek political revolution. But François Duvalier had not pursued a nationalist policy or protected Haitian national interests; he had after all offered the United States the seaport of Môle Saint-Nicolas as a replacement for its base in Guantanamo, Cuba, in April 1961. Similarly, Jean-Claude Duvalier tried to lease historic Tortuga Island to the Dupont Caribbean Corporation in the 1970s. Both Papa Doc and Baby Doc plundered the nation's resources and relentlessly pursued the acquisition of wealth. For example, the World Bank reported that in 1977 about 40 percent of the Haitian government's revenues and expenditures were unaccounted for.[33]

Neither Jean-Claude nor François Duvalier undertook any significant national projects to develop the nation's economy. Although the son allowed some private foreign initiatives to operate as part of a new technocratic image, the plight of most Haitians actually worsened under Jean-Claude's economic policies. The massive emigration from Haiti that occurred after 1977 was largely the result of these new initiatives, and the worsening economic conditions, rather than demands for abstract political democracy, led to a simple but powerful equation in the minds of the Haitian people: *Aba lan mizè, aba Duvalier* ("Down with misery, down with Duvalier").

The Carter administration, the U.S. Congress, and the French Socialist government of President François Mitterrand pressured Jean-Claude Duvalier to create a more democratic "image" for his regime. The members of the congressional Black caucus were particularly active in criticizing the Duvalier government, and they alone appeared to have understood the aspirations of the Haitian people. Carter and Mitterrand, on the other hand, were more concerned that internal Haitian dynamics were destabilizing the Duvalier regime, which had served their countries' economic interests, and that worldwide conditions were not conducive to the maintenance of such a repressive government. Indeed, the Duvalier regime appeared to be a bubble about to burst.

To create a more suitable image, the regime conducted a series of mock elections and referenda between 1971 and 1985, and these were deemed "positive steps" by the U.S. State Department. In January 1971, a constitutional referendum to allow the nineteen-year-old Jean-Claude to succeed his ailing father was approved by a vote of 2,391,916 to 1! In July 1985, six months before the government was overthrown, another referendum conducted to reaffirm the principle of the life-presidency resulted in a 99.98 percent victory for the president. In the first instance, U.S. Ambassador Clinton Knox publicly called for increased U.S. aid to Haiti in response to the regime's seeming stability;

Mme. Michèle Bennett Duvalier, First Lady, and Mgr. François Wolff-Ligondé, Archbishop of Port-au-Prince (early 1980s). Photo: CIDIHCA.

in the second, U.S. Ambassador Clayton McManaway praised the referendum as a progressive step. U.S. Ambassador Brunson McKinley told Haitian candidate Louis Déjoie II, that if disorders did not stop, both Haiti and the United States would be back to 1915. One State Department official declared that with all its flaws, the Haitian government was doing all it could.

The cynicism of these ambassadors reflected a long-standing problem in Haitian-U.S. relations. In a blatantly racist editorial that ignored the fact that François Duvalier could not remain in power without massive U.S. support, the *New York Times* on June 23, 1957, had blamed the Haitian people for their plight: "Haiti has been unfortunate in her political leadership in recent years. This was inevitable in a country with an illiteracy rate of over 90 percent. The highly emotional people, who have little but tribal rule and superstition to guide their thinking, have been notoriously susceptible to demagogic political appeal." This was not terribly different from what the *New York Times* had written on July 1, 1888: "The wealthy Haitians derive their revenues from ground rents in the cities and the spoils of office; consequently, they have little to lose by revolution, which is their occupation and amusement. By the black savages of the interior a revolution is always welcomed with fierce joy ... ready at the first note of alarm to pour into the towns by thousands, and, maddened by rum, commit every imaginable excess." Not a trace of big power politics; no economic considerations. But plenty of racism. Simply, Haiti was inept at self-rule.

A far-reaching symbolic event was the marriage of Jean-Claude Duvalier to Michèle Bennett, the daughter of an elite family, in 1980. A latter-day Marie-Antoinette or Eva Perón, she and her husband spent $3 million on the wedding. In one sense, the marriage reunited old foes, the brown and the black elites. Duvalier's "black" supporters feared that this renewed alliance of black and brown would re-establish the mulatto-elite control that had existed in Haiti before 1946, and the founder of the Social Christian party, Grégoire Eugène, wrote in *Fraternité* (Brotherhood), "Are we not handing back to the Right, on a silver platter, the political power we thought we had won in 1946?" (Prince, 1985: 33). This union did not presage a national alliance but a newly found unity between factions of an expanded ruling class. The middle class had lost its rhetorical position as the "vanguard" for urban and rural blacks, and the society was polarized further.

Traditional political parties, when they existed at all, were rarely more than an arrangement of convenience among a leader, his clients, and followers. Deviating somewhat from the aforementioned pattern, and following a Latin American trend, the late-nineteenth-century Liberal and National parties had represented variations on a theme of upper-class hegemony. Later, in the 1940s, Daniel Fignolé's Worker-Peasant movement (MOP) and the various Socialist and Communist parties were attempts to define political parties in more "institutional" terms.

Louis Déjoie's Haitian Democratic Alliance and, later, Duvalier's Sole Party of Revolutionary and Governmental Action were in the traditional Haitian mold, and so were the countless exile movements, parties, and groups that surrounded the candidacy of a presidential aspirant waiting for Duvalier to fall like a ripe mango. The most serious of these institutionalized parties was the fledgling Unified Party of Haitian Communists (PUCH), which merged many "tendencies" as it formed, or re-formed, in 1969.

In response to the political ferment of the late 1970s and early 1980s, the regime hastily organized a movement, the Conajec (National Committee of Jean-Claudist Action), in April 1978. The ferment had led to the creation of the Haitian League for Human Rights by Gérard Gourgue, Grégoire Eugène's Social Christian party, and the Christian Democratic party of Sylvio Claude, who was arrested and tortured eight times in five years.

The government seemed to lose its grip, and the last five years of the dictatorship saw an increase in political terrorism by the government. This increase was related to a further deterioration in the standard of living, which fueled political discontent. The government continually suspended constitutional guarantees, giving the president full power to rule by decree for periods of eight months when the rubber-stamp parliament, the Chamber, was not in session. Exile, prison, and torture increased during 1980–1985, and show trials, cabinet reshufflings, and the aforementioned referenda became common to assuage foreign sensibilities. But the constitution written for François Duvalier in 1957, another in 1964, another in 1971, and yet another in 1983—the last adopted by the legislature in one day—remained inoperative. In a 1982 report, the Inter-American Commission on Human Rights reached the

President and Madame Jean-Claude Duvalier at a state function (circa 1985). On the right is Dr. Roger Lafontant, Minister of the Interior and National Defense. Photo: CIDIHCA.

following conclusion: "No progress has been made, ... and there is no evidence that any government opening in the near future will re-establish [sic] free democratic life, ideological pluralism, or the free exercise of public freedom."[34]

— The Duvalier government fell relatively swiftly, and its sudden collapse came as a surprise to most people, especially foreign observers. One factor had been the government crackdown of November 1980, which was precipitated by public unrest following the Cayo Lobos incident, in which 100 Haitian "boat people" were stranded on a desolate Bahamian cay, and government indifference to the emergency had inspired widespread protests.

Forty people were killed in food riots in May 1984, and riots broke out again in November 1985. In February 1985, 60,000 youths demonstrated in Port-au-Prince with the slogan, *Pito nou mouri kanpe pase nou viv a jenou* ("We would rather die on our feet than live on our knees"). Despite foreign aid to the regime and increased private foreign investments in the Haitian economy—or perhaps because of them—

absolute poverty had increased. Military and economic aid from the United States, France, Canada, West Germany, Japan, Israel, Taiwan, and South Korea kept Jean-Claude Duvalier in for a time but could not prevent his government from ultimately sinking in the sea of its own brutality, ineptitude, and corruption. Baby Doc was bungling his economic revolution just as Papa Doc had bungled his political revolution. An important difference between the two administrations, however, was that the xenophobic father had sought to control and restrict foreign influence in Haiti whereas the son welcomed foreign interests with open arms.

The Catholic church openly supported opposition to Duvalier, and the decentralized Vodou communities also organized significant resistance to the dictatorship. In response, anti-Vodou groups assassinated about 300 Vodou priests "in the name of Christ and civilization." Although the national movement to dispose of Duvalier soon spread throughout the nation, the rebellion first took root in provincial centers and avoided Duvalier's stronghold of Port-au-Prince. The cities of Gonaïves, where Haitian independence had been proclaimed 182 years earlier, and Petit-Goâve soon emerged as the centers of the revolt.

The leaders of the anti-Duvalier movement apparently decided to resist the government apparatus peaceably. Massive unarmed demonstrations led to military repression and countless deaths followed by more demonstrations. To mollify the army, the population demanded a military government to emerge from a Duvalierist officer corps. There were few other options: No *guerrilleros* ("armed rebels") were waiting in the wings to create a revolutionary government. The fall of Duvalier's comatose government was only a matter of time, and Duvalier toppled from power as soon as the United States "pulled the plug" on his regime by ordering him to leave Haiti and by prematurely naming his successors. The White House announced that Duvalier [Jean-Claude] had left on February 1, but in fact he did not leave until February 7, 1986, after attending a lavish farewell party at the National Palace. Like the exiled Nicaraguan dictator Anastasio Somoza seven years earlier, Duvalier looted the national treasury before leaving the country.

Chapter 4

The Haitian Economy and the National Security State

Woch enba dlo pa konin jan woch enba soley soufri.
("A rock at river's bottom does not know how a rock in sun suffers.")

—Haitian proverb

AITI'S ECONOMY IS IN A SHAMBLES AND BECOMING MORE SO WITH EACH passing year. Strong interventionist policies from the International Monetary Fund (IMF) and the World Bank, foreign aid, and increased levels of "investments" have oftentimes resulted in improvement in the economy but the standard of living of most Haitians has continued to decrease nonetheless. Since the 1960s, the number of millionaires (in U.S. dollars) soared to about 200, but 90 percent of the population earned less than $120 a year. The 1987 per capita yearly income, however, was just under $300, doubling the income of 90 percent of Haitians.

The gap is awesome between the 1 percent that receives 44 percent of the total national income, owns 60 percent of the best land, but pays only 3.5 percent of the taxes and the poorest rural inhabitants who eke out a living with $50 yearly. By comparison, in the United States the richest 1 percent own about 45 percent of the national wealth.[1] A Haitian proverb comes to mind, *Si travay te bon bagay, moun rich ta pran l' lontan.* ("If work was a good thing, the rich would have grabbed it long ago"). Food imports, expensive by definition, now account for about half of all Haitian imports, with dire consequences with regard to hunger among the poor and scarce foreign exchange. This economic situation is a far cry from that of the first decade of the nineteenth century when Haiti was self-sufficient in food production and when the country was evolving a manufacturing base.[2]

The Haitian peasantry at that time had the highest standard of living of any peasantry in the Western Hemisphere after the United States, according to economist Celso Furtado.[3] Now, it has the lowest. There was no shortage of land, but there was a shortage of labor. More important, land distribution had just occurred in the context of Latin America's first land reform. Haiti's forced isolation benefited the peasantry in ways that its integration into the world market economy has not. The change from slavery and commercial agriculture to the postindependence of small peasant landholdings in much of the territory, the *minifundia*, was labeled "subsistence," a term with pejorative connotations. The peasantry ate, but since little money exchanged hands in the bartering system and the import-export trade ground to a halt after the heady "prosperity" under colonialism, little registered economically. As with social expenditures in education and health, the IMF might have labeled that kind of economic interaction "unproductive." Two reasons for the U.S. occupation in the next century were to foster commercial agriculture, and perhaps bolster a plantocracy such as the one that had existed during the colonial period, and to force a change in Haitian law to allow whites (i.e., foreigners) to own land. In this regard, the sarcasm of an officer of the king of France, in alluding to business imperatives and the logic of the import-export system, rings as true today as it did in 1773: "I do not know if coffee and sugar are essential to the happiness of Europe (or the United States), but I know well that these two products have accounted for the unhappiness of two great regions of the world: America has been depopulated so as to give land on which to plant them: Africa has been depopulated so as to have the people to cultivate them" (cited in Mintz, 1985: before title page).

APPLIED ECONOMICS: THE PUERTO RICAN MODEL OF DEVELOPMENT

The Puerto Rican model of development, as applied to Haiti, has two broad historical applications. It addresses particular processes—economic, political, and cultural—that took shape in Puerto Rico partly owing to historical accident, but it could have occurred almost as easily elsewhere. Forcibly reoriented toward the United States by a military takeover in 1898, Puerto Rico suffered political regression in the sense that the arduously negotiated autonomy from Spain would now be denied for nearly fifty years. Additionally, the United States decreed the use of the Spanish language illegal in the school system for a time and made a valiant attempt to turn the country away from Catholicism, hence attacking through political methods fundamental tenets of Puerto Rican national culture in order to facilitate the integration of that country into the United States and "speed up" the economic penetration of that society by giving it U.S. ethics and values. In forty years, the existing Puerto Rican bourgeoisie would disappear, giving way to a managerial class as the plantation replaced the hacienda and as the latter was replaced by the factory. At the same time, Puerto Rico would move from a self-sufficiency in foodstuffs and an emphasis on the domestic market to commercial agriculture and industrialization. This Puerto Rican "model" bears more than passing resemblance to conditions in Haiti as they evolved after the U.S. occupation of 1915.

But what is today referred to as the Puerto Rican model, in the economic literature and throughout the Caribbean, concerns a more contemporary phase in the economic history of Puerto Rico. The so-called Puerto Rican model refers to a form of dependent, capitalist industrialization in which a small peripheral economy is hitched to a much stronger one, with particular and specific features that heighten the dependency, a form of neomercantilism.

Operation Bootstrap was initiated by the Puerto Rican government in 1948, two years after partial autonomy came to the country. This plan, which would lead to rapid industrial development, was based on abundant cheap labor, tax "holidays," and tax incentives for new investors. The government built the infrastructure, the plants, and trained the work force for the corporations. Operation Bootstrap was a success: today the Puerto Rican economy is industrial, the per capita income is the highest in the Caribbean at $4,000 per year, and the agricultural sector accounts for a mere 4 percent of the gross national product (GNP). The model is now being widely imitated elsewhere in the Caribbean, partly institutionalized by President Reagan's Caribbean Basin Initiative of 1983, as other nations seek to undercut Puerto Rico by yet cheaper labor, more stringent control of unions, and bigger tax breaks. But certain essential Puerto Rican advantages are absent: extensive federal subsidies and large-scale migration—half of all Puerto Ricans have left their country in a form of "economic exile," unable to find work at home at the height of Operation Bootstrap's job creation. In the 1950s, 50,000 were leaving for the United States each year. The Haitian "boat people" are responding to very similar economic imperatives as shall be seen.

Further hidden from view of many mainstream economists, are the social costs wrought by the Puerto Rican economic model: an *official* unemployment rate of 25 percent, two-thirds of the population receiving some form of federal assistance, 60 percent living below the poverty line, more than 50 percent on food stamps, an illiteracy rate close to 10 percent, an obdurate drug problem, and an enormous public debt of $9 billion, one of the highest in the world on a per capita basis.[4] The Puerto Rican miracle has features that are also found in the Brazilian and Dominican miracles of the 1970s: soaring positive economic indicators and soaring poverty. According to an economist for the U.S. Agency for International Development (USAID), who would disagree with the thrust of my analysis, in Haiti "the economic growth that took place over the [1970] decade had significant but limited impacts on the welfare of the population" (Foster and Valdman, 1984: 217). Those impacts, as I see the situation, are structural inequality, inflation, and a lack of sectoral integration. U.S. assistance becomes hidden subsidies for U.S. corporations, whose overall rate of return is more than four times that of their mainland counterparts; buys domestic stability; and establishes dependent behavior that militates against a search for more permanent economic and political solutions.

One should note that the emphasis on the export sector in light industry has led to food imports—90 percent for Puerto Rico, about 100 percent in the U.S. Virgin Islands, and approximately 50 percent of Haitian food needs are now imported. This state of affairs distorts overall national development, partly by denying agriculture's multiplier effect on income, particularly as it undermines the importance of small- and medium-sized farms. This effect is particularly true in relatively capital-intensive rather than in labor-intensive industries, such as Puerto Rico's pharmaceutical sector. Based on the results, as well as the advantages that work in Puerto Rico's favor, it is doubtful that this model of economic development can succeed elsewhere in the Caribbean.

Knowing fully what would be required to make this model work, some right-wing elements in Jamaica, Grenada, and elsewhere have voiced the possibility of political integration to the United States as a prelude to economic integration. President Jean-Claude Duvalier even suggested in the mid-1980s that the United States allow heavy and systematic Haitian migration into that country in order to ensure Haiti's political stability.

Although the Haitian government, and some U.S. and international agencies, have touted Haiti as "the next Taiwan," neither the history of that island off the coast of the People's Republic of China, nor its internal sociopolitical processes over the course of a century, nor its relationship to a particular patron—Japan, or the United States—allows us to see a particular "fit" to Haiti. The point of contact was assembly manufacturing, but little else seems to augur that Haiti would be that "lucky."[5]

⌐ Haiti's 8 million inhabitants provide a sharp study in contrasts between the urban and the rural populations. No matter how desperately poor the urban workers, the rural population is even more destitute; the income ratio is ten to one in favor of the city. The only indicator that, on the surface, would imply that the countryside has an advantage is in employment, which derives from its agricultural character but carries little remuneration with it. An overall *admitted* unemployment and underemployment rate of 65 percent of the labor force infers levels of absolute poverty, the worst in the Western

The National Palace (circa 1970). Photo: Dennis Darmek.

Hemisphere. The Port-au-Prince metropolitan area, a primary city with two million inhabitants, is ten times the size of the next-largest city, Cap-Haitien, once known for its cultural life and prosperity as "the Paris of the Antilles." The capital handles 90 percent of foreign trade and monopolizes government expenditures for health, education, and all other areas with 87 percent of the budget allotment, largely for salaries, while the city accounts for only 40 percent of government revenues. Port-au-Prince is responsible for 98 percent of the energy consumption, and the Haitian elites and the foreign community of business people and diplomats live in its plush suburbs. All roads lead to Port-au-Prince, as they once did Rome, but only 600 kilometers (375 miles) of the 3,000-kilometer (1,800-mile) road network are paved.

Agriculture will remain significant well into the twenty-first century. More than 70 percent of the labor force is employed in that sector even as it becomes a declining element in the Haitian economy. Although agriculture employs more than two-thirds of the labor force, it produces one-third of the gross domestic product (GDP) and half of the export earnings. Yet the neglect of agriculture and the countryside does not augur well for the survival of the majority of the nation's inhabitants. With reference to income, rate of literacy, and access to services, the provinces lag far behind the capital.

Agriculture

More of the land area is actually cultivated than is suitable for agriculture—about 43 and 29 percent, respectively—which means that marginal lands are used extensively. The agricultural techniques are primitive, and the farm implements consist of machetes and hoes. Yet, the peasantry accounts for the production of the country's primary export, coffee, which is sold through a series of intermediaries, "speculators," and exporters who reap large profits. The product was taxed at exit, a most important source of government revenue. Coffee supplies approximately 40 percent of all export revenues. Since 1977, sugar, a hitherto important export commodity, is now *imported*, as are rice and any number of commodities that are part of the basic Haitian diet. Foreign sugar and rice undersell the Haitian products largely because they are subsidized by the U.S. and Dominican governments. These subsidies undercut local production and force Haitian farmers, whose resources are meager to start with, into dire poverty. Attendant problems are further alienation of landed property in many instances and migration.

One element that alleviates the harshness of the economic situation is that about 50 percent of the rural population owns—often without formal title—their land, in plots averaging less than half a hectare (1 acre), a residual effect of the land reform in the early nineteenth century. On the down side, these land parcels are minuscule because of overpopulation, the fact that primogeniture does not exist in Haitian law, the existence of large government-owned tracts, and the consolidation of desirable flat land into fewer hands. Population pressure is not the sole reason for land scarcity. Changes in land utilization and land maldistribution account for some of the difficulty as well, and overpopulation is a nonsensical concept unless one takes such factors into account. Overcultivated mountainous land exists side by side with idle, better-situated land. Much of the rest of the work force rents itself out to other peasants, works for relatives for no remuneration, or farms for a landlord on the principle of *de moitié* (according to which half of the production is forfeited). There are no appreciable cultural distinctions made between women and men: both sexes are equally involved in the agricultural sector. Women, however, predominate in commerce as petty traders (*mashann* or *madan sara*), which gives them a fair measure of independence. One historical reason for this predominance is that men were often inducted into the army in the nineteenth century. (See Chapters 1 and 5 for the role and status of women, family structure, and social organization as they develop from a Haitian worldview through the Vodou communities.)

Haiti suffers from what is described as an irreversible ecological disaster. First, a large population for the amount of land, of which only a part is arable, results in a density of 565 persons per arable square kilometer (1,462 per arable square mile), and overcultivation of the land is one consequence of this density. Second, charcoal is the only source of energy for home energy needs, and in the late 1980s, about 80 percent of Haiti's energy came from that source. As a result, according to the experts, the equivalent of 11 hectares (27 acres) of wood are used every day to meet that need.[6] In the mid-1950s, Haiti's forests—which up to the time of Spanish colonization had covered the whole island—were already estimated to cover only a low 7 percent of the land, and the decline continues at the rate of 5 percent of reserves yearly. A direct result of the search for both cultivable land and fuel is erosion, which is taking its toll. In the mid-1980s, an estimated 6,000 hectares (14,800 acres) of good soil was lost each year. Third, because of continuing erosion, there will be no water in Haiti in five years, and in twenty-five years the whole country will be a desert according to some scientific estimates. Numerous foreign public and private organizations are alarmed by this ecological disaster—a problem much outside the Duvalier government's concern or interests—and have been attempting to preserve what is left of the soil and trees, knowing that previous conditions are not recoverable.

In Haiti, the peasants have a saying, *Bò isit, wòch gen pitit* (here, "rocks beget rocks"), but in this case, economic necessity was responsible for the ecological disaster: immediate needs for food production, fuel, and building material could not easily be balanced against long-term land management, especially with the government's lack of concern. The story, however, began much earlier, with wholesale deforestation by the French in the seventeenth and eighteenth centuries, which led to the magnificently prosperous plantations for which Saint-Domingue was famous and the exploitation of precious tropical woods, such as mahogany. As early as the 1820s, Haitian governments passed legislation restricting the destruction of the tree cover, but as with much Haitian legislation, it had little impact: Social and economic realities and administrative corruption were more powerful. In the absence of widespread migration as an economic and political solution to landlessness and soil erosion and in the absence of large-scale industrialization, family planning and land conservation policies remain the only credible options at this point. These options cannot be exercised, however, without massive popular participation, and with the interests and the needs of the peasantry safeguarded.

Industry

Although agriculture generated about 40 percent of a GNP of $1.3 billion (G. 6.5 billion) in 1980, the manufacturing sector, largely for export, accounted for 12 percent, followed by government at 11 percent and commerce at 10 percent. Presently, the assembly industries account for approximately half of the country's exports. These figures contrast markedly from those of the pre-1967 period. Between 1960 and 1967, the economy was deeply stagnated: The GNP rose at a yearly rate of 1.3 percent, agriculture grew at a mere 0.4 percent (Garrity, 1981: 25), and dismally low investments fell further.

These were the most brutal years in which the Duvalier dictatorship consolidated itself. Thousands of Haitians were murdered, and tens of thousands fled into exile, inaugurating a "brain drain" of skilled professionals that would abate only in the mid-1970s. (It was at this time that I and my immediate family left Haiti.) Some people estimate that 85 percent of Haitian professionals and technicians live abroad (Prince, 1985: 69), for an overall total of more than 1 million Haitians. Additionally, there was a fairly continuous drop in the tourist industry because of the kind of government terrorism described in Graham Greene's novel *The Comedians*, the events that brought Haiti and the

Dominican Republic to the brink of war in 1963, and worsening poverty under "improving" economic indicators.

Between 1967 and 1980, a startling event occurred for Haiti: Jean-Claude Duvalier, at age nineteen, became the lifetime president following his father's death in April 1971, startling because the transfer of power was peaceful. Manufactured output in the mid-1970s increased sharply, though the groundwork had been laid in the final years of François Duvalier's presidency as he desired to consolidate his dynasty and thus showed flexibility. Vice President Nelson Rockefeller's visit in 1969 had also paved the way for renewed foreign penetration of the floundering Haitian economy. In 1967, there were only 7 firms engaged in assembly work; in 1970, there were 51. Three years later, in 1973, 140 corporations had settled in Haiti, and in 1986, there were about 300 U.S. corporations, all located in Port-au-Prince. Of 80 "Haitian" firms, one-third were subsidiaries of U.S. corporations (Garrity, 1981: 26), and another third were joint ventures between U.S. and Haitian business people (Foster and Valdman, 1984: 233). But despite all appearances, the actual total of U.S. investment in the Haitian economy was meager,[8] and those "investments" consisted largely of fully depreciated machinery and Haitian financial resources (Foster and Valdman, 1984: 235). Because of a volatile political situation, it is argued, U.S. corporations were unwilling to take great financial risks. The extraordinarily high profit margin afforded by a day wage of approximately $3.00, coupled with used machinery and Haitian financing, made the political risk palatable.

Meanwhile, the sudden increase in the number of U.S. firms in Haiti was accompanied, year in and year out, by a generally positive image for the dictatorship, particularly as contrasted with its first, somewhat more nationalistic phase, 1957–1969. The U.S. media and corporate spokespersons insisted that Haiti was politically stable. There was an obvious inconsistency between the image of the regime that the U.S. media and private sector were helping to build and the investment behavior of that same private sector. The meager U.S. financial investment—averaging $740,000 per installation in 1979 (Foster and Valdman, 1984: 235)—paralleled the disappointment of the Haitian commercial elites earlier in the century when the U.S.

occupation, too, failed to result in the massive levels of investment the United States made in Cuba and Puerto Rico.

Haitian manufacturing for the export market, principally in the category of objects made from imported components, rose sharply after 1971, and this secondary sector grew to account for approximately 50 percent of all exports, though many articles failed to meet the 35 percent local-component rule for duty-free entry to the United States established by the Caribbean Basin Initiative (Prince, 1985: 56). The reasons for the increase in assembly manufacturing, despite endemic political instability, are obvious. High unemployment, low wages, political repression, and high productivity—the very same factors that render the country politically unstable—make Haiti a manufacturer's paradise. Corporations "can count on a profit margin of at least 30 percent, and sometimes as much as 100 percent, from their Haitian operations."[9] The low investment rates; the absence of restriction on profit "repatriation," a primary feature of the Haitian model; and low labor costs make these high profit margins possible. Government policy has led to foreign business opportunism and a domestic lack of opportunity. Haiti had, in a sense, become the "land of opportunism." Far from the nationalist or patriotic image François Duvalier first tried to portray, the regime after 1969 was "internationalist" in its overall economic policies. Foreign business enterprises would be attracted while the means of control over these enterprises would be nonexistent.

Haiti has a good business climate. A survey found that "half the firms reported that their productivity was about equal to U.S. levels for comparable lines and activities, while about one-fifth said that it was superior" (Foster and Valdman, 1984: 237).

The sociopolitical context of the Haitian economy is made clear in an invitation to U.S. corporations from the Haitian Assembly Industry Association (Sonocoa): "U.S. firms have undoubtedly been disturbed [elsewhere] ... by mounting union pressures coupled with wage increases and new fringe benefits ... [and] run the risk of ... production faltering because of strikes and work slowdown." In Haiti, "a skilled labor force with excellent work attitudes is abundant and available at a remarkably low cost," and "union problems simply do not exist" (Garrity, 1981: 28). When about fifty unionists tried to organize in 1980, they had

Baseball factory in Port-au-Prince industrial park, utilizing a female labor force (circa 1980). Photo: CIDIHCA.

been arrested, tortured, and exiled or killed by November. That particular wave of repression took in, besides the unionists, journalists, and others—to celebrate President Reagan's electoral victory and the death of Carter's human rights concerns, to paraphrase what was said in Haiti at the time.

Since the late 1960s to the present, an urban industrial working class numbering about 60,000 has been created. Perhaps as many as 90 percent of the workers in the assembly industry are women (Garrity, 1981: 32), with a somewhat less "lopsided" mix in the import-substitution area. The rationale for this preference for women is everywhere the same: Industrialists have argued that women are more docile, "require" less income, and are more amenable to tedious yet exacting tasks—an exercise in applied sexism. Indeed, women's incomes are, on the average, 10 percent less than those of men (Foster and Valdman, 1984: 238). Haiti has one of the world's largest percentages of women in its labor force—55 percent—which may be owing to the country's extreme poverty as well as to the existence of a somewhat less sexist cultural environment. In Port-au-Prince proper, where traditionally many women and girls have moved in search of domestic employment, women outnumber men by as much as 30 percent, and women are still coming from the provinces in a steady migratory wave.

Summary

The connections among political development, political structure, and the economy are plain. Haiti's good business climate was extracted at the expense of political self-determination, particularly as the economy became more sensitive to dictates from abroad, in the 1890s and again after 1967. The popular uprisings that resulted in the 1986 overthrow of a dictatorship backed by an internal elite and its powerful foreign mentors also resulted in the loss of approximately 12,000 jobs of the 60,000 created since the late 1960s. The rise of independent trade unions and countless other organizations centered on men's and women's concerns, in all sectors and occupations, including the Vodou religious community, created "uncertainties" and made business people nervous. The vociferous demands for a democratic outcome do not augur well for business and may hurt Haiti's business prospects. One business group, the Council for the Americas, has after all suggested that "consumer democracy is more important than political democracy," though Haitians have benefited from neither.[10] Instead of helping sustain the national mood for greater freedom, investors through their actions create greater economic dislocation, which may help institute further repression. Strong political institutions without strong unions that would be the foundation for these very institutions result in less rather than in more freedom, contrary to liberal thinking that would divorce economic from political factors.

Economic hardship, on the other hand, is a primary element in political strife. Unemployment and underemployment, inflation and high consumer prices—Haiti suffers from some of the highest prices in the world, and some of the highest rates of regressive taxation—led directly to the popular dissatisfaction and disaffection that ended in the government's overthrow in 1986 and attempts to overthrow the successor regime, the National Council of Government, in 1987. Both economic factors and political dissatisfaction have led the government to become even more coercive, to extract the last pound of flesh, as it were.

What went wrong with the Haitian model of development, itself fairly typical of dependent capitalist developmental models? When one considers some of the principal difficulties of such a model, the structural dislocation of the Haitian economy simply cannot be remedied by more of the same. Restructuring rather than reform needs to occur. The cycle of borrowing to produce, producing to sell, and selling to borrow is a vicious cycle that ultimately benefits only a small percentage of the Haitian population, as is evidenced by the lopsided statistics for wealth distribution as well as worsening poverty. In the current situation, overpopulation plays a minor role. The current structure of the Haitian economy cannot support even half the present population, and the structure should be made to fit present population numbers.

Belgium's and the Netherlands' economies do support far higher populations on roughly similar space. Short of seizing colonies, as was formerly the case with these two countries, Haiti must develop internally coherent stratagems in which agriculture and industry pursue integrated national aims; in which the export market is subordinated to domestic needs; in which investments occur according to master plans laid by an "honest" government (i.e., uncontrolled by special interests); in which international relations with Western powers and the international agencies they control are benign; and in which cooperation with similarly situated countries (e.g., the Caribbean Community and its institutions) can take place in an atmosphere of trust and true equality. By true equality, I mean simply that the needs of a nation and its population are assessed in a spirit of cooperation and friendship and not, as presently done, according to the desires and greed of the dominant social classes. Stopgap reforms such as the mere creation of jobs must be measured against long-term outcomes achieved through long-range planning. Such planning is difficult if not impossible in a dependent capitalist state.

The lack of sectoral integration observed by some economists presents yet another set of difficulties, creating enclave economies where none should exist and preventing a smoother arrangement in which one sector sustains another on the road to national development. The social linkages that are sustained by such enclave economies are between a domestic elite and the country's foreign allies rather than the more traditional relationships such as those that might exist between a nation's capitalist class and the workers and peasants. Allegiances and alliances are forged internationally rather than nationally.

It must be noted that economic linkages may exist when there are no formal political linkages. Pre-independence Jamaica, formally controlled by the United Kingdom, had its economy tied to the United States after World War II, and from 1763 until 1959, the Cuban economy was primarily under U.S. control, even though Cuba was a Spanish colony or formally independent during that period. Before independence, much of Spanish America was in the British economic orbit, a fact recognized by European and U.S. leaders at the time.

The connection between political and economic spheres, and the factors that underlie that reality, is further demonstrated by the alliance between national and international elites and the difficulties the former may have in accommodating the needs of its population. Citing Antonio Gramsci, Michael Parenti wrote: "The ruling interests must act affirmatively on behalf of public interests *some* of the time. If the ruling class fails to do so, Gramsci notes, its legitimacy will falter, and its power will shrink back to its police and military capacity, leaving it with a more overtly repressive but more isolated and less secure rule."[11] In Western terms, this is the difference between democracy and dictatorship, or between Western powers and their Third World client states.

The National Security State

The net effect of having less than 1 percent of the population own almost 50 percent of the national wealth, while simultaneously increasing poverty and wealth differentials, is an increasingly powerful defense apparatus. The army, the police, the secret services, the dreaded Tontons Macoutes (Volunteers for National Security)—whose forebears were death squads in the late 1950s called *cagoulards*—all serve to rein in dissent. They do so with great effectiveness and at great cost. Foreign allies are usually obliging and extend necessary credits: weapons, ammunition, and training from the United States; fighter jets from Italy; assorted weapons and equipment from Israel. And hundreds of millions of dollars in economic aid are given to strengthen the sitting government. The net result of such measures is a bloated military well aware of its function to preserve order. Oftentimes, as was seen in Imperial Rome and more recently in Guatemala, El Salvador, and in contemporary Haiti, the military may develop corporate interests, which may not entirely coincide with the interests of the ruling social groups it is pledged to defend (this possibility is examined at greater length in Chapter 5).

Haiti's original army, a force of citizen soldiers consisting of former slaves, served Haiti well for a time. However, soon after independence, the army became the defender of the elite, of competing regional interests, and of quasi-feudal landlords. Simultaneously, the government's power was being challenged continuously by the peasantry.

The U.S. invasion and occupation of Haiti in 1915 set off a chain reaction that led to a massive popular guerrilla movement, which made a new army necessary. The U.S. Marine Corps created and officered a national guard, the Garde d'Haiti, whose objective was to fight the popular insurrection and to provide security for the new, although still meager, U.S. financial investments. Officered originally by upper-class men, the guard's leadership passed eventually to middle-class and working-class individuals who aspired to elite status. The class composition of the officer corps until the mid-1960s was the principal reason for the creation of the Tontons Macoutes and the women's branch, the Fillettes Lalo. The Forces Armées d'Haiti (FAdH), as the army is called, has become—as has the Roman Catholic church—a means for upward social mobility for working-class and lower-middle-class men and thus a source of wealth for otherwise "wealthless" people.

In the absence of competing institutions, the monopoly of force—a state prerogative—becomes the tool of an elite, and the armed forces become a power broker between segments of that elite, which they originally joined as junior partners. This situation was particularly true in Haiti from 1950, and the overthrow of President Estimé, until the rise of François Duvalier. In the absence of a foreign threat, the army's role as "guardian of the peace," as Haitian generals are wont to say, is to maintain the status quo. The great economic disequilibrium between the haves and the have-nots, and the subsequent lack of political legitimacy of the government, conspire to give the army and other security agencies leverage and power, which they exercise ruthlessly in the absence of any countervailing power. Such is the case in Haiti because of the structural arrangement that exists: the police made up a unit of the army, and the secretary of state for interior and national defense supervises all security personnel, including the secret police. National defense and the control of internal dissent are one. Never a source of pride, the army had always been a source of fear for Haitians.

Foreign Alliances and Social Crises

The correlation between hard work and a cozy life is not obvious in Haiti; indeed, there often seems to be an obverse relationship between the two. Proverbs and sayings about the working poor and the nonworking rich abound and come from keen observation and collective experience. Worsening conditions that lead to hunger and disease lead to individual-based violence in some societies and to communal strife in others, awakening military and paramilitary violence. In this sense, it is no accident that at the time of Duvalier's overthrow in February 1986, the U.S. government immediately rushed in riot gear and tear gas (*timojenn*) and started anew the training of the Leopards, Haiti's counterinsurgency troops. It was also no accident that an early symbolic act was the dumping into the ocean of a large bronze of Christopher Columbus and the renaming of Columbus Quay to Péralte Plaza.

The connection was being drawn, by these two events, between Haitian underdevelopment and lack of political control and the foreign allies of Haitian governments over a five-century span. Foreign support for the Duvalier dictatorship and the subsequent military dictatorship was perceived as instrumental in the strength and the length of tenure of the governments. Private investments and missionary societies backed these governments in words or in deeds, and "interfered" in Haitian affairs by definition. To the credit of the Haitian population, it refuses to become antiforeign, but it has learned to discriminate among behaviors, causes and effects, and outcomes.

Of the connected domestic and foreign entanglements, a British writer says:

> The immense economic weight of the United States is, however, an obstacle to building meaningful democracy in Haiti. Apart from the economic and psychological ties created by some $125 million Haitians receive annually from relatives working in the United States, total U.S. investment is around $130 million and more than half of Haiti's trade is with the United States. Perhaps a quarter of a million people depend on the earnings of some 50,000 workers at 140 light assembly plants .... Most of the U.S. plant owners consider any hint of unionism as grounds for instant dismissal.[12]

Besides the ties alluded to in the quotation, there are, additionally, consumption patterns that are imposed on the population with little regard to actual productive capacity and with little reference to the nation's control over the economy, hence over any meaningful political and cultural organization. All of these points quite logically lead to the fact that there is a correlation between social crises and foreign entanglements. Indeed, the connection is obvious, whether one speaks of inflation, the impact of tourism on national culture, or whatever.

Migration and Exile: Results of a Depressed Economy

When political power was used by a small group to achieve economic and financial preeminence, countless Haitians went into exile, and about 1.5 million Haitians live abroad, about one-fifth of Haiti's population and one of the world's highest ratios. The countries with large Haitian expatriate populations are the United States, the Dominican Republic, the Bahamas, Canada, and various other European, African, and West Indian countries. Everywhere, these exiles face a combination of racial prejudice and ethnic discrimination. In the United States, a country that had considered the Haitian government a reliable ally, the exodus proved embarrassing during the Duvalier years, because it would have to be proved that the Haitians were economic and not political refugees, notwithstanding evidence to the contrary. In the Western world, a distinction is made between economic and political refugee status. To admit that a connection may exist between dismal economic conditions and political strife may invite ideological dissonance, and indicate that all is not well in a "democratizing" capitalist country like Haiti.

Migration seemed to increase at the time when there was increased levels of aid and investments and while the U.S. media and government were praising Jean-Claude Duvalier on a regular basis. Haiti was open for business, but the successful development schemes, not so inadvertently, increased the hardships and inequality. From 1971–1979 for a period of eight years, about 15,000 Haitians fled on sailboats, and landed in U.S. jails. The grand total may have reach 40,000.[13] Meanwhile, Haiti's foreign debt grew to reach approximately $1 billion at the end of 1987.

Despite real gains in industrial output, infant malnutrition rates rose from 21 percent in 1958 to 69 percent in 1977 to 87 percent in 1980. Between 1971 and 1977, inflation reached 75 percent while purchasing power fell 45 percent. Inflation fluctuates wildly, but is said to hover at 30 percent. In May 1980, Duvalier asked Reagan to relieve pressure on the Haitian government by allowing 50,000 Haitian migrants yearly. The U.S. response was to patrol Haitian waters and the high seas and to forcibly return Haitians to their homeland, without any ethical or constitutional considerations for their safety.

A study on Haitian women shows the links between U.S.-sponsored development and Haitian poverty and migration: "Since it started anew in 1971, under Jean-Claude Duvalier, the Office of Development of the Artibonite Valley (ODVA) is the primary agent for underdevelopment in the region. Without scruples whatever, ODVA expropriates lands from peasants and burdens them with irrigation fees and taxes, forcing them to become 'boat people' to avoid prison."[14] The rise in land value, owing to improvements of various kinds, was accompanied by a land grab by landlords, urbanites, and foreigners.

Politics and economic hardships created political refugees. Simultaneously, between 1971 and 1977, the population of Port-au-Prince increased by 145,000 to approximately 1 million inhabitants, largely because of people having been thrown off the land by rural schemes of development. These new residents were not absorbed by foreign-owned industries, however.

The contemporary picture bears some resemblance to what occurred during the period of the U.S. occupation. At that time, about 50,000 Haitians died, hundreds of thousand of acres were transferred to U.S. corporations, and maybe 300,000 peasants migrated to U.S.-owned sugar plantations in Cuba and the Dominican Republic.[15] According to one U.S. anthropologist, Haitian migration is unlikely to stop now:

> Forces beyond Haiti's borders largely demand some continuance of the flow. The Dominican sugar harvest ... cannot exist without Haitian labor. The Bahamas, in spite of its ambivalence and vacillation toward Haitians, is just as dependent upon them for low wage labor, and I predict that soon Florida agriculture interests will prefer Haitian labor, as some Miami Beach hotels already do. Regardless of events internal to Haiti, these forces will continue to demand Haitian labor. [Foster and Valdman, 1984: 348]

The Dominican Republic represents a particularly difficult case in light of widespread mistreatment suffered by Haitians there for the past two generations. Following a massacre of 30,000 Haitians ordered by Dominican President Rafael Trujillo in 1937, because he worried about the Africanizing of his mulatto country, an arrangement was made whereby Haitian cane cutters would satisfy the needs of the sugar industry. The contract for economic cooperation between the two neighboring countries was expanded in 1978: Haitian officials received $1.5 million per annum as well as guarantees that anti-Duvalier activity would be banned and that workers would be monitored for their political views. The arrangement was particularly severe on the women, who either were left behind in Haiti or followed their men illegally. According to Dominican newspapers, a number of women were forcibly sterilized, and bonuses were paid to management for such action.[16] In 1979 and 1982, the London-based Anti-Slavery Society and the United Nations Working Group on Slavery denounced the agreement between the two states as disguised slavery. Under enormous popular pressure, the Haitian government was forced to abrogate the contract in 1986.

The assassination of presidential candidate Louis-Eugène Athis in August 1987 may have occurred because he had spent years organizing Haitian labor in the Dominican Republic. Head of the Democratic Movement for the Liberation of Haiti (MODELH), Athis's death was additionally a signal to other candidates that the army would not allow Duvalierism to be uprooted.

Popular demands for unionization, political parties, and a free press increased political repression during the Duvalier dictatorship as well as under the military dictatorship that followed Baby Doc to power. A crackdown in November 1987 echoed the crackdown of November 1980 in which 200 persons in the media, labor unions, political parties, and church groups were muzzled, exiled, or murdered. Between the two dates, a change of government, a "revolution," had taken place in February 1986, according to the Western media. The situation has deteriorated further since 2000.

If remittances of Haitians abroad to families left behind are contributions to daily survival, bilateral and multilateral aid given by foreign governments, international organizations, and nongovernmental organizations is also necessary for the survival of the Haitian regime. One should note that much multilateral assistance—notably from the World Bank group and the Interamerican Development Bank (IDB)— is in fact U.S. controlled in its disbursement. Under the guise of helping attenuate the suffering of the population, foreign assistance allows the government a certain latitude of action and options it would not otherwise have. Foreign aid, which accounts for between 40 and 75 percent of Haitian development program expenditures, additionally occurs where it will have the greatest impact in support of private investment, with far-reaching consequences on what one may want to call the U.S./U.S. rather than the Haiti/U.S. trade.

One U.S. economist wrote that "the Government's first five year plan (1972–1976) gave priority to rebuilding the country's infrastructure" (Foster and Valdman, 1984: 211). Roads, electric power, and expansion of the Port-au-Prince harbor were the key elements of that plan, and these improvements directly benefited the U.S. corporations that were being established to take advantage of the cheap work force. There was no overall, integrated development blueprint, and few if any intersectoral links existed between the various segments of the economy. In the second plan (1977–1981), increased investments were to occur in agriculture and industry, but in reality, a tighter link between Haiti and the international market was to be developed, hence a continuation of the status quo and not development that would necessarily benefit the majority of the people. A later statement by another U.S. expert, with quotations from a U.S. official document, is most significant and deserves to be quoted fully:

> Haiti's "attractiveness" and "untapped possibilities" have not been lost on Washington, which also recognizes the island's strategic military importance. "First, the U.S. has significant security interests in Haiti which shares the Windward passage to the Caribbean sea and the Panama Canal with Cuba. Haiti is strategically located only 700 miles [1,125 kilometers] from Florida and the existence of a non-hostile government and populace in Haiti is a fundamental security interest."[17]

The statement continues, citing an incredible admission on the part of a U.S. official:

> According to plans laid in 1982, "AID proposes to shift 30% of all cultivated land from the production of food for local consumption to the production of export crops .... AID anticipates that such a drastic reorientation of agriculture will cause a decline in income and nutritional status, especially for small farmers and peasants .... Even if transition to export agriculture is successful, AID anticipates a 'massive' displacement of peasant farmers and migration to urban centers."[18]

He might have added, migration to the United States as well. This is economic change engineered by political means. The economic priorities of the U.S. government with regard to Haiti are the same as those of the Haitian government. For example, Finance Minister Leslie Delatour had closed numerous enterprises and increased unemployment in an effort to make the country more "competitive" in world markets during his tenure in the Namphy government. Much along the same lines, a British writer said:

> Some schemes, like certain hydro-electric projects or the eradication of the pig population [which suffered from African swine fever], have severely damaged the peasant economy to the benefit of the growing industrial and agribusiness interests. In 1982, more than 200 Canadian missionaries in Haiti protested to the Canadian government over its support for a [U.S.] scheme to build two hydro-electric plants in the Artibonite Valley, the country's most fertile region. The plans involved flooding 4,000 hectares and dispossessing 60,000 people to provide power for the Port-au-Prince industrial zone. A USAID report in the same year stated that the final goal of its development aid was a "historic change to a greater commercial interdependence with the U.S.A." [Prince, 1985: 72]

Foreign aid commitments, in the public sector, totaled $676 million for the period covered by Haiti's first two five-year plans, 1972–1981, though actual disbursements were lower (Foster and Valdman, 1984: 207). As further assistance, 130 private voluntary organizations were to provide food and health care to alleviate conditions created by foreign aid and relentless development, supplementing food provided by Public Law #480, "food for peace" (Foster and Valdman, 1984: 208). Fifty or so U.S. fundamentalist Protestant missions were to attempt to restructure the Haitian psyche, norms, and values to fit a new "Americanized" country.

The presence of about 300 U.S. corporations on Haitian soil, at the close of the Duvalier regime, all of which are financially more secure than the host government, did not augur well for non-interference in future electoral or extra-electoral contests. The military governments that took over between 1991 and 1994, and subsequent economic dislocation since then, have resulted in further deterioration of the economic sphere, as we shall see later. In the words of one U.S. business person, stability was the primary achievement of the Duvalier decades and proved a boon for investors.[19] A USAID official concluded optimistically that "although worldwide recession has effectively blocked growth of the Haitian economy since 1981, it is anticipated that with the U.S. recovery the Haitian economy will return to the growth path of the 1970's" (Foster and Valdman, 1984: 214).

According to a former U.S. ambassador to Haiti, tourism forms the third leg, with industry and agriculture, of Haiti's development. But tourism requires comforts that are unavailable to Haitians, and the introduction of luxury goods and services stimulates demands in the Haitian society that can never be satisfied. The goods must often be imported from the country of the tourists' origin. Tourism can be costly, and like the assembly plants, relies on cheap labor, largely that of women; exemption from local taxes; the climate, of course; and the state of health of the world, especially U.S., economy. Major operations—hotels, airlines, public relations firms, travel agencies, consultants—are foreign owned and subsidized by the Haitian government, which spends scarce hard currency on costly infrastructure rather than on basic needs. English becomes the sole language. Tourism in Haiti contrasts with tourism in developed Western societies, such as the United States, where linguistic and cultural integrity are not at stake and where infrastructural development responds to overall needs.

The costs are largely cultural and psychological. As a service-oriented industry, tourism according to many scholars can foster servility, which may lead to an inferiority complex, and it may aggravate racism and ethnocentrism on the part of the visitors. Because of Haiti's stark poverty, the image of paradise required for tourism is often unobtainable, and contact between the two national cultures is difficult in view of the unequal power relationship. The trade could institutionalize the cultural gap to the detriment of the economically weaker group. The head of the Caribbean Development Bank, an economist, summarized the problem in these words: "We welcome

Young children in Haiti face the *restavèk* phenomenon of virtual slavery (a kreyol term for working as domestic help outside the home) circa 1980. Photo: CIDIHCA.

foreigners, we ape foreigners, we give away the national patrimony to foreigners .... It is a state of psychological, cultural, and intellectual dependence on the outside world."[20]

In many instances, a large proportion of the work force in the service sector in general, as well as in the tourist industry, is female. The work includes more "formal" occupations such as chambermaid, waitress and receptionist work as well as more "informal" occupations such as prostitution. Male prostitution is widely practiced in Port-au-Prince and the elegant suburb of Pétion-Ville. If female prostitution is often "domestic"—individual women involved with primarily an upper- and middle-class Haitian clientele—there are bordellos, which cater to foreign employees of corporations, to some of the 15,000 Americans living in Haiti, and countless other foreigners. Male prostitution is primarily with the foreigners in Haiti. The availability of males is a matter of individual or family survival. Often times bisexual or homosexual, some are heterosexual whose dire financial straits have led them to prostitution. The seeming prevalence of bisexuality, rather than strict homosexuality, may well be a pattern in the Afro-world and in Latin America.

As a result of these sustained contacts with the exterior, and without prejudging the question of origin, AIDS has developed into a major disease since the first case was diagnosed in 1979. Haiti was rapidly stigmatized, and other tourist-dependent countries in the Caribbean took measures to hide their cases. In 1982, the Atlanta-based Center for Disease Control (CDC) listed four categories or groups at risk: homosexuals, hemophiliacs, individuals with a drug habit who used an intravenous mode, and Haitians. Removed from the CDC list in April 1985, the Haitians were placed back on the list in August 1986 as a group at risk via heterosexual transmission. Haitians protested energetically. It is well worth noting that the Haitian boat people and the AIDS panic coincided and that U.S. government officials released information about the connection between AIDS and Haiti when scientific data was dubious.

In Haiti, as in Africa and Afro-America, the disease very rapidly affected women and children as well as men. From the beginning, in Haiti, about 30 percent of the cases were female, and that percentage has steadily increased. For much of the world, the disease spreads through heterosexual behavior.

AIDS presents Haiti with an impossible situation. With about 600 physicians, maybe 600 nurses, and fewer than 2,000 hospital beds for a population of almost 7 million, the country is faced with endemic diseases and illnesses brought about by malnutrition; cases of tuberculosis, malaria, and salmonellosis; and venereal diseases, all of which take precedence over AIDS.

Conclusion

The proliferation of problems since 1971 has its genesis in earlier decades and is the result of an interplay of elements and forces in the society. These elements and forces have not come together to resolve Haitian crises and set the nation on the path of development. On the economic side, a combination of foreign aid and investments working within a particular model of development has led to some success statistically, yet the level of impoverishment is greater than ever before. On the social side, many foreign missionaries have accompanied the technical experts and complemented their skills: The missionaries are supposed to affect Haitian culture by introducing permanent changes in norms and values that will facilitate economic change. Inherent in their attitude is the premise of an uncivilized Haiti and the certitude of their own civilized status.

Since 1971, statistical evidence has revealed some improvement in certain areas, in terms of criteria that define development as generally understood in Western Europe and North America. But simultaneously with an improved infrastructure; an increase in investments, which are smaller than they appear at first blush; and the growth of light industry of the assembly variety for the export market, not the national market, the population has become increasingly restless. Thirty years of dictatorship represented thirty years of political struggle, and an increasingly harsh political environment in which short periods of liberalization could not hide an overall downward trend. The stakes simply became too high for any of the players to willingly step aside, without a major conflagration ensuing. The events that have transpired since February 1986 simply confirm this trend.

The heavy transfer of scarce financial resources to security forces, whose function has never been external defense but internal control, ensures that the "peace and stability" spoken about by business people so publicly may occur. One anthropologist has noted that sometimes "a successful development project can increase local inequalities, creating further migration" (Foster and Valdman, 1984: 345). Successful development—based on a given definition of development—can lead to increased disparities internationally as well, and to dependence, which affects national and individual pride.

Migration from the countryside to Port-au-Prince, and to foreign countries, indicates a deep-seated dissatisfaction with the political and economic state of affairs, and particularly with the policies that have generated the kind of development responsible for the creation of so much wealth for so few people. The necessary linkages between the three legs of Haitian development are absent. Industry relies on imported materials and the immediate exportation of local production. If agriculture is to be developed, it is to be reoriented toward exportable crops even as landlessness and hunger increase. Labor policy must ensure a docile, if not servile, work force with few protections and safeguards lest it lose its competitive edge. As a result, paramilitary agencies must be strengthened to meet any disruption or any challenge, hence the delivery of additional weaponry after the departure of Duvalier. Tourism—in a weak society—can easily lead to a dislocation of the national culture, particularly when that society faces traditional racism and has a large resident foreign population.

Can any of these policies lead to development? Alice in *Alice in Wonderland* asks, "Would you tell me, please, which way I ought to go from here?" "That depends a good deal on where you want to get to," answers the Cat. One might say that the answer to the above question depends on what is meant by development. Not that Haiti is unique, far from it. Although more stark in Haiti, similar failures are apparent in the United States, too, as that country has problems of a nagging "underclass," hunger, homelessness, crime, and illiteracy—none of which can be easily resolved.

Haitian migration illustrates further the juxtaposition between Haiti's political economy and the country's political repression, the connection between the economy and national security. In more developed societies, a distinction is established between the twin concepts of national security and the national interest. In Haiti, the second concept never appears, partly because a national consensus has not yet emerged, and class divisions and antagonisms necessitate the application of the first concept. Seemingly absent from consideration is the idea that national security may be better served by a more equitable economic system. The failure to understand the connection between the economy and national security has led to a rejection of Haitian refugees abroad. Intuitively, perhaps, some of these refugees had thought of democracy as an economic concept.

Chapter 5

Politics and Government

Kreyon Bondye pa gin gom.
("God's pencil has no eraser.")

—Haitian proverb

HAITI HAS HAD TWO DOZEN CONSTITUTIONS SINCE 1801, AND AN examination of them is useful. First, they indicate which ideas predominated at what particular time in Haiti's small upper class and the extent of the level of its integration into Western culture. Second, these constitutions, though honored in the breach, represented the intellectuals' vision of an ideal society they ardently desired. Indeed, the 1987 constitution states in its first article that "Haiti is an indivisible, sovereign, independent, cooperative, free, democratic, and social republic," when in fact Haiti is few of these things. The fact that constitutional principles were at odds with political practices was a source of frustration and despair for enlightened members of the elite. What many people failed to realize is that far from being a "young society," Haiti is an old society whose roots are deep in the African soil but whose more immediate political traditions are anchored in the colonial heritage of slavery and color and class.

Furthermore, all Haitian constitutions have been liberal, in the classical sense of the word, because of the social base of the elite that arose from the Haitian and French Revolutions of 1791 and 1789, respectively. In Haiti, the constitutions of 1843, 1889, 1902, and 1950 stand out as having been particularly advanced for their times when compared to other constitutions around the world. Perhaps because "practice makes perfect," Haitian constitutions are often small literary *chefs d'oeuvre*.

THE CONSTITUTION OF 1987 AND NATIONAL INSTITUTIONS

The constitution adopted by referendum on March 29, 1987, broke with tradition in most regards. Although less than 7 percent of the electorate had cast their ballots to name forty-one members of the constitutional assembly in October 1986 (nineteen others were named by the government), approximately 50 percent of the voters participated in the constitutional referendum, voting 1,268,980 yes and 2,167 no, an approval rate of 99.8 percent. Virtually all groupings had called for ratification: labor unions, peasant organizations, the Roman Catholic and Protestant churches, and most political parties and groups, including the Haitian Communist Party (PUCH), which was legalized by the passage of the document.

These organizations had been active and had established study groups throughout the country, and the constitution had been studied line by line by the population. Duvalierist groups, on the other hand, fought against the constitution, which they labeled "Communist." Although it was not expected that the vote would transform Haiti, the common people placed their hope in a symbolic act against the dictatorship. One voter said, "If we said 'no' today, it would mean that we wanted to go back to slavery under the Duvaliers." Another: "Nothing will change, really, they [the government] will do their part, and we'll do our part. If we want them to respect this constitution, we'll have to make them."[1]

Inherent in the debate on the constitution was an indication that the level of political awareness was indeed high in all classes of society. But political consciousness alone does not change a political culture or centuries of bad government. In fact, political repression usually accompanies such a display of awareness everywhere in the world. The statement about making the government respect the constitution is echoed in two traditional Kreyol sayings: *Konstitisyon sé papié, bayonet sé fè* ("The constitution is made of paper, bayonets are of steel") and *Fè koupé fè* ("Iron cuts iron"). This realistic assessment goes beyond cynicism to become a call for struggle and optimism. Otherwise, why vote? Eight months later, on November 29, 1987, the death of about 150 women and men at the hand of government forces who stopped the national election did not mute the cry in the street, "We know, we know, but we still have to show them!" As a personal example, my eighty-four-year-old aunt tried to vote for the second time in her life (women's suffrage had been granted by the constitutional assembly of 1950, which her father had chaired). This behavior on the part of the people was not a case of naiveté.

The lengthy constitution of 1987, 298 articles drafted by fifty-seven men and two women, was profuse in its minutiae and thoroughgoing in its coverage. Its effectiveness was in doubt, since it went against "tradition," which admits that dictatorship is a 400-year-old Haitian tradition. What compromised the constitution further, in the eyes of the Western media in particular, was its violation of sacrosanct tenets of free market ideology when it assigned to the government a number of tasks under the rubric of "basic rights" such as education and health care. What the analysts failed to understand, however, were the changes that had taken place in the popular psyche, changes that had led to the events of February 1986 and that made the violent government response all but inevitable. It was no longer a matter of "good" versus "bad" presidents but of a rotten system in need of fundamental change.

The constitution of 1987 represented one such change. It digressed enough from earlier constitutions to indicate the future possibility for change, but it was still a liberal document, profoundly reformist, and came from the wellspring of upper- and middle-class society. Political awareness may not have heralded a different "political culture," but the beginning possibility for such a cultural change.

Fine-tuning to avoid a cataclysm of the sort Duvalierism represented was necessary. The elite desires reform, not revolution, but all classes desire guarantees against the return of Duvalierism. It is in this sense that the authority of the executive—long dominant over the legislative and judicial branches of government—was divided between a president and a prime minister, even though a political paralysis might ensue, which could lead to a dictatorship to break a deadlock. Although the prime minister was head of government, he or she was not to be elected by the national constituency; the president, whose powers were reduced considerably remained the only official elected nationwide. The procedure was somewhat dissonant in view of the expectations, though the objective was the strengthening of political parties.

Further guarantees against Duvalierism led to an independent Permanent Electoral Council (KEP), an Office for Citizen Protection, and stringent guidelines for public finance and for the courts. A plethora of decentralized territorial jurisdictions accompanied by a "gridlock" of age requirements and duration of tenure marked the new constitution. Although the age of majority is eighteen, one has to be twenty-five to fill lesser offices, thirty for the Senate and the prime minister, thirty-five for the presidency, and forty for the KEP. Men and women who meet these requirements and those of residency, must meet yet another: that of property ownership. This requirement prevents countless Haitians from seeking local or national office. Meanwhile, the term of office is three years at the local and national levels, four years for the Chamber of Deputies, five years for a nonrenewable presidential term, six years for the Senate, seven to ten years for judgeships, and nine for members of the KEP. The overlap of terms of office was to ensure that the president and the prime minister were denied areas of critical control that they might have used to restore a dictatorship.

Civil and political rights were enshrined in Title 3, Chapter 2, sections B, C, D, E, H, I, and J. Individual and personal freedoms were to be an expansion of the ideas expressed in the Preamble: "The Haitian people proclaims this Constitution ... To guarantee its inalienable and indefeasible rights to life, liberty, and the pursuit of happiness, in conformity with its Act of Independence of 1804 and the Universal Declaration of Human Rights of 1948." Included in these rights were the freedoms of expression, association, and assembly; of thought and access to information; and of property and security.

More significant, however, were the sections of the constitution devoted to human rights. In the Preamble, it is stated that the constitution was

- To re-establish a strong and stable State, capable of protecting norms and traditions, sovereignty, independence, and a nationalist vision.
- To fortify national unity in eliminating all distinction between urban and rural populations, through the acceptance of a linguistic and cultural commonality, and the recognition of the right to progress, knowledge, education, health, work, and leisure for all citizens.

In order to anchor human rights on economic equity—and to establish what can be defined broadly as economic democracy—several sections were devoted to the issue. Title 3, Chapter 2, sections A, F, and G abolished capital punishment, defined access to health care as a Haitian right, reasserted nineteenth-century Haitian laws about free education at all levels, spoke of freedom from hunger, and addressed the issues of housing, social welfare, security, and—only obliquely—women's equality. Articles 52, 53, and 268 established compulsory civic and military service for men and women under army supervision. Title 9, Chapters 1 and 2 defined economic rights and a safe environment as basic. The constitution realized that agriculture is the country's source of wealth but that the peasantry is desperately poor. Therefore, the National Institute of Agrarian Reform was created "to reorganize the structures of real property and to implement an agrarian reform to benefit those who actually work the land." An ombudsman was created in the Office of Citizen Protection whose sole function was to intervene on behalf of a citizen's complaint against the government.

The two most important changes, however, came as a result of lobbying by peasant groups, notably from Zentray (Entrails)—Zenfan Tradisyon Ayisyen (Children of Haitian Tradition). Both changes were major reversals of previously stated policy. The first was the recognition of Kreyol as Haiti's national language and its new status as the official language, listed ahead of French. This change was incorporated in Article 5. Syntactically and grammatically related to West African languages, with mostly a French-derived vocabulary, Kreyol is spoken by all Haitians while French is spoken fluently by approximately 10 percent. Article 213 created a Haitian Academy, on the model of the

Académie Française founded in 1635, to standardize Kreyol as its French counterpart standardizes the French language.

The second change, in Article 257, was the decriminalization of Vodou by repealing the decree-law of September 5, 1935, on superstitious beliefs, and the disappearance of the special role for Roman Catholicism, a role it had had since the concordat was signed in 1860. No state religion is recognized. Vodou is practiced by most Haitians, and the significance of the traditional religion was recognized in the following passage from Article 215, which reinforces the Preamble:

> Archaeological, historical, cultural, and folkloric treasures of the country as well as architectural wealth which bear witness to the grandeur of our past are part of the national patrimony. Consequently, monuments, ruins, the sites of our ancestors' great feats of arms, the high religious sites of our African beliefs, and all vestiges of the past are placed under the protection of the state.

All things being equal, Vodou might play the role that Shinto exercises in Japan, as the spiritual essence and emanation of a people and a culture. A number of progressive groups now open their debates with prayers offered by a priest, a pastor, and a *houngan*.

The final issue to be discussed here concerns the disposition of the armed forces. The military, from its creation by the U.S. Marine Corps, continues to play a major role as "arbiter," save for a brief period under François Duvalier until it could be "macoutized," which was easily accomplished through a system of rapid promotions from segments of the population best described as a shade or two above the lumpen proletariat. The question that arose after February 1986 and which persists to date was, how does one purge the military of Duvalierism and reconstitute its cadres while "it" is watching? Events in late September 1988 seem to have offered a partial answer: The dissatisfaction of sergeants and corporals could lead to a *coup d'état* whose purpose might just be to rid the army of unsavory officers. This scenario, however, was preempted by the dissolution of the Haitian army in April 1995.

It was hoped that the constitution would set in motion the elements to create a professional and a political force. Removed from direct control of the president and the minister of the interior, the new Force Publique would consist of two separate bodies: the police forces, operating under the Ministry of Justice, and the armed forces, subdivided into land, sea, and air forces and the technical services, under a general officer selected for a period of three years. The army made it abundantly clear that it did not intend to accept any of the constitutional provisions that affected it when it began a massive internal overhaul in August 1987.

Easily the most discussed—and possibly the most popular— constitutional provision was Article 291, which forbids for a period of ten years participation by "any person well known for having been, by excess zeal, one of the architects of the dictatorship and of its maintenance during the last twenty-nine (29) years." This provision applied to those people who had benefited financially as well as to those who are commonly known to have tortured and killed political prisoners during the Duvalier regime. (The particular effect of this prohibition is discussed a little later.)

From the beginning, the specific structures established by the Haitian state have been particularly weak, partly as a result of a lack of any real connection between them and national institutions and partly because of a lack of any real consensus among Haitians. At one end of the spectrum, the objective is to control the state apparatus in order to reap financial rewards and to dominate a vast work force. At the other end, the objective is freedom, however defined. This pattern was set early during French rule and has survived, modified, to the present day. There is as yet no emerging consensus on basic definition, let alone on what is to be done. Each group reserves the right to create the "national vision," to use a phrase actually used in the constitution.

The 1987 constitution was an intentional attempt to bridge these divergent visions, and the composition of the assembly that brought it forth consisted of individuals as diverse in their social origins as could be expected. In a sense, they created a document that established structures which are more faithful to the hopes of Haitians, but they also realized that it could not but be a transitory tool, since the nation itself is in transition. On June 20, 1988, when General Henri Namphy deposed the civilian president, who had only been in office five months, Namphy declared the 1987 constitution dead, inappropriate, and out of tune with Haitian historical realities. On March 13, 1989, General Prosper Avril, who had overthrown General Namphy, reinstated the constitution of 1987, but it remained inoperative.

THE MILITARY DICTATORSHIP AND THE ELECTORAL CAMPAIGNS OF 1987–1988

The election of January 17, 1988, represented the end of a flawed process set in motion with Duvalier's overthrow in February 1986. The election also indicated a new beginning in the struggle for justice and freedom as well as the continuation of a dictatorship. If the means justified the end, democracy was to have represented a stage leading to justice and freedom, which it subsumes. But Duvalier's ouster released popular forces that had seemed dormant. There were suddenly about 200 presidential candidates, who had waited impatiently for an opening in the presidency. By October 1987, this number had dwindled to three dozen, and there were two dozen a month later.

There seemed to be a discrepancy between the popular uprising and the sophisticated arguments heard in the street and on the radio, on the one hand, and the expectations of the presidential aspirants, on the other. The latter were largely replaying the last campaign, in 1957, which made little sense because the Duvalier years had irremediably altered the fabric of Haitian social and political life. It is in this context that the words of an illiterate woman I overheard in the street are explained: "The [common] people will have to educate [instruct] the elite." The people one calls *gwo chabrak* ("those who wear big Western suits")! These were ominous words that would reverberate all the way to Washington, DC.

Each new political era in Haiti is inaugurated by the time-honored tradition of drafting yet another constitution. In 1987, the new constitution, as seen in the previous section, had taken a different course. That constitution was easily the most far-reaching in all Haitian history, and most of its major provisions came about as a result of intense lobbying efforts by peasant groups. Until 1946, Haitian politics had been the preserve of a small elite, the top 1 percent, and then the middle classes, another 5 percent of the population, entered the political stage. Today, the rural peasantry and the urban working class are demanding access, but the elite and their foreign allies insist that the peasantry is not ready. As examples, "General Namphy ... has often said he believes his impoverished country ... is not ready for full democracy, but needs the army to gradually lead to a more open way,"[2] and sectors of the Haitian Catholic church have accused the United States of doing all in its power to stop the poor from taking over.[3] More than seventy years ago, the United States intervened militarily in the name of stability to prevent a similar demand, then labeled anarchy.

The idea that a popular government is not so much unstable as it is predictable in its demands seems generally absent from the rhetoric and from the analysis. David Rockefeller's strong correlation between democratic governments and hostility to foreign interests speaks for itself.[4] So does the declaration of a founder of the Haitian-American Chamber of Commerce: Haiti "has an authoritarian style of government but there are more freedoms and opportunities in private enterprise [in Haiti] than in many Western style democracies."[5] Democracy as "style," rather than as substance or process, leads to show elections, which are acceptable to foreign patrons.

If the first phase of the process of democratization was the ouster of Duvalier and the second phase, the selection of the constitutional assembly, the third phase ended with the massive approval of the constitution in March 1987. More than half the electorate voted, and the approval rate approached 100 percent. The referendum occurred with the orderliness and decorum befitting the historical moment, tempered by unabashed joy. The Duvalierists alone had asked for a "no" vote, and they received less than 0.2 percent of the votes cast.

The National Council of Government (KNG) was furious. It delayed the promulgation of the constitution, and it delayed the formation of the mandated independent Provisional Electoral Council (KEP), thus damaging the mechanism that would allow for the implementation of phase four, the establishment of electoral structures and processes. Precious time was lost. Later, in June 1987, the KNG overrode the KEP by shifting effective control of the electoral apparatus into its own hands, but the government was forced to rescind that decision after massive street protests in which many died when army troops opened fire.

Earlier, in January 1987, the original KNG had taken a decisive turn to the right when four of the more "liberal" cabinet ministers were dismissed under pressure from hardline Duvalierists. Even earlier, Gérard Gourgue—head of the Haitian League for Human Rights— had lasted a bit more than a month as minister of justice before being replaced by the former exile François Latortue, who himself was forced out in the purge of January 5. Still, Duvalierists had lost a round in October 1986, three months before, when they attempted to form a political party in violation of a constitutional ban against their participation in politics until 1997 and street protests forced the movement underground. (A Duvalierist party was as popular in Haiti as an avowed Nazi party in Israel.)

Phase five of the process of political democratization was to have been local elections for the smallest territorial units, the *sections communales*, in July 1987. Postponed twice, they were finally held at the same time as the mock election of January 1988. Ostensibly, the reason for the delay was the nationwide upheaval that followed the government's efforts to subvert the constitution. In June, besides attempting to seize control of the electoral process from the independent and highly respected KEP, the KNG banned the most representative of Haiti's three trade unions, the Autonomous Central of Haitian Workers (CATH), looted its offices, and arrested its officers. Additionally, some public corporations were closed because they were "inefficient," and some private companies also closed because of a "lack of profits," throwing thousands of Haitians out of work. These closures included all three of the country's sugar mills—while sugar was being smuggled into the country by high officials. Efforts to unionize were accompanied by massive firings, lockouts, and intimidation of workers by groups close to the army. At least 14,000 laborers in one assembly zone were locked out or fired in one particular instance. One U.S. observer noted that "companies producing goods for the U.S.

market, including shoe, sportswear, and electronic assembly operations, have been among the first to fire scores of employees attempting to unionize. The U.S. Embassy has remained silent, despite Caribbean Basin Initiative requirements that internationally recognized labor rights be respected."[6]

Additionally, the government was implicated in the stoning death and the hacking and burning of the body of centrist presidential aspirant Louis-Eugène Athis, along with the deaths of two campaign workers, in August. A similar event occurred in October 1987, when a minor presidential candidate, Yves Volel, was murdered at point-blank range by government security forces while speaking to reporters in front of police headquarters, a few hundred yards from the presidential palace.

Death squads roamed the street at night in army vehicles and uniforms, and each morning bodies of people who had been executed "gangstyle" were found. On July 29, more than ten bodies were found in Port-au-Prince alone, all executed with their hands and feet bound to their back. Recent U.S. State Department statements have "placed" these death squads in the Casernes Dessalines, the army's main barracks abutting the president's palace, and the commander of these barracks, and many other top army officers, have been implicated in the Colombian cocaine trade, which often passes through Haiti on the way to the United States.

These death-squad activities—which had the effect of imposing a curfew at 9:00 P.M.—were supplemented during the day by army sweeps of slum neighborhoods, in which dozens of people perished, and by the killing of demonstrators in large peaceful marches protesting government actions. Between June and August 1987, there may have been hundreds of casualties among the demonstrators and more than forty deaths. Typically, the U.S.-trained counterinsurgency unit, the Leopards, would ambush the demonstrators and benefit from the element of surprise. In no instance were the marchers armed and belligerent.

Haitian and foreign journalists were also attacked by security forces. They were fired upon repeatedly and suffered casualties. Routine armed attacks against political headquarters and radio stations also occurred throughout the period between June and September 1987. On the night of July 30, seven radio stations were attacked simultaneously, seemingly by army personnel. The attack lasted all night, and the shells found in the morning matched the calibers of military ammunition.

Despite the new, liberal constitution, the decree-laws enacted by the KNG concerning press and political party control were similar if not identical to those of the Duvalier regime in 1980 and 1985. The laws extended the definition of the press to include bookstores and printing presses so that booksellers and printers were made responsible for their subversive actions as much as journalists. The latter were required to reveal their sources, and informants were equally liable for prosecution or persecution.

Each demonstration was accompanied by killings at the hand of the army, and each series of killings gave rise to further protests and demonstrations. In frustration, political parties and movements, labor unions, student and women's groups, and particularly the left-of-center umbrella organization, the Committee of 57, called general, nationwide strikes that would shut the country down for days at a time and effectively paralyze trade and commercial activity for one or two weeks. The fact that these strikes occurred at all—despite their failure to reach their objective, the overthrow of the government—showed that anti-government sentiment was widespread. Strikes are a weapon to be used sparingly in a poor country, where income might be obtained daily and where no personal money reserves are available.

The Lessons of Jean-Rabel

Between 800 and 1,000 peasants may have lost their lives in the vicinity of the township of Jean-Rabel, the greatest such massacre since the Dominican government massacre of 30,000 Haitians in 1937. On Thursday, July 23, 1987, approximately 2,500 peasant members of the cooperative Tet Ansanm (Heads Together), a Roman Catholic group established four years earlier, headed out to join "antagonistic" peasants for what has been described as a reconciliation party. On the way, they were ambushed in a well-planned assault from which there was no escape, and at a spot where mass graves had already been dug. For four years, Tet Ansanm had been a thorn in the side of members of the landed oligarchy, the *grandons*, and a number of clashes had already occurred.

Jean-Rabel is located in the North-West department, a territorial subdivision long-accustomed to lengthy and devastating drought. Facing Cuba, and the Guantanamo naval base, the North-West has long been considered as an alternative location for a U.S. military station, and only desperate Haitian diplomatic maneuvers had forestalled that outcome. Under the Duvaliers, offers seemed to have been made that resulted in a preemptive 1987 constitutional ban on the cession of any part of the territory (Article 8-1). The North-West is easily one of the driest parts of the country, a fact that together with a grossly unequal social structure has led to widespread starvation and a situation close to actual famine. These conditions had led the Duvalier dictatorship to close access to the region for a period of years, except to some Americans.

The social structure is feudal. At the top, an oligarchy consisting of four families—Lucas, Poitevien, Richardson, and Marrhones—has controlled the politics, economy, commerce, transportation, and military and legal affairs of the region since the 1930s, when they made an alliance with the central government in Port-au-Prince. At the bottom, there are tens of thousands of sharecropping peasants whose lives have become more precarious as land consolidation has worsened with each passing government.

The method for land acquisition was deceptively simple. In the absence of any cadastral survey, land the oligarchy rented from the state was automatically extended to spill over onto peasant-rented lands, particularly in areas close to water. This was particularly true of the Lucas family, who owned thousands of acres, and three-fourths of the land irrigated by the Jean-Rabel River. Any protests brought swift retribution by local army units and the mobilization of the judiciary, which was headed by family members of the oligarchical group or their allies.

Any land improvements made by the peasants or infrastructural improvements, in terms of road construction or irrigation resulting from foreign developmental aid, rendered the land immensely more valuable and led to further "land-grabbing" by the powerful. Food crops

leave the region for Port-au-Prince and the Bahamas—leaving little
for local consumption—and commerce and transportation are
monopolies of the *grandons*. Land and population pressures have little
to do with the worsening political and economic situation, which could
be defined as the result of market forces. Overpopulation is a tricky
matter often used to disguise dismal conditions. A large number of the
Haitian boat people who made the voyage to Florida came from the
North-West, and they were promptly defined by U.S. authorities as
nonpolitical refugees. Nicol Poitevien declared on state national
television that his troops had killed "1,040 Communists"[7]—the Tet
Ansanm community was never interviewed by the state-owned media.

Even a Haitian government report speaks candidly about the region:

> From the socio-economic standpoint, the Jean-Rabel commune
> belongs to this most desolate region of the country commonly
> called "Le Far-West." In this mountainous and rural zone, the
> majority lives miserably from subsistence agriculture and
> charcoal production. On the other hand, one finds a local
> bourgeoisie—in some cases exceedingly rich—which controls
> agricultural production, public transportation, commerce, and
> political power. Curiously, this small elite quite rich, is the big
> beneficiary of government-owned lands which it obtains by
> lease at prices that vary between [US$4.00 to US$10.00] per
> *carreau* [1.2 hectares/3 acres] which it sublets, in certain cases,
> at very high prices to small peasants for a season. According
> to statistics recorded by the local office of the DGI [Secret
> Police], 84.5% of state lands as assessed by the census in 1984
> are found concentrated into the hands of three people.[8]

Being the most destitute of all regions in a destitute country, and
politically sensitive because it faces Oriente Province in Cuba where
tens of thousands of Haitians have settled over time, the North-West
became the recipient of charitable efforts by U.S. groups and the Haitian
Catholic church. These efforts were the antecedents of the events
that led to the massacre.

Once the Haitian Catholic church had achieved a modicum of
success in helping the rural communities in Jean-Rabel, it soon ran

into conflict with the power structure and its foreign allies. To resolve the "land question," peasant cooperative groupings, which would collaborate on all fronts, were formed. Besides sharing successful agricultural methods and techniques, Tet Ansanm established clinics, a drainage system, electrification, leisure centers, fisheries, and other elements that were analyzed correctly by the oligarchy as sapping its power. In time, approximately 10,000 peasants became members of the association. Conservative elements of the church, sustained by the Port-de-Paix bishop, started to fret. The church became divided, but Tet Ansanm merrily went down the path of confident defiance of a century-old tradition of subservience to the local oligarchy. The peasants started to question the government tax structure, the prices paid for goods and services, the land tenure system, and the prices paid for local produce by the *speculateur*, the middleman-buyer who has traditionally exploited the peasantry mercilessly. Adding insult to injury, Tet Ansanm developed several projects, including successful marketing projects, that bode ill for the future of the oligarchy. The *grandons* complained about their abandonment by the church, activities that could lead to their failing fortunes, and the lack of respect exhibited by a more proud peasantry, which had previously been subservient.

Together with land consolidation and the exportation of food production out of the region toward the capital and foreign countries, particularly the Bahamas, Protestant missions in the area deliberately tried to teach a gospel of resignation, and outer-worldliness, and aligned themselves with the oligarchy against the activism of the Roman Catholic peasant groups. In addition to these private missionary groups, controlled by parent bodies in the United States, other players weighed in on the side of the status quo. One of these was the U.S. government, which made available—among other things—"free" food under the food-for-work plan. This plan was strenuously opposed by the cooperatives, because, they argued, free food would destroy the regional economy by forcing laborers off their fields for lack of profit. Derisively calling it *manje sinistre*—approximately "victims' food," in the sense of a cataclysmic disaster—Tet Ansanm bought locally produced food and rejected the free U.S. food as the true disaster, the creator of real *sinistre*. Free food was distributed to landless peasants for infrastructural improvements, which increased the value of land, which was then seized by the *grandons*, creating more landless peasants—a never-ending cycle that would spin out of control.

Free food, or *manje sinistre*, eventually led directly to contraband, *biznis sinistre*—an almost untranslatable Haitian expression connoting a business venture that preys on the famished by selling not-for-sale U.S. staples. Such ventures increase dependence and dislocate the national economy. The dynamic "ingredient" that made it all possible was a venal officialdom operating in a corrupt system.

Once it was feared that Tet Ansanm was becoming too successful, yet another organism came to the fore to try to rechannel the energy of the peasantry away from a confrontation with the power structure, by limiting the scope of their activity to complaints *within* the power structure, in areas such as rent rather than agrarian reform. In the name of labor unionism, a splinter group of the Autonomous Central of Haitian Workers (CATH/CLAT) moved aggressively into the region of Jean-Rabel. It was backed by the most conservative union allowed to operate under Duvalier, the Federation of Unionized Workers (FOS), which in turn was sustained by the U.S. National Endowment for Democracy and the CIA-linked American Institute for Free Labor Development (AISLD). The stage was set for a confrontation between Tet Ansanm members and the *grandons*, their domestic and foreign allies, the Tontons Macoutes, which still roamed the countryside, and the military government in Port-au-Prince.

Three months after the fall of Duvalier, in May 1986, Tet Ansanm held a massive demonstration demanding the return of 690 hectares (1,700 acres) it said had been stolen by the Lucas family. Nine days later, Rémy Lucas and his men marched to the village of Gros Sable and set fire to the village and to fields in broad daylight. Sixteen peasants were murdered. When the peasants complained to the local constable, the *chef de section*, they were told that "one does not arrest a *grandon*." A similar answer was made by the justice of the peace. Several requests for help were made in subsequent months by Tet Ansanm, but no response was forthcoming from any quarter.

A month before the July massacre, General Namphy, the president, and General Williams Régala, the most powerful member of the military government (KNG), visited the area and left behind $20,000 for "organizing." On June 22, fifty members of Tet Ansanm were killed in a clash at La Montagne. Immediately before the "big event" in July, Haitian army units were removed from the area, and it was many days after the massacre before units of the army reentered the region—to destroy all physical evidence of the existence of Tet Ansanm as well as clinics, schools, churches, homes, and various factories. The mainstream Haitian New York City newspaper, *Haiti-Observateur*, analyzed the situation as follows:

> In summary, Tet Ansanm directly opposes the fiefdom of the Lucas and Poitevien families. Feeling their interests threatened, pushed around, the traditional authorities reacted violently. Using as an excuse a new initiative from the missionary group [Tet Ansanm], the authorities went directly to the offense. The "antimissionary" coalition is composed of sectors whose ideologies, interests, and ideals are clearly different. In fact, the Protestants join those described as Macoutes, *grandons*, and reactionaries. It is said that the "people of the Tet Ansanm movement" have connected the Protestants to the American CIA.[9]

So on July 23, 1987, 2,500 Tet Ansanm peasants were ambushed, encircled, and attacked with machetes, pikes, stones, and some firearms, which presumably belonged to Tontons Macoutes whose weapons had never been collected. Ditches dug ahead of time for the occasion were used for mass graves. The carnage lasted well into the next day, with no interference from military or civilian authorities. Those peasants who did flee were pursued and "arrested" by the pursuers. Some were beaten after they found refuge in the Jean-Rabel Hospital or in the prison. Only Tet Ansanm members were imprisoned, and none was interviewed by the media at the time. New machetes and $3.00 were distributed, it appears, to all individuals who had taken part in the massacre.

That summer, similar though lesser conflicts erupted elsewhere in the country, all in places where the local authorities and oligarchies were confident of government support in moving against peasant organizations. The U.S. media chose to ignore the social and economic dimensions of these struggles, choosing instead to call them a "civil war."

Role of the Church

The role of the church in the Jean-Rabel massacre was ambivalent. Once intensely reactionary while under French leadership, François Duvalier's expulsion of the archbishop, bishops, and prominent priests had paved the way for an indigenous hierarchy under his control in the early 1960s. The president had weathered several years of excommunication by the Vatican but had also named the prelates of his choice, as allowed by the concordat of 1860. The change from foreigners to nationals eventually made possible an overall transformation that was otherwise nearly impossible: the evolution of a praxis that would favor the poor and validate their life experiences and culture in the eyes of the church.

The divisions remained, however. A fairly conservative hierarchy was led by the de facto head of the church, the Cap-Haitien archbishop, François Gayot. The Port-au-Prince archbishop, François Wolff-Ligondé, had been shunned by colleagues for his close association with the former regime, and most of his functions were now carried out by his two auxiliary bishops. At the other end of the ideological divide was the Jérémie bishop, Willy Romélus, one of Haiti's best-liked figures. He, in a sense, symbolizes the significant changes seen in the church since the late 1960s. The changes, at one level, were connected with Vatican II, the recommendations of the 1968 Latin American Conference of Bishops (CELAM) held in Medellin, Colombia, and the admonishing of Pope John Paul II during his visit to Haiti in 1983. More significant, however, were the pressures from below, from clergy and laity, and particularly from the Ti Légliz movement of basic ecclesiastical communities. Early in 1986, one Ti Légliz group in Gonaïves issued a document which said in part: "There have been, at all levels, members of the Church who have agreed with the dictatorship and who profited by it: today, these must publicly apologize. Complicity with power must cease immediately. Only in this way shall we begin to see that the Church is not a pyramid, but a genuine communion."[10]

That kind of language indicated a rift in the church between progressive and conservative factions, between hierarchy and lower clergy, and among the hierarchy. Bishop Romélus's *Raché manyok, bay tè a blanch* ("Uproot the manioc, and clear the land") elicited a strong popular reaction on the part of a population frustrated by the tenacity of Duvalierist macoutism.[11] Romélus's statement is wonderfully ambiguous and subject to many interpretations, as is customary in Kreyol speech. However, everyone took it to mean that the *dechoukaj*, the uprooting of the dictatorial structures, should continue until the overthrow of the military junta.

The cry was picked up by one of the country's most-beloved priests, Jean-Bertrand Aristide, while the prelates were retreating into guarded support for the military dictatorship, the KNG. When the Haitian Catholic hierarchy, the Vatican, and the KNG tried to silence Father Aristide, or "Titide" as he is called affectionately by slum dwellers, in August 1987, their actions set in motion far-reaching events that specified the relationship as well as the interaction between the powerful and the relatively powerless. Hundreds of Catholics, most of them youths, invaded and occupied Port-au-Prince's cathedral, the Notre Dame basilica. Seven students went on a hunger strike for five days, demanding that Aristide be returned to his parish in Cité Soleil rather than banished to the countryside or exiled in Rome as planned. The striking students added the demand that the Jean-Rabel massacre be condemned, something church authorities had failed to do.

The first phase of this particular struggle ended when three bishops went to the cathedral on August 19 and read a statement that gave in to the students' demands. It also ended what might have been the only hunger strike ever undertaken against the Roman Catholic church anywhere in the world. At a press conference on August 20, Father Aristide stated, "We have the steering wheel of Haitian history in our hands ... and we must take a left turn." He continued, "A socialist Haiti ... alone can allow each and everyone to be fed and to find justice, liberty, and respect." At a morning mass on August 23, with about 5,000 in attendance, Aristide asked, "If I die, will you cease the struggle?" That night at 9:00 P.M. 100 kilometers (60 miles) from Port-au-Prince and 75 meters (250 feet) from an army post, an ambush to assassinate Aristide and three other well-known Haitian priests took place. The attempt was bungled, and the priests escaped alive, though not unharmed. There would be twelve more attempts against Aristide's life, all unsuccessful.

If the Roman Catholic church has traditionally been on the side of the power structure, and if large segments of it have had second thoughts, a very different picture emerges concerning the Protestants. The latter group is subdivided into denominations whose ideological positions are intricately linked to the social class ascription of their communicants, to their longevity in Haiti, and to their connections with foreign governments.

The most telling distinction is between pre-U.S. occupation churches—Episcopal African Methodist Episcopal (AME), and Methodist—and churches that have been established in Haiti during the occupation. The earlier churches, from their inception in the Haitian milieu, have tended to see a symbiosis between evangelization and conversion and social action. This attitude had tended to set them apart from the Roman Catholic conservatism of the time. An Episcopalian bishop, Alfred Voegeli, was unceremoniously thrown out of Haiti at the same time Catholic bishops were asked to leave, and in both instances, the cause was the link between these churches and the upper class, and the challenge they presented to an embattled middle-class regime. In the contemporary period, these "mainstream" Protestant denominations have encouraged change, promoted ecumenical dialogue with the Catholic church, and participated in the challenge to Duvalierist power. Since the mid-1960s, the Methodist church has been involved in adult literacy, health, reforestation, and general rural rehabilitation programs.

The picture changes, however, with the more recently established evangelical and fundamentalist sects in Haiti, whose genesis was the U.S. occupation and whose reactionary social and political message and challenge of the mainstream churches were welcomed by the Duvalier regime. In a letter to the U.S. Council of Churches, Navy Under-Secretary Edwin Denby had argued for establishing plans to evangelize Haiti in the first years of the century: "Nothing accords better with my own ideas .... I am familiar with the function of missions in foreign lands, and the advantages they give .... Haiti is enclosed in the United States' sphere; its relations with the United States are a vital question for us ... and in my estimation, the churches and missionary societies can be of very real help .... The Navy Department will be happy to facilitate your work in any way possible." The Roman Catholic bishop Jean-Marie Jan detailed the results of this suggestion: "Following the suggestion of the navy secretary, Protestant missions certain of U.S. government support have spread to the entire territory of the republic, and have multiplied down the years. The most generous American churches and missionary societies send numerous missionaries ... giving them enormous subsidies."[12]

The fundamentalist and evangelical groups are controlled by their churches in the United States, and in a report published in 1987, the Caribbean Council of Churches wrote that "the post-occupation group was also foreign-based, entirely American. As the religious support-system for a very unpopular military operation [the government] with political, social, economic and cultural objectives, it was seen to promote an anti-political, anti-Catholic, anti-Haitian pro-American message."[13] And one may add, antiblack since some Haitians are now defining the difference between Americans and Haitians as, "We are the black sons of Satan, and poor, and the Americans the white sons of God, and rich."

Because fundamentalist sects faithfully reflect U.S. ideological and racial biases and U.S. positions internationally, the United States has gained immensely from this "private sector" while France has been the great loser from this battle for the hearts and minds and work of Haitians. The influence of that country is now restricted to bilateral government interaction and pressure and the leverage accorded by its foreign assistance.

The connections among religion, politics, and economic exploitation are made clear in this passage of the 1987 report of the Caribbean Council of Churches fact-finding mission to Haiti:

Most powerful among the Churches is the Conservative Baptist Church which has come to be seen as the church of "Pastor Wallace." Pastor Wallace Turnbull is an American [white]

Southern Baptist of the extreme fundamentalist type .... His Church became involved in the North-West of Haiti, the region from which the great majority of "Boat People" have come. That section of the country has suffered most from the ill-effects of erosion, low rainfall, endemic and abject poverty and the serfdom of the "share-cropper" system. This is the region where Jean-Rabel is situated. And the very unfortunate commentaries on relationships between Protestants and Catholics has been the fact that the two groups which clashed were broadly comprised of Catholic *"Tet Ansanm"* on the one hand, and on the other hand, the land-owners, *tontons macoutes* and others—all driven by deep passions aroused by a widely distributed tract published by Pastor Wallace in which he portrays as "communist" all who have developed an awareness of their situation and who would take action for change.[14]

The Protestant sects increased Haitian dependence upon the United States, while simultaneously becoming a mainstay of support for the Duvalier dictatorship, as the Catholic church was becoming more liberal and playing out its "preferential option for the poor." This heavy, yet subtle, penetration of Haitian culture has served U.S. international interests, displacing other Western powers in the process.

One area in which the Catholic hierarchy and the fundamentalists agreed was about the persecution and eradication of the Vodou religion. The Protestant radio station, Radio Lumière, called it a "national curse" that should be "uprooted." About 300 Vodou priests were murdered in 1986, but little coverage was given to that massacre. A British journalist wrote that "those who hunted them down were sometimes led by youthful zealots egged on by Christians, mainly Protestant pastors, but some Catholics, many of them white and foreign."[15] Although many *houngans* were part of the Tontons Macoutes, probably as many Catholic priests and Protestant pastors were involved with the regime as *houngans* according to Max Paul, director of the Bureau of Ethnology of the University of Haiti. He continued: "Equating Voodoo with Duvalier's reign is a pretext for the massacres. It's an excuse used by those Catholics and Protestants who want to reduce Voodoo to a less significant role in Haitian culture."[16]

Coming from churches that had been notorious for the support of the dictatorship, the anti-Vodou position appeared self-serving. All three religions had had priests who were identified as card-carrying and gun-toting macoutes.[17]

The political influence of the Catholic Church increased with its social activism and in direct proportion to its involvement in schemes for communal development through more than 500 base communities, the Ti Légliz. The church's more ancient role as a supporter of the status quo was taken over by evangelical Protestant sects. Although seen as an upper-class church because of its membership and pro-Western ideology, the Catholic church has countered that reality in its role since the 1970s, particularly after the government repression of November 1980. The church's Radio Soley, founded in 1978, became the primary outlet for dissent after twenty-three leading dissidents largely from the influential radio media, were exiled. In this sense, the church has been one of the few organized alternatives for dissidence. Haitians wished to use all avenues to redefine the political situation, and the church obliged. But when the popular movement went beyond the church's politics of reformism, the latter felt it necessary to slow down the movement. More recently, the ten or eleven prelates forming the National Conference of Haitian Bishops have sought a delicate balance between popular demands and the conservative Duvalierist governments in place since February 7, 1986.

> The Church hierarchy, despite its insistence that it was "non-political," flew to the defense of the KNG to denounce the "communist" danger—in effect its own radical priests. Radio Soleil softened its broadcasts. Some recalled the frequent visits by the papal nuncio to the U.S. Embassy as the Duvalier regime crumbled. "The Church hierarchy has no interest in real change," says trade union leader Yves Richard. "After all, the Church is the second biggest landowner in the country."[18]

Popular Action and Candidates

The radio stations that broadcast in Kreyol had been instrumental in bridging the gap between town and country, and that medium—together with the popular theater—was an important element in the political consciousness that developed within the context of an overwhelming illiteracy rate. The popular movement had a chance to develop further and organize into a plethora of diverse groups after the departure of Duvalier all pushing and pulling in a same direction: the "demacoutization" of Haiti. The uprising that led to Duvalier's ouster had not been disorganized or spontaneous, but in the atmosphere of relative freedom created while the Duvalierists were regrouping, better possibilities were present. And though the hope and enthusiasm were palpable from February 1986 until September 1987, in fact few structural changes, if any, had taken place in Haiti. Two civilian justice ministers—Gérard Gourgue and François Latortue—were forced to resign their posts once it was realized that they intended to indict officials involved in the torture of prisoners and diversion of public funds, and the "citizens' arrest" by thousands at the Port-au-Prince international airport of secret police chief Luc Désyr resulted in a show trial of no consequence.

The government's inaction was met by popular action. A number of low-level Duvalier officials were executed summarily by lynching or stoning, mansions were looted and burned. Better-known Duvalierists went calmly into exile or continue to live peacefully as officials or on the margin of officialdom. Peasants demanded services and planned tax boycotts; they repossessed, if they could, land seized by Duvalierists, especially in the Artibonite Valley, the Plaine du Nord, and in the Jean-Rabel region. When serious flooding occurred near Haiti's third-largest city, Les Cayes, in June 1986, peasants rejected offers of food and demanded land instead—that region had made a similar demand almost a century and a half before in 1844.

The National Congress of Democratic Movements was formed in January 1987, during the atmosphere of relative freedom. In what was a turning point in Haitian politics, approximately 1,000 participants representing nearly 300 popular organizations met for five days. Speaking Kreyol, the debates were opened by prayers by a Catholic priest, a Protestant minister, and a *houngan*. Some of the demands and suggestions of this congress were met in the new constitution. It also set up a standing body, Konakom, which in turn indirectly spawned

Pharmacy in Les Cayes (1980). Photo: Howard Goldbaum.

the Comité des 57 (Committee of 57), representing fifty-seven key organizations, that took the lead in opposing the junta starting in June 1987. Although generally successful in the general strikes and demonstrations it called throughout the bloody summer of 1987, the Comité des 57 was unable to stem government killings or to reach its goal: the government's overthrow.

If a number of organizations emerged in the peasantry and urban work force as a result of the popular movement, meaningful political parties did not arise. Perhaps the only exception is the Unified Party of Haitian Communists (PUCH), formed in 1969 by a merger of the Popular Unity Party and the Popular Party for National Liberation and led by the charismatic René Théodore. It is the successor to Haiti's first socialist party founded by Jacques Roumain, the nation's most prominent writer, and Max Hudicourt in 1930 and briefly legalized by the "revolution of 1946." Another possible exception is the Popular

Unity Bloc (BIP), a coalition of three smaller parties led by Serge Gilles who has a strong connection with the French Socialist party.

Other parties follow a model established in the nineteenth century of being a mere vehicle for one man's ambitions. It is in this sense that most of the numerous presidential candidates in 1987 seemed to "replay" the campaign of 1957. This statement seems to apply particularly to Louis Déjoie II—whose father was François Duvalier's most formidable opponent in 1957—who represented the bourgeoisie. The son, a wealthy building contractor and considered one of the four major candidates, played on the nostalgia of simpler times and gathered his strength in daddy's old southern bastions: Les Cayes, Jérémie, and Jacmel. Déjoie's National Agricultural and Industrial Party (PAIN ["bread" in French and Kreyol]) is similar to other one-man parties, notably those of the former U.S. favorite, World Bank official Marc Bazin's Movement to Install Democracy in Haiti (MIDH), and of the Baptist minister and populist Sylvio Claude's Haitian Christian Democratic Party (PDCH). These three candidates represented the political right. Together with former justice minister and human rights activist Gérard Gourgue—a center-right candidate representing a center-left coalition—these four were said to account for 80 percent of the support nationwide. Gourgue became the compromise candidate of the Comité des 57, which had transmogrified into the Front National de Concertation (FNC, National Front of Consultation).

Further down the scale were Professor Leslie F. Manigat's Assembly of National Progressive Democrats (RDNP), founded in Caracas, Venezuela; former Duvalier minister and professor Hubert de Ronceray's Mobilization Party for National Development (MDN); the late Louis-Eugène Athis's Democratic Movement for the Liberation of Haiti (MODELH); Thomas Désulmé's National Labor party (PNT); and law professor and constitutional law expert Grégoire Eugène's Haitian Social Christian party (PSCH). All of these parties were center-right, indistinguishable from those of the first group as well as from one another. Somewhat more distinctive was the late President Daniel Fignolé's party, the old MOP, founded in 1946 as the Worker-Peasant Movement and rebaptized, with the same initials, as the Movement for the Country's Organization. The MOP retained its populist platform and support among slum dwellers.

The fact that there were originally 200 or so presidential candidates, some heading parties, some not, seems to indicate that anyone could become president—or thought so. There seemed a discordant inconsistency between politicians practicing their craft "as usual" and the mass movement. None of the candidates seized the popular imagination. Most of them seemed to want to be the "army's candidate," believing that the individual who would satisfy the generals and the United States would become the president, as François Duvalier had in 1957.

The laws that regulated the parties were similar to those devised by the Duvalier government. Among other requirements, parties had to submit 5,000 signatures to be legal, and they could not have a trade union or religious affiliation. The government could dissolve them and seize their property; moreover, extra-legal machinery could be put into place quickly for more effective control during an emergency.

Duvalierists of note were forbidden by Article 291 of the constitution to run for office, yet within hours of the banning of twelve Duvalierist presidential candidates, violent reprisals took place against members of the KEP, their homes and businesses and against nondisqualified political headquarters and candidates. The buildings marked for destruction were often within a few blocks of army barracks, police stations, or the National Palace. The rampage started early on November 3. The KEP national headquarters, the nerve center for all operations for the November 29 election, was set ablaze. Voter registration bureaus were attacked throughout the country, and a printing plant in charge of election ballots was burned. The government did nothing. On the contrary, it had told the KEP that little funding would be available. Goods and services had been borrowed domestically, and tens of thousands of volunteers had donated their time. Meanwhile, the United States, France, Canada, and Venezuela had given $7 million of the $9 million necessary to hold the election.

Although the presidential field was crowded, and the Senate and Chamber of Deputies moderately so, candidates for local offices were wanting. For 1,695 elected positions in the smallest territorial division, the communal sections, there were only 242 candidates; for 411 municipal posts, 54 candidates. Scheduled for July, these elections had been postponed because of the macoutes' stranglehold on the countryside: Duvalierists were running for these posts, despite the constitutional ban, and had managed to intimidate the local populations.

Role of the United States

Even by summer's end, well before the terrorism that began on November 3, all democratic sectors were having second thoughts about the feasibility of elections under the KNG. A push from the United States might have been sufficient for the government to fall, but despite all evidence to the contrary, the United States calculated that the military dictatorship ensured a modicum of "stability" and that a well-liked popular government could not. (That argument had previously ensured U.S. support for the Duvalier regime until the bitter end.) In 1986 and 1987, Washington praised the generals for "liberalizing" Haiti, doubled financial aid, and provided military advisers to train the Haitian army in riot control. The lessons seemed lost, for it was the army that rioted. General Williams Régala—allegedly implicated in the 1964 Jérémie massacre and the 1969 massacre in which hundreds accused of being Communists died—visited the United States three times, secretly, in the summer and fall of 1987 and made additional visits to Venezuela, the Dominican Republic, Israel, and South Korea for which no explanations were ever given.

> On June 30 Assistant Secretary of State for Inter-American Affairs Elliott Abrams spoke at length about the sanctity of the electoral calendar in Haiti without once mentioning the recent wave of killings. The Haitian military seems to have interpreted this as a sign that U.S. support is unflagging, so long as elections are delivered. The United States is seen in Haiti as promoting the forms of democracy—symbolic elections—without encouraging significant efforts to promote the democratic institutions required to give substance to these forms.[19]

Any kind of elections were therefore acceptable. And while the democratic sector was attempting to overthrow the government, the

U.S. deputy assistant secretary of state for Caribbean affairs threatened to cut U.S. aid if that government stepped aside.[20] Having had a hand in selecting the officers that controlled Haiti, the United States saw no alternatives to these not-so trusted men, despite the absence of a left-wing threat.

The Caribbean Council of Churches had this to say about the U.S. role in Haiti at the end of August 1987:

> With the advantage of hindsight, there is a more widely shared view among Haitians that the United States "intervention" of February 1986 in combination with the Haitian army which finally helped to oust Duvalier served to "avoid the full victory of the people and to slow down the process of change," in the words of a Haitian presidential candidate of the moderate centre. What is clearly apparent is the often documented fact of a distinctive and rising tide of anti-Americanism.[21]

With reference to the economy, the United States was blamed as well. The church report continued: "Economic resentments of the United States are especially marked among broad segments of the Haitian peasantry. A major cause is the dislocation of local market prices by the U.S. food aid programme .... Another lingering economic antagonism is the unsuitability to the Haitian peasant and tropical environment of imported American [white] pigs to replace the more hardy Haitian [black] pigs." The conclusions Haitians had drawn, according to the report, were that U.S. military assistance and training of the Haitian military were viewed "as U.S. complicity in an increasingly repressive climate." Hence the inescapable belief both by Haitian conservatives and radicals that the KNG is "totally in the hands of the United States."

Meanwhile, the U.S. congressional Black caucus and lobbying groups, such as the Washington-based Black lobby TransAfrica, were seen favorably by Haitians as trying to tilt U.S. policy away from its traditional concerns for stability, and for U.S. economic and security interests, and toward a concern for the Haitian national interest. The role played by African-Americans and liberal whites in 1986–1988 was precisely the role these same groups had played during the U.S. occupation of Haiti in 1915–1934.

Terrorism and Elections

The level of government terrorism increased once more a week before the elections set for November 29. Radio stations were attacked and destroyed once more. An urban market located a short distance away from a police station was set ablaze. A slum neighborhood with a police station in its midst was attacked. Churches were sacked and parishioners were brutalized. The Departmental Electoral Bureau (BED), which was being converted to house the central offices for the elections after the KEP building was torched, was set on fire; so was the Communal Electoral Bureau (BEC), for the third time. The army was seen crisscrossing the streets all night long while these acts were committed.[22] One day after the canceled elections and the carnage, the *New York Times* in an article dated December 1, 1987, printed the following headline, "Comrades in Terror: Soldiers and Thugs Are Reportedly Allied in the Campaign in Haiti to Cancel Elections." The article continued:

> Finally, after months of killing and terror attacks by unidentified gunmen, there was evidence that these people were working in concert with the armed forces, the institution that the United States had counted on to bring Haiti to democracy .... [A]s an observer of the disrupted elections, [former Ambassador Robert B. White said] he witnessed soldiers cooperating with civilian thugs .... There were many similar reports. "It seems clear to me," Mr. White said, "that there is a reciprocal relationship between the military and the Macoutes."[23]

It had taken the *New York Times* almost two years to believe the evidence. But then, again, Haiti was an ally of the United States.

The election of November 29 promised to draw record crowds, as had the constitutional referendum of March 29, 1987. About 150 may have died—having been shot, beaten, or hacked to death—and hundreds were injured, by men in army uniforms and in civilian clothes.[24] Dozens died at the Argentine Bellegarde school, named after my great-great-great aunt, a few blocks away from the National Palace. During the short hours of the election, machine-gun fire erupted from speeding cars, and grenades were thrown.

Although the campaign of terror had been continuous since November 3, the latest carnage lasted about thirty-six hours. The election-day massacre was carried out and synchronized with military precision. Death squads were active, particularly in the slum areas of Cité Soleil and Carrefour-Feuilles, which had organized grass-roots *brigades de vigilance* ("vigilantes") in self-defense. These brigades met the ire of the army, which arrested individuals who had formed these groups, and there is some evidence that more than forty were executed at the infamous macoute prison of Fort Dimanche. After canceling the elections, the military government accomplished what it had been unable to do in June 1987. It dissolved the independent electoral commission (KEP) and sent its nine members and many presidential candidates into hiding or asylum at foreign embassies.

Other cities had suffered the fate of Port-au-Prince. Although Cap-Haitien and Fort Liberté ballots had been ambushed and destroyed in transit, ballotless stations were attacked and destroyed all the same. A similar situation existed in the south. The ballots that made it through the blockade had to reach their destination by road. When the KEP asked for the use of military helicopters to deliver the ballots, the government said no. When the KEP rented two helicopters from Miami, they were not allowed to enter Haitian air space.[25]

Enough was known before the balloting to have anticipated some government violence against voters, and comments by citizens in the streets days before indicated that they feared some violence. The KEP was blamed by some people for having sent voters to their death. When General Namphy canceled the election and dissolved the KEP, he did so because that body had "imperiled the unity of the nation"—one presumes for having rejected the Duvalierist candidates. One day after the aborted elections, Generals Namphy and Régala are said to have met secretly with four Duvalierist candidates to discuss the future.[26] A "death list" of 103 to 152 names was said to exist.[27]

Next, the KNG seized control of the electoral machinery in violation of the constitution. It named nine unknown individuals to a new KEP, and new elections were set for January 17, 1988. New electoral procedures were issued that denied access of polling stations to anyone but the military and government officials who would see a ballot before it was deposited. Liberals in the U.S. Congress and the press called for military intervention, preferably by the Organization of American States (OAS) or the Organization of Eastern Caribbean States (OECS), which had been enlisted to give "legitimacy" to the U.S. invasion of Grenada in 1983.[28]

A delegation of Caribbean prime ministers headed by Edward Seaga of Jamaica—who appeared to be representing the United States—declared on December 10 that bygones should be bygones and that there still was time for new elections. The massacre was "history," Seaga said, and the KNG was acting "in a manner consistent with the constitution as they see it."[29] Early in January 1988, at a meeting of the heads of states of the Caribbean Community (Caricom), held in Heywoods, Barbados, that view was upheld. It is worth noting that the man who would emerge two weeks later as the president of Haiti had a personal relationship with some of these leaders, whom he had known while a professor of international relations at the University of the West Indies in St. Augustine, Trinidad. Seaga's representative said later that the elections of January 17th were "fair and traditionally Haitian."[30]

Meanwhile, the United States felt obliged to suspend its aid but did so reluctantly, and forty warships and 2,400 marines were on exercise near Haitian waters. Eleven Canadian warships were also nearby. This was an exercise in "gunboat diplomacy," which frightened Haitians more than it did their government. The four leading candidates—Déjoie, Bazin, Claude, and Gourgue—joined forces in a Democratic Front and refused, as did most other candidates, to participate in new elections unless the KNG resigned and the old KEP was reinstated. They called for a boycott instead.

The United States, though stunned and embarrassed by events, continued to send positive signals to the Haitian military. Throughout the summer, the United States had shown its unwillingness to "alienate or undermine" that group.[31] The deputy assistant secretary of state for the Caribbean, Richard Holwill, offered the Democratic Front an unconstitutional "Korean" formula, which was rejected promptly: select one candidate from among yourselves to compete head-on with one Duvalierist.[32] In fact, the United States, recognizing its limitations over its client state, was admitting its support for new elections organized by the KNG, hence support for the KNG itself. It was asking the Haitian government to do in less than twenty days what it had failed to do in twenty-three months.

The Duvalierists, shunned by the old KEP, restarted their candidacies confident of a positive outcome this time. In a very unexpected development, all these candidates, except for one, were rejected once more by the new KEP on constitutional grounds. The strategy started to emerge. The four popular candidates of the Democratic Front were boycotting the election. The democratic sector was out of the competition and represented what the military feared the most: indictments and trials for violations of human rights as had occurred in Argentina with President Raul Alfonsín. The civilian Duvalierist sector was unacceptable to the United States and to Duvalierist officers in an army that had come into its own. Of the eleven candidates that remained, only one was "presidential," with the necessary stature, education, and international contacts—Leslie F. Manigat. A former Duvalierist, with connections with politicians in Venezuela and the English-speaking Caribbean, he was personally impressive to none other than Secretary of State George Shultz.

The *New York Times* reported that "Mr. Shultz said that he had been impressed with Mr. Manigat's credentials as a scholar and author who has studied and taught in the United States, France and Latin America."[33] Bazin, widely believed to be the U.S. choice until November 29, announced more than a week before the election that Manigat would be selected as part of a deal between the United States and the Haitian army. Bazin added: "The Americans want stability at any price. But they'll pay for it later."[34]

President Leslie F. Manigat was "selected" formally on January 17, 1988, to serve a five-year term of office, in an "election" in which only 2–5 percent of the electorate "voted." Children voted by the handful. Young girls were transported from polling station to polling station, voting each time. Young men hid at a distance, to rush in to vote every time a white journalist happened by. Votes were purchased for the sum of $0.30. Ballot boxes were stuffed. Before the election, the U.S. government had declared that it could accept a 35 percent level of participation, and the Haitian government obliged by insisting that, indeed, 35 percent of the electorate had voted. This action is reminiscent of an admission of the State Department, made decades after the fact, that it had evidence that François Duvalier had been elected fraudulently in 1957.

Reading between the lines, the *New York Times* reported ahead of the election that "at the heart of the plan advanced by the Government is a series of compromises in which candidates identified with the deposed Duvalier dictatorship as well as candidates feared by the army would forsake election bids in the interest of national unity."[35] The national unity, and the "national integration" Manigat spoke about in his inaugural speech on February 7, 1988, had little to do with democracy and popular will but a great deal to do with not upsetting macoutism as a system. For its part, the United States had had nothing to fear from any of the candidates.

The Haitian army, with its eleven generals and about 12,000 soldiers, looked forward to a Guatemalan, Honduran, or the well-known "Panamanian solution," in which President Manigat would serve at the pleasure of Commander-in-Chief Namphy as President Arturo Eric Delvalle served under General Manuel Antonio Noriega. The United States, in the meantime, was searching for a "Haitian solution" to the Panamanian crisis: "General Noriega, the civilian opposition here and the United States and several Latin American countries were discussing what was being called 'a Duvalier solution' to Panama's crisis. The reference was to *the arrangement that permitted the Haitian dictator ... to go into exile in 1986 with his personal fortune intact and no criminal charges pending*."[36]

With the selection of Manigat, the Duvalierists had won a two-year struggle to maintain their power. There had been no revolution of 1986, only an uprising and hopes that were later dashed. The military government revealed more results of the election: 95 percent of Senate, Chamber of Deputy, and local government seats had been won by known Duvalierists, without benefit of a formal political party, a fight they had lost in October 1986.[37] The Duvalierists had lost that fight, but they won the war—temporarily. A Haitian businessman declared: "Nothing much has changed. It's still the old system. There's no way the army or the Americans would allow the democratic cleaning up of the whole country."[38]

PEASANT ORGANIZATIONS, STRUCTURES, AND INSTITUTIONS

Although there is ample evidence that the peasantry has been dissatisfied over the course of centuries, particular and specific causes have led to the contemporary upheavals. In no way do these detract from the centuries-old endemic suffering and misery, but they do represent the proverbial straw that broke the donkey's back.

One such cause was the detection of African swine fever in 1981 and the destruction of Haiti's entire porcine population of 1 million between 1981 and 1983. The Haitian "black" pig had occupied an important role in the rural Haitian economy, and pork had satisfied 50 percent of the annual protein consumption. The traditional dish "griots" consists of highly spiced and fried morsels of pork. Moreover, in the absence of a "banking system," the pig represented a savings capacity and insurance for the peasant faced with an extraordinary expense. This situation gave meaning to the words "piggy bank": pigs as capital.

The black pigs, said to be a cross between European pigs introduced by the French and an undomesticated indigenous variety introduced earlier by the Spanish, were incredibly hardy and demanded no particular care. Arguably, they are said to have consumed excrement and thus helped overall sanitation needs in the countryside.

Under explicit pressure from the United States, the Haitian government embarked on the destruction of these pigs. The partial compensation that was promised never came, and 500 Iowa pigs were sent in what appeared to many agronomists to be the willful start of an agribusiness concern. Some people questioned whether the pigs were destroyed out of necessity or to benefit the U.S. market. This situation, among many others, fueled popular anti-Americanism.

The Haitian black pig was replaced by the "white" American pig but its delicate constitution in tropical conditions demands treatment that is literally unavailable to 90 percent of Haitians: a balanced diet laced with proteins and vitamins, a potable water supply and regular showers, a cement floor in the pen. Promptly nicknamed American or white princes, these pigs came under heavy verbal abuse from a population that threatened to kill the foreign interlopers. Gone were the black pigs who ate anything and roamed anywhere, never needing any care.

The Association of Haitian Agronomists helped the peasants collect more than 25,000 signatures asking that new black pigs be brought in from other Caribbean countries such as Jamaica. Although France made an offer to bring in 3,000 black pigs from Martinique and Guadeloupe, its Caribbean possessions, nothing has occurred to date, reinforcing the view that there might have been ulterior motives and business considerations hanging in the balance.

The African swine fever episode left a bitter taste and was but one such episode that defined the power relationship between the Haitian people and its government and foreign allies. The U.S. distribution of free food was yet another example, proving costly to peasant farmers and to the Haitian economy. The Jean-Rabel massacre in the summer of 1987 was another illustration of the unequal power relationships that, ostensibly, were to result in the modernization of Haitian agriculture. However, that modernization was to be accomplished by means of a reverse agrarian land reform that would benefit big farmers and increase the "proletarianization" of the peasantry as wage earners rather than as proprietors. The U.S. emphasis on an "export economy," which increased landlessness and malnutrition, was seen as a necessary hardship by USAID and Haitian Finance Minister Leslie Delatour. Similarly, the closing of inefficient and corrupt state industries at the urging of the U.S. government and international banking interests by the Haitian military government was done for the same outcome: a better "fit" in the international economic system through increased trade. Thousands of sugarcane farmers and thousands more who had been employed in the sugar mills were faced with suddenly altered living conditions for themselves and their families.

Although it is much too early to see if "modern" economic structures will emerge, what has ensued so far is a defense of the status quo and the strengthening of a system that, in the countryside,

Peasant family, near Gonaïves, in their kitchen (c. 1980). Photo: Howard Goldbaum.

is largely feudal in nature. Parallel efforts have taken place through religious conversions to "restructure" Haiti along modern and Western lines, away from "archaic" thought systems and "superstition" that seemed to reinforce the desire of small farmers to remain independent. Cultural and economic dependence are two sides of one coin. It is in this sense that the two statements below reach down the centuries to explain the present. The first, by the Ethiopian emperor Tewodros II (1818–1868), who committed suicide after the defeat of his armies by the British, was a cry of anguish: "I know their game, first the traders and the missionaries, then the ambassadors, then the cannon. It's better to go straight to the cannon." The second is by the French philosopher Charles de Montesquieu (1689–1755): "The idea in colonies is to do commerce under much better conditions than is done with neighboring peoples [other European states] with which the advantages [agreements] are [for] reciprocity."

Roughly 45 percent of the rural labor force in Haiti consists of independent farmers, and the rest are sharecroppers and wage laborers earning, on the average, $1.45 a day, less than half the minimum wage—honored in the breach—established by the government. These statistics will change under the impact of population and land erosion but even more—and this point is usually neglected in foreign analyses— under willful policies of the Haitian government, rural oligarchic interests, and foreign private- and government-sector interests in a quest for profits and a ready supply of cheap labor.

The idea may be, as one anthropologist told me approvingly, to bring the Kreyol language as the official language and the Vodou religion "up into the sunlight" so they can be destroyed more effectively. Presumably they would be replaced by the English language and fundamentalist Protestantism. The French language and Roman Catholicism "failed" in their historic mission to transform Haiti, and Haitians have been too resilient in their attachment to Haitian culture.

One should distinguish between land monopolization by oligarchs, and Duvalierists in the last generation, and land consolidation that occurs *inside* the peasantry through inheritance sale, migration, and population pressures of various kind. Although the Haitian peasantry has been generally successful in maintaining precarious control of its lands, especially when compared to the rest of Latin America, could this pattern survive exogenous pressures?

With regard to endogenous factors, one U.S. anthropologist, Gerald F. Murray, argued that

> in a society such as Haiti, where even at the "grassroots" level land has traditionally been alienable, the danger is especially great [that land concentration may occur]. For where there is land purchase, there must be also land sale and—ipso facto— the emergence of at least temporary resource differentials. And where land is further transmitted via inheritance ... these differentials will easily be intergenerationally perpetuated.[39]

But a Swedish economist argued that "this has not occurred so far, however, because there is another mechanism which serves as a periodic regulator of the distribution of land, namely, voodoo."[40] Although legal deeds to land may be hard to come by, verbal agreements and unwritten property rights are widely recognized in peasant society, reinforced and enforced against interlopers—such as those peasants who have migrated and have some legitimate claims—by Vodou, "sorcery," and rulings by Haiti's peasant secret societies.

With reference to Vodou as a "periodic regulator of the distribution of land," Mats Lundhal wrote: "For reasons connected with need to finance voodoo ceremonies at various times over the life cycle, land has to be put on the market for sale. Murray found that a majority of all land sales in the community were motivated by these needs."[41] In conclusion, Murray argued that "the mechanism has not eliminated differentials, but it has kept them within the basic confines of a life-cycle modality of resource management, and has prevented the emergence of intergenerationally perpetuated local strata."[42] Although economists—and economics—are sometimes unlikely to agree with anthropologists' assertions, the dispute on this issue points to the reality of a sociocultural, political, and economic dimension in religion, religious ideology, and ritual that not only has a powerful impact on rural Haiti but is seen by some people as a hindrance for their plans for the country, hence the restructuring of minds that needs to accompany transformations on the terrain.

Harold Cruse, an African-American historian, has maintained that "as long as the cultural identity is in question or open to self-doubt, then there can be no positive identification with the real demands of their [Black] political and economic existence."[43] He has also argued that, in the words of another African-American scholar, "cultural oppression is tightly interlocked with political and economic oppression, for cultural control facilitates political control which in turn insures economic control."[44] T.O. Beidelman has argued that religious conversion—particularly in the eyes of the missionary—constitutes a theory of social change (Foster and Valdman, 1984: 52). Similarly, the Black church in the United States has been the center of African-American cultural life, its arts, ethics, economic "clout," a source of political dissent.[45]

Thus the strong interest of the U.S. Navy in the 1920s in the growth of Protestant missions in Haiti and elsewhere in the Caribbean is explained, as well as the economic interests of Harry L. Roosevelt, a cousin of Franklin Delano Roosevelt, in establishing his plantation on the Haitian island of La Gonâve (Schmidt, 1971: 111). The Belgian minister for colonies, Monsieur Renquin, had similar concerns as he sent Belgian priests into the Congo, also in 1920:

> The task which is given you is a very delicate one and demands great tact. As priests, you certainly come to preach the gospel, but this preaching must be imbued with our great principle, "everything first and foremost for the metropole." ... Essentially, your role consists in facilitating the task of the administration and of business. This is to say that you will interpret the Bible in a fashion that serves our interests in this part of the world best .... Your knowledge of the Gospel will help you find the passages that approve of and render poverty likable, for instance, "Blessed are the meek, for the kingdom of heaven belongs to them; it is harder for a rich man to enter the kingdom of heaven than for a camel to pass through the eye of a needle ...." Thus you will do all in your power so that the Negroes fear getting rich in order to merit heaven. To contain them, to avoid that they rebel, the administrators and businessmen will find themselves obliged, from time to time, in order to instill fear, to resort to violence .... It would not be appropriate that the Negroes retaliate or nurse feelings of vengeance .... You will comment upon and invite them to emulate all the saints who have extended the other cheek, who have forgiven offenses, who have received—without wincing—the spittle and the insults .... Long live the king, long live Belgium.[46]

As early as the late 1950s, the Tontons Macoutes, a system of Conseils d'Action Communautaires (Community Councils), and foreign charity groups (nongovernmental organizations) were working in tandem to increase central government control over the countryside (Brinkerhoff and Garcia Zamor, 1986: 102). This work was reinforced by the 1962 Code Rural of François Duvalier and was similar to a plan proposed by a pro-Western Haitian statesman in the 1920s, Dantès Bellegarde, when he suggested that the church, the school, and business be at the center of rural progress. The *noiriste*, or Pan-Africanist, position of Duvalier and the position of Bellegarde, a pro-Western liberal, were identical in their political and economic agendas. Education and commerce were joined (Bellegarde-Smith, 1985: 51).

Before the fall of Duvalier, and particularly after it, the peasantry organized itself into several hundred organizations through autonomous groups, churches, and other affiliations such as labor unions and women's groups. Between February 1986 and February 1987, one can note the following actions taken by the peasantry:

1. Jean-Rabel peasants organize demonstrations against landlords of the region.
2. La Chapelle peasants protest against policies of the military government.
3. Sarrazin peasants by the thousands demand the importation of black pigs to replace those killed by the government in the African swine fever episode.
4. Artibonite Valley peasants organize to oppose the importation of U.S. rice, which competes with their product.
5. Desdunes peasants meet to form a local association in defense of their interests.

At any given time between 1980 and 1988, one can see a similar level of activity, implying an extraordinary level of organization. Although most Protestant fundamentalist groups tried to dampen any crisis erupting in their geographic areas, the Catholic organizations alone— Ti Légliz and others—cannot account for all the commotion. Ten years ago, a colleague who had just returned from a CIA-sponsored meeting suggested that I get "into the bonanza," since the CIA wanted to finance studies on the "revolutionary potential of voodoo." Presumably, the calculation was that in the absence of a left-wing movement, other popular organizations or institutions would fill the void and give voice to Haitian grievances.

The lobbying by peasant and working-class organizations of the 1986–1987 constitutional assembly was both intensive and fairly successful, and the results of specific areas of emphasis can be found throughout the document adopted in March 1987. It is a "hybrid" constitution, reformist in tone yet sensitive to the demands of the population. That sensitivity was well-rewarded by the massive interest in the national debates that surrounded the adoption of the constitution and the massive "yes" vote it received. Peasant organizations had insisted on the broadest public discussion in the drafting of the new constitution, that it be written in Kreyol and that all government business be conducted in that language.

The Haitian National Language: Kreyol

Although Kreyol is spoken by all Haitians, that language had no official status before the 1983 Duvalier constitution. A national symbol despised by many people, Kreyol was supplanted by the French language for a number of highly complex socio-economic and psychological reasons. In other words, the power elite and the dichotomous class division of the society, together with questions of self-esteem and self-hatred present in any given "minority" as a result of colonialism, rendered an appreciation of Kreyol all but impossible. French, on the other hand, spoken by about 10 percent of the population and spoken well by less than that, is the language of power and prestige—so defined, not in Haitian, but in foreign terms and reflecting norms and values alien to the country. In working-class and rural Haiti, the attitude toward French has been ambivalent in "cultural" terms, to the extent that elements of self-hatred have penetrated that population. The adoption of Kreyol as the official state language and the recognition of its status as the national language by the constitution of 1987 represent a far-reaching ideological stance and a blow against cultural dependence.

The adoption of a "definitive" orthography in 1979, replacing earlier forms, and the eventual creation of the Haitian Academy will stabilize the language further. A very important number of written works in Kreyol now exist: poetry, novels, plays, and adaptations of foreign works such as the fables of La Fontaine (by Georges Sylvain in 1901) and *Antigone* (by Félix Morisseau-Leroy, 1953). These works— such as those of Frankétienne, Paul Laraque, Madlen Payè, and Jan

Mapou—build on an incredibly rich oral culture that is millennia old. Kreyol has always been both a language of communication and a literary language.

It was relatively easy for the Duvalier regime to "favor" Kreyol, notably in the 1980 and 1983 constitution, in the adoption of an official orthography in 1979 because the middle class from which that government came did not have the same degree of virulent animosity toward Kreyol that the upper class had. Levels of ambivalence remain. Oftentimes, when people unilingual in Kreyol are asked what language they speak in the presence of foreigners, they answer, "French." But Kreyol proverbs and sayings tend to show a different reality: *Palé fransé pa lespri* ("Speaking French is not the same as being smart"); *li palé fransé* ("the powers of deception of those who speak French"); and *Kréyol palé Kréyol Konprann* ("Speak plainly, don't try to confuse or deceive").

Although independent for nearly 200 years, Haiti faces the linguistic situation of some newly created states that must ponder whether to retain or cut the umbilical cord to the colonial language. Haiti's linguistic "problem" is simple: there is but one language spoken throughout the territory. Kreyol is recognized as a language derived from West African grammatical and syntactical sources, using a large French-derived lexicon with important word contributions from English, Spanish, and other languages, much as English is a Germanic language with much of its vocabulary from Norman French, Latin, and Greek sources.

The peasant groups did not lobby just for the adoption of the Kreyol language as the official language, which meant that for the first time in history, 90 percent of the population could understand judicial proceedings, parliamentary debates, and discussions of trade policy and high finance at cabinet meetings. They fought to decriminalize the national religion, Vodou, as well, and that point was also carried in the constitutional assembly.

The same kind of ambivalence that exists with regard to Kreyol exists for Vodou, which, in fact, forms a coherent Haitian world view. Notwithstanding Vodou's political importance in the slave uprisings of the seventeenth and eighteenth centuries, in the wars of independence, in the armed resistance against the United States, and

in the downfall of the Duvalier regime—or perhaps because of it—
Haitian governments have found it difficult to coexist with a power
they could not ultimately control. With reference to these historical
events, could Haitian resistance have occurred without Vodou's
ideological conceptualization? Not likely. Could Haitians have acted
outside of their faith, particularly when the actions they took were
distinctly different from those of the elite? Haiti's national history has
yet to be told properly. One is hard put to find a single Haitian president
who did not adhere to the Vodou "mind-set" even if he was not himself
a practitioner. Before the massive effort to Protestantize the country,
it was said that Haiti was 90 percent Catholic and 100 percent Vodou,
and in this spirit, an anthropologist asserts: "As a belief system, the
Voodoo religion crosses class boundaries; it is truly a national religion.
In terms of ritual practice, Voodoo is largely a folk religion .... Middle-
and upper-class families also participate, but rarely in public settings"
(Foster and Valdman, 1984: 37). A member of the Haitian upper class
wrote: "Voodoo is a very, very old religion. It is a religion in the same
sense that Islam, Buddhism, or Christianity are religions. [It] is an integral
part of the mental, political and moral structure of the West Indies
and Central and South America" (Paquin, 1983: 246). The latter might
have mentioned some African-Americans in North America as well,
traditionally in places like New Orleans and more recently in others
after the influx of middle-class Cuban refugees in the mid-1960s.

In the Haitian countryside, away from the direct control of the
Port-au-Prince government, the Vodou communities and secret
societies patterned after those of West Africa are institutions that are
respected more than feared, and they mete out justice in a "democratic"
setting (if democracy is defined as being of and for the people). They
run what is a parallel judicial structure to that of the elite-controlled
government and are the repository for Haitian folk medicine, control
the lineage system, work associations, and are the source of all the
arts for which Haiti has become justly famous. Peasant leaders even
suggested to the constitutional assembly that this traditional system
of justice be incorporated in the new constitution and Haiti's legal
framework. It was not.

Vodou, though hierarchical, is not centralized and thus difficult to
control. There is, however, a national association of priests, both

houngans and *manbos*, which could play as important a role in the religious arena as the Haitian Academy will play in the standardization of Kreyol. Although the Catholic church did not celebrate a Te Deum for the newly selected president in 1988, a Vodou ceremony was held and televised, sending a powerful message of yet another possible accord between a dictatorship and a religion. Just possibly, however, the ceremony also indicated a break from the "shame" in which Vodou has been held for so long in Haiti, a view that came from Western countries.

It is easy to see why both Vodou and Kreyol are feared by the Haitian elite and their foreign allies, as both indicate an ideological coherence and potential power that could be exercised by the peasantry and the urban poor.

Conclusion

These essential elements of culture, language, and religion are not so much powerful tools for "democracy" as they are a sign of independence, perhaps a move away from the crippling economic dependence that has been imposed on Haiti because economic dependence works best in a state of cultural dependence. Besides economic dependency, foreigners have brought racial bigotry to Haiti, along with a heavy dosage of ethnocentrism and the belief that Christianity is a universal religion. Vodou is "primitive" because it emanates from Negroes, a "primitive" people. It is on that basis that the Haitians have been asked to abandon an ancestral religion, and perhaps to distance themselves from "African-ness" and adopt the European concept that nonwhites are inferior. It is in this light that one needs to understand the Western liberal concepts of assimilation or integration. These concepts have been, more often than not, a "one-way street," black into white, never European merging into African civilization.

Arguing about what would bring a change in the plight of African-Americans, the Black scholar Harold Cruse wrote in 1967: "There can be no real Black revolution in the U.S. without a cultural revolution as a corollary to the scheme of 'agencies for social change.'"[47] In other words, "deculturation" is the *sine qua non* of continued control of any given population, and this fact was well understood by all colonial administrations everywhere. Culture, the totality of thought and practice, is an important part, according to Maulana Karenga, of several essential areas: sacred and secular mythology; social, economic, and political organizations; arts and sciences; and ethos defined as collective self-definition.[48] Any weakening of the fabric in one area critically weakens the whole tapestry, perhaps beyond repair. This fact is well understood by Third World peoples whose societies have been penetrated heavily and whose defenses have been breached. As an illustration of the opposite effect, Japanese culture has been able to maintain its integrity; the country, its religious and political independence.

In imitation of the extraordinarily useful decentralization of Vodou, the Haitian Constitution of 1987, in an effort to forestall the development of yet another dictatorship, introduced institutions that would decentralize, and diffuse power: weakening the presidency by adding a prime-ministership, distinguishing between army and police, and reinstituting a bicameral legislature. But more important, local governments were established, and taxes were to be spent in local communities by an elected civilian leadership. One hopes the result, a welcomed local autonomy in constitutional law, can stem the tide toward centralization introduced by the United States in the name of law and order and efficiency in 1915.

The Haitian Constitution of 1987—one of the most democratic in the world—is all things to all people. It does respond to the concerns of a Western liberal state by ensuring civil and political rights. But more important, it responds to the appeals of the peasantry and the urban poor by also addressing human rights concerns. Full employment, education, health care, housing, and protection accorded to the "family" are now in the purview of government action, not the private sector. Democracy is as much an economic as it is a political concept. There is ample evidence that peasant organizations favor "indigenous" methods toward a modernization that would take into account their own cultural traditions. This preference is illustrated by the declaration of a rural cooperative member after February 7, 1986: "Tell *Monsieur* George Shultz [the U.S. Secretary of State] that we don't care about

American democracy. We want Haitian democracy." Over the last eighty years, the speaker argued, there had been ample time to appreciate the kind of democracy the United States had in mind for Haiti.

Democracy as generally understood in the Afro-world has meant political consensus, cultural homogeneity—agreement on myths and symbols that undergird political consensus—and decentralized political and economic structures. The rulers are authorized to rule, often as despots, but within agreed limits and with reciprocal obligations and responsibilities placed on those concerned by traditional law. This form is called legitimacy, which produces stability in its wake. Wealth serves sociopolitical functions as much as it does economic functions, and a sense of noblesse oblige is thereby established. Haitian national security will be better served by stable political institutions and a more equitable access to national resources. In the final analysis, Haitian democracy will occur only when state institutions are made to reflect the national culture.

Chapter 6

Heralding the Bicentennial:
Breaks and Continuity

Si w manje pitit tig, ou pa fèt pou dòmi di.
("Eat the tiger's cub, don't think to sleep too soundly.")

—Haitian proverb

A LACK OF TIGERS, LIONS, AND MONKEYS IN HAITI'S FAUNA DOES NOT MEAN their absence in the dense metaphorical jungle of Haitian society and in political discourse. Similarly, sheep and wolves, cats and rats play dangerous and complicated games of "one-upmanship," in which the victor and the vanquished are not always obvious. In much the same way that such beasts long-gone are a part of West African lore, they reappear in Haitian art ... and in politics.

The situation had worsened after Leslie F. Manigat's selection by the army leadership in January 1988. Death squad activity had continued to occur daily. In response to a question about these killings, the President asserted that such occurrences were found "in all the great countries," wishing to compare Haiti to the murder rate in the United States. One observed a new routinization of repression as the system reasserted itself, achieving a new institutionalization of terror as found in El Salvador in the 1930s, Guatemala after the coup in 1954, Argentina during its "Dirty Little War," Brazil under military rule, and Chile's Pinochet.

The militarization of Haiti had followed a predictable course, occurring under the aegis of the United States as it did elsewhere. Since the early part of the twentieth century, American foreign policy had desired political stability to usher in economic opportunity for its citizens and corporations. That militarization took place anticipating domestic disturbances and revolts, not extra-territorial entanglements with European or other American states. In Haiti, that process had started soon after the U.S. occupation in 1915, with the creation of the *Garde d'Haiti*, a centralized and efficient army officered by Marine Corps personnel. It would, as is the case with National Guard units in the United States proper and similar institutions created by the United States in Central America, respond to domestic insurgencies, having a domestic police function alone. The concern was less "national defense" than the defense of the status quo defined as stability.

The American military intervention of 1994 to restore Haiti's constitutional government to power had, in the final analysis, a similar outcome as those of yesteryear. Alex Dupuy wrote that "[B]y intervening as it did in Haiti, [in 1994] ... the United States had radically altered the terrain of politics and political conflicts in Haiti" (Dupuy 1997: 164), just as the United States had done in 1915. As expressed in chapter 3, the American anthropologist Sidney W. Mintz had argued "[that] the occupation was notable for its failure to make any alterations in the economic structure ... of the country. But most significantly, the United States institutionalized the army and police forces [one and the same] ...." (Leyburn 1966 [1941]: xvii). It may not have escaped this prescient observer of Haitian society that the U.S. had not wished to change the economic structure, but to buttress the Haitian bourgeoisie under siege at that time by pandemic rural revolts, retaining the *status quo ante*. Mintz had continued, "[a]nother political effect of the occupation was the importance it imparted to the United States ambassador, whose political opinions thereafter would matter significantly in the transmission of power of the Haitian governmental system" (Ibid.).

The creation of the Haitian army by the U.S. Senate in 1916 and subsequent efforts to "save" that army and the general officers who had been paid "CIA assets," in the delicate period of 1991–94 for the better part of twenty years, led Haitians in the street, concerned about an American military intervention yet desperate enough to want it to get relief from the severe repression, to say: "come take away the caca you created."[1] The American government was disconcerted when

President Aristide disbanded the army on April 19, 1995, and on the eve of transmitting power to his elected successor, René G. Préval, he recognized the Republic of Cuba as had all Caribbean states much earlier. The latter measure was adopted to spare Préval the fallout from the United States. As shall be seen later, Aristide operated "at the margins," subverting U.S. influence where he could, the very embodiment of Haitian *marronage,* the ability to survive *tant bien que mal*, with a modicum of independence as the escaped maroons had done during the French colonial period.

The situation was vastly complicated by the "arrangements" of forces arrayed at the departure of President-for-Life Jean-Claude Duvalier in 1986. First, a rogue military whose structure and membership had been macoutized, seriously compromised as a praetorian guard, since it had corporate interests of its own; a "noiriste" middle-class who came of age in the 1940s, angry by American predilection for upper-class mulattoes; and finally, some of the tenants of large rural landowners who did not visualize a future apart from that of their landlords, had given the Duvalier regime a minority, but powerful political support for the brute force exercised against a hapless population. The period after February 7, 1986 had become an opportunity to consolidate a system—remarkably similar to what preceded and to what would follow—jettisoning a government while preserving all its elements, duvalierism *sans* Duvalier, as had been tried elsewhere, notably in Nicaragua after Anastasio Somoza Debayle and in the Dominican Republic after Rafael Leonidas Trujillo y Molina.

The first military junta having been selected by Duvalier in consultation with the United States, the successive provisional governments were elaborated through similar methods, including the more "permanent" selection of Manigat, forcing Haitians of all social classes to reflect upon the traditional role played by the United States in domestic politics since the latter part of the nineteenth century, or the role played by the United Kingdom, Germany, and France before that. Haitian international power had existed but for a fleeting moment, when—as expressed in chapter 2—the Haitian Revolution and its aftermath had created real anguish amongst all white nations. Sidney W. Mintz wrote, "[T]he time when a Pétion could aid, protect, and politically influence a sick and tired Simon Bolívar was long gone. The world had changed, while Haiti, the Haitians learned, under their North American masters, had nearly stood still. In effect, the United States occupation compelled Haitian scholars to rediscover what it meant to be Haitian" (Leyburn 1966 [1941]: xi–xii) and to create "negritude," facing the unreconstructed American racism of the early twentieth century.[2]

In a statement before a subcommittee of the U.S. House of Representatives' Foreign Affairs Committee in early March 1988, I argued that Manigat's days were numbered unless he were to deliver foreign aid, and if he tried to enhance his power and prerogatives against the military establishment. At that hearing, a senior fellow at the conservative Center for Strategic and International Studies, asserted that Manigat was an excellent outcome of a flawed process. His government, he argued, should be engaged "constructively," and U.S. aid renewed at once. He continued: "Democracy in Haiti? The nation lacks the most basic elements for this most difficult of political regimes to take root: (1) basic political consensus; (2) established and representative political parties; (3) rule of law; and (4) some degree of economic equality .... One should realistically expect the bare minimum. In fact, that a candidate [Manigat] with democratic credentials made it through Haiti's recent convoluted and very violent electoral process to become the nation's chief executive is to be applauded."[3]

Aside from the paternalism and condescension implied in these remarks, the statement brought to the fore a peculiarly American definition of democracy, homegrown and inapplicable elsewhere, a myopic view even for the United States, where slavery and racism could coexist with, and not damage "democracy." Meanwhile, the broad sweep of Haitian history, from the first great slave revolt in Hispaniola in 1522 to the constitution of 1987, showed Haiti's obsession with both freedom and democracy, anchored in Afro-Haitian cultural ethos and constructs.[4] Since the early 1980s, the formation of thousands of rural and urban associations; the intellectual ferment in Haiti and in its diaspora, and a vigorous media; concerns for religious freedom in the decriminalization of Vodou in 1987, and its full recognition as a religion equal to Christianity and all others, in early April 2003; the tens of thousands of Haitians killed over a period of thirty years resisting the Duvalier regime and subsequent military governments; the massive "yes" vote in the plebiscite on the constitution, in March 1987, which had been debated article by article by the majority of Haitians in all venues; and that constitution's provision granting access to health, education, housing, and employment—makes one wonder if, judging U.S. history and politics, a Haitian scholar could not conclude, based on some ideal Haitian standard, that American democracy is found wanting, and undemocratic. The lack of a political consensus in Haiti would seem obvious, since discrepancies between Haitian political culture writ large and the political regimen, between Haitian national and state interests, and between differing concepts of reality, added to international hegemonic realities particularly after the fall of the Soviet Union, would tend to handicap the country. The "selling" of a middle-class ethos to all classes in the United States, that allowed for consensus and a national vision, could not take place in Haiti. Oppressive conditions always lead to repressive governments.

Impediments to democracy might be defined differently. The fear of democracy exists, by definitional necessity, in elite groups who monopolize economic and political power. That fear exists also in elite structures of the hegemonic power whose interest benefits from a tight relationship and broad alliances with local national elites. Relinquishing political power while maintaining absolute economic power and privileges based on money and skin color—as is the case in the United States—would indicate the strength of other structures presently absent from Haiti. In no case is this to be confused or conflated with democracy. In both the United States and Haiti, the top 1 percent owns approximately 45 percent of national wealth.

Haitian sociologist Alex Dupuy expressed U.S. goals and objectives for Haiti in these words: "... there was the United States, which, after the fall of communism, sought to change its ugly image as the defender of dictatorship by promoting an 'ersatz of democracy' in the poor countries. In Haiti, the problem for Washington was how to compel its traditional allies—the bourgeoisie and the military establishment—to accept a minimal democracy ... while at the same time preserving Haiti as a source of cheap labor for the assembly industries and the multinational agribusinesses. The solution [for the United States] lay in electing a candidate who accepted the new game plan and who was supported by the local oligarchies and the United States. Unfortunately, the Haitian masses ... spoiled it by voting for their own unexpected and unpredictable candidate [Aristide]" (Dupuy 1997: 133). In similar fashion, American President Gerald Ford and Secretary of State Henry Kissinger had expressed the thought, rendered public, that since the Chilean people would not vote the way the United States wanted, it would be denied the right to vote. And it was, via the Chilean military.

The broad view is that Haiti, like the rest of the Caribbean and the Western hemisphere, must remain within the political orbit of the United States. For a more complete picture of Haitian-American relations, one would have to study, besides diplomacy, the action of multinational companies, international lending agencies, U.S. churches and missionary societies and other private U.S. organizations—all of which share a certain American vision of the world and the place of the United States in that world.

When the army deposed Leslie F. Manigat on June 20, 1988, five months into a five-year presidency, there was a painful sense of déjà-vu. Nothing about Manigat—not his behavior in the early 1960s as a duvalierist or his behavior abroad while in exile—convinces one that he was a sheep in wolf's clothing, able to "play" the army, or waiting for a propitious moment to expose himself as a democrat. The army "played" him.

General Henry Namphy, once more President Namphy, was surrounded by those military officers who had been a part of the original cast of characters. The twenty-one gun salute, the raising of the flag, the playing of the national anthem, "La Dessalinienne," and the happy grins of the army chiefs made one wonder whether the calendar, in a time warp, had not gone back to February 7, 1986.

On September 17, 1988, army sergeants had arrested Namphy and replaced him by General Prosper Avril. A collective of about thirty non-commissioned officers was ostensibly in charge, and their demands for a transition to democracy resonated favorably with the citizenry. That generals, colonels, majors, and some "Tonton Macoutes" were removed from high office, gave credibility to Sergeant Joseph Heubreux and his cohort. These men were members of Haiti's urban and rural lower classes, using the army to raise their social capital as had done their superiors since the accession of François Duvalier to power in September 1957. Contrary to the Cuban and Dominican armies, also established by the United States in incursions into these countries, the Haitian army officer corps had remained the bastion of elite, mostly mulatto men. The Church, as we shall see with Jean-Bertrand Aristide, was the other avenue for social mobility for lower class men. Army and Church became the means to achieve status for the middle and lower classes—for men—who were "déclassé," outside the traditional class system.

General Avril, who was a millionaire and financial advisor to the Duvalier family, talked about instilling a process of "irreversible democracy." He named a civilian cabinet, purged about fifty senior officers, including Colonel Jean-Claude Paul who had been indicted on drug charges in the United States and who later died poisoned under mysterious circumstances. In its edition of October 9, 1988, the *New York Times* wrote: "One of the most difficult steps taken by General Avril was dismissing a powerful military commander, Col. Jean-Claude Paul. Immediately after General Avril seized power, the colonel appeared with him at the Presidential Palace, and there were reports that the general would name the colonel commander-in-chief of the army. That was ruled out by the United States ambassador, Brunson McKinley, when General Avril telephoned the diplomat in the hours after the coup, as decisions were being made about who would hold the major positions in the new government." *Realpolitik*—in the guise of a general, Duvalierists, and the U.S. ambassador—asserted itself against a popular movement of sergeants and corporals, "les petits soldats" as they were affectionately called, and like a common Haitian, democracy laid bloody on the sidewalk. These little soldiers, as so many little "red hiding hoods," had been the pawns of the big bad general. Failure to live up to the incipient populist agenda led Avril's countrymen to say that they had experienced a *"poisson d'Avril"* (April fool's day), and a *poison d'Avril*, Avril's poison, a double play on words. Avril's administration had also meted out beatings, prison terms, deportations, and assassinations against persons from the political left and center.

Three Generals and a Lady

General Namphy had acted decisively when President Manigat had tried to consolidate his power, threatening army unity as Duvalier had done earlier. He abrogated the constitution, arguing that democracy was contrary to Haitian "tradition."

Much earlier, from exile, Manigat had written that "the support of the police-army is needed to overthrow a government, and police-army opposition makes the election of any candidate insecure" (Manigat 1964: 28). However, the army is unlikely to intervene without the support of other powerful sectors, usually the commercial-industrial complex consisting of Haitian and non-Haitian wings. Haitian anthropologist Michel S. Laguerre made a convincing argument that the army seldom acts alone (Laguerre 1993). Rather, it acts and reacts in accordance with other foci of power, both domestic and foreign, and in accord with its own corporatist interests. It must be noted that the vagaries of Haitian politics, starting with the end of the nineteenth century, made it certain that many Haitian *commerçants* had double or triple citizenships—just to be on the safe side (Plummer 1984). Manigat had had unofficial support from prominent members of President George W. H. Bush's administration in the United States, but principled opposition from the congressional Black Caucus and a fairly recalcitrant U.S. Congress.

The army remained fractious. Avril weathered a coup led by the Leopards, a counter insurgency unit created at the behest of the United States, and the Casernes Dessalines battalion. The plotters seemed heartened by what they perceived to be weakening support from the United States for the general. Eight key U.S. Representatives came to Avril's support in a letter sent to President Bush. "In addition to urgent humanitarian assistance we believe prompt consideration should be given to an immediate transfer of sufficient Economic Support Funds to quickly stabilize the economy and encourage a similar return to political stability .... We realize that a limited amount of military assistance may be needed on an urgent basis to permit the Haitian armed forces to maintain public order."[5] Avril nonetheless resigned after a late night chat with the new U.S. ambassador Alvin P. Adams, and turned over the government to the army Chief of Staff, Major General Hérard Abraham, retiring to his palatial home in the Miami suburbs on March 12, 1990.

Writing about these events, American historian Brenda Gayle Plummer wrote that "the Bush administration appeared at first to continue Reagan-era diplomacy, accepting the notion that democracy could occur in Haiti under a military dictatorship." She cited a confused U.S. reporter who declared that, "in relying upon the military the United States compromised the support it could have otherwise given to the creation of alternative popular democratic movements and civilian democratic institutions" (Plummer 1992: 228).

The country was united in the belief that national elections could not take place under a military dictatorship. The opposition drew up plans to re-establish constitutional order by negotiating with Judge Ertha Pascal-Trouillot of the Cour de Cassation, Haiti's Supreme Court. She was the first woman named to the Court. To help her not to stray, the democratic opposition established a 19-member Conseil d'Etat, a Council of State, as an advisory and quasi-legislative body representing major Haitian institutions, political parties and the popular movement. But first, she would need the benign neutrality of the army and proactive assistance from the American embassy if her government was to survive. She got both. Three days after the resignation of Avril, and one day after his departure for a golden exile in the United States, Pascal-Trouillot took the oath of office on March 13, 1990. Her sole task, as she herself described it, was to organize general elections after which she would retire from public life.

At this point, Haiti had had seven governments in four years since the overthrow of Jean-Claude Duvalier in February 1986. This "anarchic" situation had presented itself at key periods of Haitian history, when there was popular dissatisfaction with the status quo, when social groups attempted to insert themselves into the body politic to create ostensibly a more democratic state with equitable access to societal resources and access to political power. The period 1843–1847 with six presidents, was the period framed by the *Piquets' "l'Armée Souffrante,"* peasant insurgents from the south, who demanded economic restructuring and "black" presidents at the helm; there were eight

presidents between 1911 and 1915, when pandemic insurgencies, largely
from the north, attempted to wrestle power from a socio-political elite
ensconced in the capital to the detriment of the provinces, generally
called the "Cacos"; there were six presidents again, between 1956 and
1957, when the middle-classes, "la classe," tried to recover what was
lost in the hiatus presented by General Paul-Eugène Magloire who
had put an end to the first "radical" middle-class government of
President Dumarsais Estimé in 1950. These periods, when certain
sectors attempted to re-define themselves—or merely wanted to access
political power as the key to unfettered economic wealth—were
followed by strong dictatorial leadership, President (then Emperor)
Faustin Soulouque in 1847, the U.S. occupation in 1915, President
François Duvalier in 1957, and President Jean-Bertrand Aristide in
1991.

President Pascal-Trouillot delivered on her promise by holding
national elections on December 16, 1991 that were witnessed by more
than 800 international observers. These elections were proclaimed free,
fair, and honest.

But to these intense national struggles were attached international
concerns. Several foreign governments had vested interests in
deteriorating conditions in Haiti, among which were the United States,
France, Canada, the Vatican, Venezuela, and the Dominican Republic.
These interests and the concerns held by these foreign powers
transcended clearly one particular leader, remaining consistent
throughout the unstable period between 1986 and 2004, representing
a protracted period of political transition in Haiti.

In terms of the United States, important considerations played in
its policies toward Haiti, notwithstanding that country's overall
insignificance in the scheme of things internationally. Foremost was
an overarching principle applied with particular emphasis to the
Caribbean basin, the quest for political stability, pursued since the
beginning of the twentieth century. At stake were the safety of private
investments, the repatriation of capital, unfettered access to national
resources. In the contemporary period, political repression, poverty,
and overpopulation in that order, led to refugees, mostly by boat and
mostly lower-class and "black," creating a potential crisis for domestic

politics in the United States in ethnic terms, but also in foreign affairs with having to admit that all was not well in American support for right-wing dictatorships. These considerations became a sufficient cause for favoring certain options, such as the choice of one politician over another, one faction over others, one labor union—preferably one over which one had control—and for distrusting all popular movements and organizations as inherently destabilizing. It is in this sense that, generally, American definitions of what constitutes stability or democracy can be unduly narrow and short-sighted in ways that would not be tolerable inside the United States proper. Each state within its federal structure is given more freedom and more leeway than it grants sovereign national states around the world.

France's agenda in broad terms, seems to be the quest to re-establish its cultural and commercial influence where it can, as befits a middle-sized and middle-aged power in full retreat. That President François Mitterand shared a socialist ideology with some Haitian political sectors and later, with President Aristide, may have heightened the desire to assist Haiti as it devised structures and institutions by which it would be governed in the early part of the twenty-first century. In fact, the constitution of 1987 owes much to the constitution of the Fifth Republic, including the tendency to "freeze" all action when cohabitation occurs—when different political parties are in control of the presidency and the parliament then has to form a government that represents that fact.

France's geographic and historical "distance" from Haiti, and its waning influence worldwide makes that influence seem benign, desirable even. When I expressed such thoughts at a colloquium on Haiti in Paris in February 1991, a representative of the French Foreign Ministry responded by reminding me and other Haitian scholars present, that Haiti must come to terms with the awesome presence of the United States in the Western hemisphere, and that France could do little to alleviate that situation. He was booed. The tactic of opposing France to the United States had been tried before, albeit with no appreciable success, by Haitian diplomats, notably at the League of Nations and other international forums in the 1920s (Bellegarde-Smith 1985: 68).

Venezuela and the Dominican Republic are two Latin American states with historical, but divergent interests in Haitian politics. The former's influence as an oil-rich sub-paramount power in the region, can be exercised easily in the Caribbean basin as a Caribbean power in its own right—and it has done so in its diplomacy and assistance of a general nature to Central America and the Antilles. Venezuelan interest in Haiti preceded its own political independence as that country seemed genuinely grateful for Haitian military assistance in the first years of the nineteenth century.

The fate of the Dominican Republic, on the other hand, is intertwined with Haiti and shall remain so forever, a fact of geography, history, economics, and ethnicity. Haitian power in the nineteenth century and Dominican power in the twentieth—a reversal of fortunes—also reversed the direction of political interference in the domestic affairs of one over the other, but the mutual impact on these countries is awesome. Economic reverses in Santo Domingo, with its attendant political upheavals, lead some Dominican scholars to label the phenomenon, wrongly, as the "haitianization" of the Dominican Republic. The fact remains that that country is stronger economically, and politically far more stable—it has had, since the U.S. occupation of 1963, a string of presidential elections with no *coups d'état*. In addition, there is generally a visceral dislike of all things "Haitian" in the country, largely anchored in the fear of the strength of Haitian culture, poverty, and demographics, based on historical antecedents of numerous Haitian army invasions, but also a rejection of "African-ness." Both countries share a similar African ethnic heritage, one that goes largely unrecognized in eastern Hispaniola. The Dominican governments that succeeded the U.S. invasion of 1963—that would forestall the restoration to power of leftist President Juan Bosch—have tended to support the most conservative political sectors in Haiti.

Haitian poverty is a critical issue for the Dominican Republic. There are perhaps one million Haitians living and working in a juridical limbo in that country, operating in the critical sugar industry and in other industries, operating at the margins of Dominican society. Recent Haitian governments have proven to be too weak to negotiate effectively for better treatment for its citizens, or for Dominican-Haitians. There is, of course, a vexing stigma based on historical factors and race that remains constant in the equation.

Canada's emerging presence on the world scene counteracts, in effect, the long-standing relationship between Haiti and the United States. Canadian interest in Haiti is due partly to a massive Haitian migration into Quebec, with a very high concentration in Montreal— perhaps as many as 70,000 Haitians or Haitian-Canadians reside in that city alone. Though that country recognizes U.S. preeminence in the Haitian quagmire, it has played a powerful supportive role in terms of both government and private agencies in the field of development assistance.

The Vatican has had a long relationship with Haiti and its national elites since the signing of the Concordat in 1860. The Vatican does not have armed divisions to enforce its will at present, but is nonetheless influential. The hierarchical nature of the Church, its ideology and discipline are stronger still in a Haitian context of institutional disarray. Pope John Paul II was given credit for a statement he made in March 1983 at the François Duvalier International Airport (now the Toussaint Louverture International Airport), that "something in this country must change." He was giving permission to Church authorities—whose hierarchy had been named largely by François Duvalier—to participate in impending social change, lest it be left behind. A timid Haitian episcopate could now help manage the crisis. But the true impact of the Church came with Liberation Theology, not through the official Church. The philosopher Antonio Gramsci argued that "religion, for any society, constitutes the most important element of the people's 'common sense'" (Marable, 1991: 211). In Haiti, the philosophical underpinnings and ideological superstructure for most Haitians lie in the majoritarian religion Vodou, not Christianity. The Church's real intentions were rendered clear, however, when the Vatican recognized the *de facto* military dictatorship in March 1992, six months after the overthrow of President Jean-Bertrand Aristide. The Holy See was the only government to take such a step, and this action had strong implications and dire consequences in the mind of the public.

In Haiti, the Church was much slower to act. It was only toward the end of the 1980s that the Haitian Conference of Haitian Religious Persons (CHR) took to heart the "preferential option for the poor." The Haitian Episcopate Conference (CEH) the bishops assembled, took seriously the role of stemming the flow toward the radicalism of lesser clerics and the Ti Legliz—the base communities of grassroot Roman Catholics.

The role of the Ti Legliz, however powerful, was somewhat exaggerated to the detriment of other social formations stemming from the peasantry. The Haitian anthropologist Rénald Clérismé, at a conference on Vodou at the University of California, Santa Barbara, had delineated three major peasant groups and hundreds of others connected to Vodou and to the secret societies, that were crucial in organizing the countryside against the Duvalier regime.[6]

THE FAILED ERA: ARISTIDE AND THE ANATOMY OF A COUP

A defining moment within a significant period in Haitian history occurred on December 16, 1990. Haiti held national elections as scheduled. Father Jean-Bertrand Aristide, a 37-year-old Roman Catholic of the Salesian order, won with 67.7 percent of the votes. His victory was achieved with overwhelming margins in all nine administrative *départements*; he would not have to face a run-off election. The next highest vote getter, with the largest campaign expenditures (reportedly $3 million, mostly from American sources), was former World Bank official Marc L. Bazin. He garnered 14.2 percent of the votes in the eleven-man field. 60 percent of the electorate had voted under intense international scrutiny to ensure that the elections were fair.

Aristide seemed to have entered the race reluctantly in October 1990, partly to counteract a Duvalierist resurgence. Roger Lafontant, a major architect of the Duvalierist regime, had presented himself as a candidate to the presidency despite article 291 of the constitution that forbade individuals who had played a significant role in Duvalierism to take part in the electoral process for a period of ten years. The provisional government of President Ertha Pascal-Trouillot was unable or unwilling to prevent his return from exile and to have him arrested. After the elections, he pledged that he would not allow Aristide to take power. Two weeks later, on January 7, 1991, Lafontant took over the National Palace in a *coup d'état* that lasted twelve hours. A watched plot never boils.

Of the eleven presidential candidates, only Aristide had had an unequivocal position against macoutism. The *dechoukaj,* the violent uprooting of men and structures of the *ancien régime,* was the highest priority of most Haitians. Aristide had emerged as the conscience of the nation in this issue. Many had failed to appreciate the tenacity of Duvalierism after three decades of harsh rule. The new president was an unlikely leader for these tumultuous times, when the country felt the need to reinvent itself and desired radical change. No political party had kindled the interest or piqued the curiosity of the peasantry and the urban working class. Perhaps none really tried, or knew how to accomplish the task. In a deeply conflicted society, and in the absence of hegemonic control of information—state or private—the electoral process is dangerous to the status quo.

The electoral process, as distinct from democracy, is predicated on the existence of certain structures, among which are political parties that buttress the system that sustains them. Narrowly defined, parties may tend to isolate as they specify certain class interests, enhancing the status quo in which they have developed a stake. Haiti's forty-odd chiefs of state and twenty-five constitutions had represented, at best, 10 percent of the population. When existing at all, parties vehicled the ambitions of one man, and were in the habit of dying with him if not sooner. This fact of political life made the study of parties somewhat unhelpful and problematic. And because the formal structure of the state has been at odds with the national culture, social movements offer a more precise instrument, defining popular tendencies and trends in the context of historical moments. Political repression is typically severe against mass movements, far less so against political parties that are the "playthings" of elites and are thus protected from state-sponsored repression.

The Haitian political scientist Sabine Manigat suggests that the 1986–1993 interregnum was caused by a gap between social movements and political parties, as the latter struggled to conquer political legitimacy, while the population remained guarded and suspicious. She argues,

Democracy [as understood through political parties] ... does not make reference ... to those structures that undergird the power of land and commercial oligarchies, to the networks of concentration of social wealth erected from a dual economy [and] the persistence of social relations that ignore—in concrete application of the law, legislation and citizens' responsibilities, that can only emerge and consolidate from practices rather than from speeches or from voluntary [personal] behavioral changes.[7]

Aristide entered the race essentially without the benefit of party. The National Front for Change and Democracy (FNCD), an umbrella of center-left parties, had selected Aristide, and came to control both the Chamber of Deputies and the Senate, when two houses replaced the Duvalierist unicameral legislature. The FNCD achieved a mere plurality after the run-off election in January 1991. Some of its leaders had questioned the wisdom of holding elections so soon, when Duvalierists still controlled the bureaucratic apparatus and the army. There were, however, no obvious alternatives. The attempted *coup d'état* in January 1990 and the later coup that overthrew the Aristide government on September 30, 1991 showed how prescient the FNCD leadership had been about lingering Duvalierist strength. But Haiti is not unique. Eastern and central Europe faced similar conditions after the fall of communism, and fascism survives its defeat in the West after World War II.

That only 15 to 25 percent of the electorate had voted in the second round, denied the President a majority in the legislature. Aristide would have had to develop political skills he simply did not have, and would have been inconsistent with recent political history. There are some interesting possibilities as to why only a small fraction of the electors had participated in the run-off. The President elected, many Haitians simply did not realize the importance of the second vote in this new context, or simply did not believe in the importance of the parliament. People were saying openly that, now that they had a President, they saw no reason to go back and vote. That new context derived from the institutional safeguards introduced in the new constitution to prevent a recurring dictatorship. It may be remembered that whenever bourgeois control went unchallenged in the nineteenth century, the legislature in Port-au-Prince had played a significant role.

The popular reaction did not preclude a yearning for democracy. As I have explained in other writings, the Haitian people seemed to be defining democracy away from its Western moorings, understanding that party and electoral process can be subverted by elite groups that appropriate for themselves the style and the symbols of democracy, and not its substance. The rekindling of political consciousness would seem to tend toward newer (and perhaps, simultaneously traditional) forms of democratic consent reminiscent of the Haitian countryside and the African past, as amended by the authoritarianism found in colonialism—one in which the chief rules autocratically, but with safeguards and constraints applied against him or her. Political anthropology may have something to teach us in this regard. In its ideal form, this model could represent the triumph of content over an alien style; at its worst, abject dictatorship. Political culture and tradition alone could infuse the political system with the means to maintain such a political regimen. Whether "indigenous" institutions are strong enough remain to be seen (Rotberg, 1997: 27–46).

The idea of competing ideological paradigms and pluralism would seem alien in such a context. American ideologues might have concluded that such a political course of action would conflict with pluralist characteristics central to modern democratic government. Perhaps. Some have written about a predisposition toward violence, almost as if speaking of congenital malformations, with not a word about the inherent violence of the system itself under which more that 90 percent of Haitians live. Gone is an understanding of the impact of one's culture on academic disciplines proper. Pluralism easily eschews the concept of social class, so that American scholars could and did argue that many groups opposed Aristide. Thus we have a dual problem; that scholarship is often both ahistorical and sociologically flawed.

As is the case in many polities, legislators are elected by a local constituency largely concerned about local issues and personalities. These have their own dynamics. In Haiti, the national stage overwhelms localities, and national politics seems to take precedence over other

factors, especially as Port-au-Prince overwhelms provincial cities and
the countryside. The President's mandate was to bring about change.
The squabbles in both chambers made it easy for Aristide to bypass
the legislature when he could. Because no party had a majority, the
President named his alter ego, René Garcia Préval, a Belgium-trained
agronomist, as Prime Minister. Préval had no political base of his own,
and thus found it difficult to coalesce with the FNCD. This created a
situation that was aggravated when Préval later became president in
1996–2001. Shortly into Aristide's presidency, the FNCD was in
conflict with the administration and the "Lavalas" movement, the
"cleansing flood" that had deposited Aristide on the littoral of the
National Palace.

When Aristide took the oath of office in Haitian (Kreyol), a first,
on January 7, 1991, Haiti's chronic despair turned to hope though the
President had submitted no platform, had formulated no policy, and
long after the election, had remained without a ministerial cabinet.
But he had promised "justice, transparency, and participation." The
President was despised by the upper-classes (a peasant in the
presidency), feared by the middle-classes (he might move against
bureaucratic corruption and nepotism), disliked by the Church (he had
challenged the episcopate repeatedly), distrusted by the business sector
(he might raise wages and enforce tax laws), worried the army (he
might move against the drug trade and contraband at the borders),
and opposed by the United States (he was a socialist). In brief, his
presence was no comfort to the power brokers. In fact, in his seven
months in office, he justified the judgments of the aforementioned
sectors by moving in all these areas.

Born in the peasantry at Port Salut in 1953, Aristide did not see
that particular social class as a special interest group, but as the marrow
from which all things Haitian originated. He saw the political classes—
the others—as "the locus of Haiti's culture of poverty," to use an
American economist's judgment (Fass, 1988: 301). In July 1990,
Aristide had claimed, "This is a political revolution, but it's not a social
revolution. Now we are trying to achieve a social revolution. If we
don't do that, the political revolution will not go anywhere" (NACLA,
1995: 58). A social revolution could, in turn, lead to an economic

revolution which might mean a redistribution of wealth—less than 1 percent of Haiti's now 8 million inhabitants own about 45 percent of all national wealth, roughly the same as in the United States. No one wanted that, except perhaps 90 percent of all Haitians. But they do not matter. Anything less than a socio-economic revolution would be "reformist" and not address the issues that truly mattered: social justice, economic opportunity, and equality.

Unlike many others who individually escape their social station in life by joining the priesthood or the ministry or the military, Aristide never seemed to have denied, denounced, or denigrated his origins nor his culture. He could have, and indeed, might have been expected to do so. He spoke perhaps seven languages, traveled abroad, and earned degrees in theology, biblical archeology, and psychology, and published several books. Class ascription and life experiences seemed to have marked Aristide's politics. He raised the issue of social violence inherent in generalized poverty. He would not forego making connections with factors in the international system that seemed to create the underdevelopment of Haiti. There were several assassination attempts against his life.

During his inaugural speech, Jean-Bertrand Aristide asked the army chief of staff for the resignation of most of the officers of the *Haut Etat Major*, the army's high command, and he declared a symbolic marriage between the army and the people. An adroit orator in the Haitian language, the President used that language's double and triple meanings and colorful nuances to full effect, creating moods and attempting to alter realities. He received the presidential sash from an elderly peasant woman rumored to be a *manbo*, a Vodou priest. He invited beggars into the grounds of the National Palace, and helped feed them. Watching those events with Haitian upper-class families in Port-au-Prince, I was well aware of their tortured facial expressions. I had returned home to witness an extraordinary moment in Haitian history.

That same week, hundreds of officials of previous administrations, including Madame Pascal-Trouillot, were forbidden to leave the territory pending a review of the disbursement of state funds entrusted to them. When it came time to form a cabinet, women were appointed to three powerful ministries, external affairs, finance and economic development, and information. Other women were named to key ambassadorial posts in Europe, and a ministry for women's affairs created, headquartered where the army's chiefs of staff had had their offices, after the army was disbanded soon after the President returned from exile at the end of 1994. The population was enthralled by these changes; the mistrust of the elites grew. But while Aristide drew the enmity of the power brokers, he garnered support from individual persons connected to all these groups. Administrative positions were, of course, not filled by peasants, but with members of these elites who were not tainted by the previous three decades, who might have come back to the country from exile in Europe, the United States, Canada, or Mexico. Some came from university ranks. Many seemed far removed from Haitian realities, steeped in Western models of governance. Other administrators came from the Lavalas movement, the circle of activists who may have had a different "take" on reality, and on what change meant at this juncture. But soon dissension arose between sectors of the governing alliance, between parliamentary and executive branches of the government, between the Lavalas movement and its offshoots, the FNCD and diasporic elements, as those who had come from abroad were called.

In the area of human rights violations, during the first Aristide administration, Haitians saw a marked decrease. If statistics are good evidence, violations went from a total of 73 and 59 per month under the presidencies of General Avril and Pascal-Trouillot respectively, to 24 per month under Aristide. A State Department report stated that there were 75 violations in the seven months before the coup, for an average of 10.7 a month. All the while, one must keep in mind the ultimate source for some of these violations, that the army had paramilitary groups operating throughout these periods. Anger and frustration, and mob violence against agents of repression, largely in response to the absence of judicial procedures, should be placed in a different category altogether. Since the start of President Aristide's second term in February 2001, there has been a clear augmentation of cases of human rights violations targeted at members of the political opposition, and against journalists. It must be noted, that many if not most intellectuals and activist cadres that were a part of Aristide's first administration have become members of the opposition. All bets seemed to be off.

Gone are the socialist statements. Also gone are all reference to Haiti's hero Charlemagne Péralte who fought the U.S. Marine Corps during the first American occupation of 1915–1934. Aristide would have to depend heavily upon the kindness of strangers who would extract their pound of flesh in the process. Returning at the good graces of the U.S. government with more than 20,000 American soldiers, he would now speak of privatizing public sector industries under the euphemism "democratization." The connections could not be made clearer. Yet, from the struggle to approve the constitution in 1987, into Aristide's return from exile in October 1994, one finds that popular grievances were seldom expressed in economic terms. A Haitianist from Guadeloupe, Jacky Dahomay, summarized the situation succinctly when he stated, "what amazes one during that whole period are fairly non-existent social grievances, of strikes about work conditions. All the movements ... are articulated directly to political grievances, specifically towards political rights, citizenship and democracy. It is in this context that one must understand the massive vote for the constitution. Every time the population took to the street, always leaving behind some dead, it is never a riot for hunger, but a highly political protest. Hence the extreme politicization of the Haitian masses which never cease to amaze foreign observers."[8]

Economic hardship did not result in any boat people seeking refuge abroad during the first seven months before the coup. Hope reigned supreme. Hope has changed to despair. In response to an intelligent question about the economic situation, President Préval (1996–2001) responded unintelligently with an aphorism of his own making that carried a multiplicity of meanings: *se pou n naje pou n soti,* we must swim to get out [of our predicament, sink or swim]. But the phrase bore to strong a resemblance to an admonition to flee on boats for foreign shores. Some took that advice.

There are some dangers in adopting the trappings of Western democracy in nation-states of the periphery. After all, capitalist states in dependency are more likely than not to be dictatorships. This comes from the very nature of oppression, always more brutal and naked than at the imperial "center" where the institutions are stronger and populations more assuaged. At the center, that fate is reserved for marginalized populations such as Blacks in the United States and Algerians in France. General Henri Namphy had declared ex-cathedra, that Haitians were not ready for democracy as he abrogated the constitution. A Haitian business leader said that neither the local bourgeoisie nor the United States would allow the democratic cleaning up of the country. A conservative U.S. writer had said that one could realistically expect only the bare minimum from Haiti under the circumstances.[9]

What transpired from these positions—that of a general officer, of a noted businessman, a well-connected American academic—were conflicting and antagonistic definitions of democracy and the means to achieve it. What was missed or resisted, was the seminal idea that Haiti may have been trying to reinvent itself. It had tried the ballot box, and the majority had not prevailed, but the system did. The risks were in the absence of "choice control." One is reminded of Henry A. Kissinger's statement as he prepared U.S. intervention against Chile in 1970: "I do not see why we have to let a country go Marxist [sic] just because the people are irresponsible." U.S. President Gerald Ford had echoed these sentiments. On a news item on National Public Radio's "Morning Edition," dated February 25 1996, CIA Director Deutsch said that he intended to continue the practice of using American journalists and clergymen abroad, in response to a question posed to him. There was no follow up from the wise reporter.[10] A prominent Haitian reporter who had survived many governments, said on camera: "You cannot depend on the people to make a good choice." Peasants are revolting!

Inside Haiti, the issue was not about majority rule and minority rights, nor about civil rights, or even about pluralism, but about control of the state apparatus and access to both wealth and power, a control that is maintained through cultural, socio-economic, religious, and linguistic hegemony. Though weak, the Haitian state has been a powerful tool to impose a "vision," a state against the people for the use of a predatory elite. At heart is a struggle and a continuing cultural war between Franco-Haitian and Afro-Haitian variants of that culture.

Democracy, I argued three decades ago, would be an Africanizing process in Haiti as state structures would come to harmonize with national cultural institutions.[11]

There is increasing evidence that foreign powers knew of the impending coup, according to Haitian government officials I spoke to at the time. In an attempt to save his government from the coup that cost Haitian businessmen $40 million to mount, Aristide made some statements that approved of vigilante violence. Though used *ex post facto* by coup leaders, the overthrow would have taken place, even if these statements had not been made by the President. To reclaim control of the state, Haitian military leaders and army-sponsored terrorist groups killed approximately 4,000 individuals, largely from the working class. In U.S. terms, this would have meant 164,000 dead. Another 300,000 persons were displaced in internal exile, 12.3 millions in U.S. terms. A U.S. analyst opposed to Aristide described the slaughter as a case of "pre-emptive butchery."[12] Over the following twenty-five months, assassinations targeted populist leaders, trade unionists, student activists, religious and lay persons of the Ti Legliz (Catholic base communities), peasant leaders, the media, in an effort to decapitate the popular movement.

A perspicacious scholar of the Haitian scene summarized the particular impact of each social formation as follows: "The bourgeoisie is ... a lumpenbourgeoisie ... [that] gets a part of its wealth from a situation of injustice and social apartheid that country knows. As for the petite bourgeoisie, and the whole of the middle classes, ... if it had been able to support, for a brief moment, the candidacy of Aristide, with the coming to power of the latter, the social question substituted itself ... to the political question, and the anguish of the middle classes increased incrementally as the urgency of an overhaul of Haitian society became explicit. It is probably this social category that lives most tragically the opposing political/social question. It says yes to the State of Laws, but remains divided about the reduction of social inequalities. As concerns the army ... it lives essentially from plundering and from drug trafficking ... a veritable army of occupation whose primary function is not to defend this country against an invasion or to defend citizens against insecurity. Insecurity comes from that army itself."[13]

This was not quite the army that had fought the wars of independence, then abrogated for itself all powers and the role of a national arbiter between 1804 and 1915. It was the new army created as a police force by the United States, and approved by the U.S. Senate in 1916. That institution had remained true to itself. At heart a praetorian guard and a predatory institution, the army had developed corporatist interests of its own, and allowed—since the rise of the Duvaliers in 1957—for upward social mobility for young men of the urban lower-middle class and the peasantry under some circumstances. Though it could act on its own, it seldom did entirely, having developed webs of alliances with particular groups, such as the business sector or the Pentagon.[14]

The overthrow of Aristide was not a simple matter. In the past fifty years, one elite president was replaced by another, all effected with a minimum of fuss and very little bloodshed by elite officers in control of the army. This time, repressive measures proved necessary to prevent a powerful popular reaction as had been the case in the earlier coup attempt by Roger Lafontant in January 1991. But neither the military, nor its civilian allies nor for that matter the "Daddy" Bush administration appreciated the depth of feelings for Aristide, the willingness to accept a crippling embargo that coming later would punish the masses far more than the elites, or that support for President Aristide would grow stronger over each passing year.

The Organization of American States (OAS), the United Nations (UN), and all governments—except for the Vatican—denounced the *coup d'état.* At first, the United States had little choice but to deplore the overthrow of a democratically elected constitutional government it never favored. But the signals in Washington to the junta were mixed and confused, particularly when the U.S. government tried to dissociate "democracy" from Aristide. The Haitian military, business sector, Duvalierist groups and other elite groups were dismayed by Washington's very public rebuke, but pleased by other signals sent *sub rosa,* that "democracy" could survive *sans* Aristide as Duvalierism had survived the downfall of Jean-Claude Duvalier. Haiti's relative insignificance was shown when the U.S. government turned to the OAS. The end of the Cold War had made this possible. In the Santiago (Chile) Accord of June 1991, the OAS had been erected into an instrument of multilateral diplomacy. And the American governments throughout the Hemisphere were bound by law not to recognize a government that came to power by extra-legal methods.

Haitian popular reaction proved markedly strong. Thousands were murdered within the weeks and months of the overthrow. By late October 1991, some 40,000 Haitians "boat people" sought to escape the repression by fleeing to the United States where they were labeled economic migrants and not given political refugee status. All, except for a handful, were returned to Haiti. The United States government seemed to be violating its own laws on asylum and its international obligation on *refoulement* contracted under the UN Protocol of 1968, where governments had pledged not to "push back," *refouler*, refugees to a place where they might face political persecution.

Former U.S. Ambassador to Haiti, Ernest H. Preeg, spoke about an agreement between Haiti and the Unites States that prejudged Haitians as economic migrants when he wrote, "The 1981 bilateral agreement for migrant interdiction on the high seas by the U.S. Coast Guard is unprecedented, raising controversial questions of international law."[15] He went on to specify, "This leads to the final, longest-standing unique dimension of the Haitian challenge—namely, the overwhelming dominant position of the U.S. relationship from the Haitian point of view. The United States normally accounts for close to 90 percent of Haitian exports, provides the largest share of economic aid, and is highly integrated at the family and business levels through the million Haitians in the United States. This special relationship extends to the political domain, from the period of U.S. Marine occupation of 1915 to 1934 to the varying forms of close bilateral relations since that time."[16]

The UN, OAS, and U.S. renewed their efforts to "reconcile" the elected president with those who overthrew him, urging them to build a national consensus in which various elite groups would work together—but not the masses—to establish a framework for a new government of national reconciliation. To achieve these goals, President Aristide would relinquish some of his powers and prerogatives. In the absence of these goals, the United States made it clear that Aristide would not return to power in Port-au-Prince. This had been the "liberal" position assumed by the William J. Clinton administration. The conservative position had been more severe and unbending. The embargo had no appreciable effect on the political discourse, except that it further impoverished Haitians, breaking the back of the economy in several more places. Goods were readily available via the land route from the Dominican Republic; prices on essential products raised; several more millionaires were created, for a grand total of approximately 600. The more stringent worldwide embargo applied by the UN in mid-June 1993, coupled with accelerated negotiations led the *putschists* to the table. Meanwhile, fearing assassination in Venezuela at the hand of the Americans, Aristide had moved early to Washington, DC where he had established a government in exile.

In late June and early July 1993, the Accord of Governor's Island in New York came into being. No direct negotiations had taken place between President Aristide and his government in exile and the generals' *de facto* government. The pressures were applied almost exclusively on the Aristide camp that searched for guarantees in the area of human rights to no avail. The Haitian army and the police function that sprung from it were to be reorganized under UN supervision, but none of the principals involved in the overthrow would be punished. These had been *"interlocuteurs valables,"* worthy actors, opponents with valid grievances who would have to be trusted. No mass organization was consulted, and none participated officially in the negotiations. The Peasant Movement of Papaye (MPP) said that the international community had legitimized the "de facto," [government], and that the Accord was but the visible part of the iceberg (NACLA, 1995: 189). The mass-based peasant organizations were not pleased.

When the Aristide delegation expressed satisfaction that the constitutional government had made inroads among small businessmen in Haiti, a U.S. official declared that popular support was not nearly as important as that of a dozen multimillionaires, and he proceeded to name these "big men."[17] He seemed to understand social class, economic hegemony, and class struggle even as American scholars in academic settings would deny their existence in the world or in the United States.

Despite the Accord, Aristide would not be allowed to return for another year and a half, on October 15, 1994.

Could Aristide reaffirm his mandate and re-establish his constitutional powers? Or might he become a president *de doublure*, a figurehead controlled by powers in the shadow, giving the population a "black" leader and few reforms as was the case in the nineteenth century? This had indeed been the pattern established after peasant uprisings in 1844–1846 and the demands for change from the insurgents. The American government had insisted on a new government of national unity under Prime Minister Marc L. Bazin, the unsuccessful "American candidate" for the presidency, or René Théodore, the head of the Haitian Communist Party (PUCH). Aristide got away with naming a successful publisher, a member of the Haitian aristocracy, Robert Malval, who selected in early September 1993 ministers representing many political tendencies, men and women of real talent. Economic assistance of $1 billion promised over five years that would double Haiti's foreign debt, has yet to materialize thirteen years later.

On Wings of Eagles: Continuity and Uncertainties

President Jean-Bertrand Aristide returned to the National Palace on October 15, 1994, after three years in exile in Venezuela and in the United States. His return inaugurated a period of uncertainty, rather than the hoped for certainty, lasting to date. The assassination planned for September 1991 (but never carried out), would have "resolved" a nasty situation for his opponents, until the next social upheaval would have led them to other drastic measures. The forces that had conspired to overthrow the president were still in place after his return to Port-au-Prince. There was to be no *tabula rasa*, and no revolution as had been the case in 1804. In fact, those forces had grown stronger in the interim, after the murder of about 5,000 men and women, leaders of the popular movement that had backed the Aristide government. After Aristide had abolished what remained of the Armed Forces of Haiti

From left: René G. Préval, President, 1996–2001; Robert Malval, Prime Minister; President Aristide (Washington, 1993). Photo: Haitian Embassy in Washington, DC.

(FAdH) in April 1995, he eliminated but one of the power centers that had opposed social change.

There is serious doubt about President Aristide's ability to govern and his overall effectiveness, particularly after his prerogatives were circumscribed by the very process that allowed his return to power. There had been severe conditions imposed on him by the U.S. government, the Haitian army, and the bourgeoisie, a whole range of new expectations and implied threats which Aristide had to accept as preconditions for being returned on an American aircraft. His own wings had been clipped, as it were. As the story proceeds, Aristide did respond in all the predictable ways of Haitian autocrats by strengthening his power where he could, buoyed by the considerable popular support he still held. Stymied, unable to come to agreement with the opposition, bereft of significant financial means, but retaining the love and affection of perhaps 80 percent of the peasant and urban working classes— those who did not count formally—Aristide seemed to retreat in a form of *"marronage"* in which, as with the maroons of yore, he would resist against all odds rather than become the *president de doublure* as expected. The latter term expressed a Haitian concept when elites had sought to govern through a "black" president who looked like the masses in an attempt to assuage them. The corresponding method in the United States perhaps, would be the hegemonic control of the economy by certain elites, while politics became the purview of the middle classes. One notes the lowly social origins of such contemporary presidents as Richard M. Nixon and Ronald Reagan in that scheme.

"*Le peuple*," the people were feared as they demanded a share in the political leadership and a more equitable division of wealth after two centuries of national independence. In the upper and middle-classes that fear translated in fairly simple terms, that Aristide would become a dictator, albeit an ineffectual one, as occurred in the late 1950s with three decades of Duvalierism. That situation had arisen because of the intransigence of the ruling groups that had opposed the first middle-class experiment of President Dumarsais Estimé in 1946–1950. Now both groups saw a common ground in opposing the large contingent of peasants wanting to accede to power.[18] Aristide had already proven to be a challenge to the body politic. Indeed, when it was obvious that Aristide would have to be returned to power, the army and right-wing militias increased the assassinations and the terror which included the widespread use of rape.[19]

The role of the paramount and sub-paramount powers—the United States, Canada, France, Venezuela—was key. As concerns the United States, it would attempt to "spread democracy" as the surest way to install modernity and civilization. But cold butter tears the toast; forcing foreign values upon a polity that had had enough of foreign interventions has little chance of success. The industrialist David Rockefeller had once stated that democracy, by definition, would be anti-capitalist in the underdeveloped countries.[20] Indeed, the political conditions in most Third World states, within the capitalist system, consist of subtle and not so-subtle political repression and gross economic inequality.

A U.S. army Psychological Operations officer stated that the United States would not countenance the popular movement, and that the objective was "to see that the Haitians 'don't get the idea that they can do whatever they want.'" He then added, "you publicize that you're simply not going to tolerate that kind of stuff." Another U.S. intelligence official described a Haitian CIA asset, Emmanuel (Toto) Constant, the founder of FRAPH, a paramilitary squad, as a key "young, pro-Western intellectual ... no further right than a young Republican; he would be center-right in the United States."[21] And this in Haiti where a small right-wing had moved much of the country to the "left" since the 1920s, partly because of the U.S. military occupation and pervasive American efforts to develop a middle-class, and helped by the intromission of Protestantism.

Some of these American operatives were "particularly interested in voodoo priests" in leading popular movements as they had been in 1757, 1791, 1915, and in the 1980s. In the most perceptive contemporary work on early Haitian history, U.S. historian Carolyn E. Fick wrote, "... voodoo was indeed one of the few areas of totally autonomous activity for the Haitian slaves. As a religion and a vital spiritual force, it was a source of psychological liberation .... Indeed, the sheer tenacity and vigor with which the slaves worshipped ... eloquently attests to voodoo as a driving force of resistance in the daily lives of the slaves" (Fick, 1990: 44–25). Opening a parenthesis here, the "Black Church" and Black Christianity fulfilled a similar function in the lives of African Americans in the United States, though these institutions were not meant to do so by those who christianized them. The reality expressed by Fick did not elude the CIA or the DIA, but seemed to have escaped other scholars who saw liberation from Duvalierism as solely the work of Roman Catholic grassroot organizations and Christianity writ large. This seems to have been connected to "spreading democracy" which does not allow for indigenous movements and initiatives from "natives." Furthermore, culture would replace "race" as the locus, though the analysis remained curiously the same. A USAID director in Haiti wrote, "I believe that culture is the only possible explanation for Haiti's unending tragedy; the values and attitudes of the average Haitian are profoundly influenced by traditional African culture, particularly the voodoo religion .... The imprint of African culture, particularly vodun [sic] ... sustained by long years of isolation from progressive ideas, open political systems, and economic dynamism is ... the only possible explanation for the continuing Haitian tragedy."[22] Not exactly eloquent, this passage could have been written a hundred years ago by a follower of Arthur de Gobineau. Of course, Haitians are not saints and some share the blame for their failings; but not a single mention is made of an international system, of the web of interaction between states, about capitalism and its efforts toward globalization, or about colonization and slavery and purposeful discrimination. Nothing. As if Haiti was "*en vase clos*," impervious to all that occurred beyond its borders over long stretches of time. Culture had replaced race, but we were no further along in terms of the analysis. Then again, little in actual practice had changed the world over in any significant way.

One notes that, in furthering cultural transfers, another U.S. observer had stated "[Vodou priests] were victims of a zealous Haitian [Protestant] clergy eager to exploit public anger at the Tontons Macoutes ... to resume their long standing inquisition to eradicate Vodou's power altogether. For while many who died [between 500 and 2,000] were houngan and manbo, they were not necessarily Macoute" (Fatton, 2002: 72 n. 15). Haitian sociologist Alex Dupuy concluded, "for the foreign policy intelligentsia [in the United States], the defense and promotion of democracy and the free market serve as the 'grander vision' of U.S. policy objectives in the new world order" (Dupuy, 1997: 7). Indeed, the objective so dear to all colonialisms is the alteration of cultural systems under the guise of a helping hand, and the spread of capital.

A new, improved, refreshed Aristide was sent back to Haiti in order not to complete the job he had started. He was expected to accept neo-liberal economic imperatives while facing the reluctance or outright opposition of most Haitians to embark on such a course. Prime Minister Michael Manley in Jamaica, and Presidents Cheddi Jagan and Janet Jagan in Guyana had had similar constraints imposed on them, with a marked definition between the two terms in office of the first two Caribbean leaders.

Privatizing all major government assets was dubbed "democratization" to render the process more palatable to Haitians. It did not work. "Shortly after Aristide's return last October [1994], a peasant woman in the Central Plateau talked about the new economic policies. 'I do not know,' she mused, 'these World Bank and IMF plans do not sound too good for us. Titid [Aristide] says they must be good, but he says it surrounded by many tall Americans. I wonder if he wants us to object.'"[23] *Marronage*, again, is the keen art of obfuscation adopted by subaltern people.

The articulation of the shift of power as it occurred in the summer of 1993 was indicated by Alex Dupuy. About Aristide, he wrote: "Now he was completely dependent on the goodwill of the United States ... and he was dealing with the Haitian bourgeoisie and the foreign investors from a weakened position. He, not they, had to make all the concessions. They signaled a decisive shift in the balance of class forces: the Haitian bourgeoisie, under Washington's hegemony and the full weight of the U.S. government and the international financial institutions behind it, had regained the upper hand. Aristide understood ... and he modified his discourse and behavior accordingly" (Dupuy, 1997: 147). The embargo adopted by the Organization of American States and the United Nations against the Haitian military junta in the hope of re-establishing Aristide to the presidency, remained seemingly purposefully ineffective, becoming enforced only after May 1994. The Agreement of Governors' Island in New York bay negotiated between the generals and the constitutional government, from the end of June till mid-July 1993, proved a disaster for Aristide (Malone, 1998: 86–88). Later, the three "Wise Men" bearing gifts for the Haitian military to induce them to leave, former President Jimmy Carter, U.S. Senator Sam Nunn, and—representing King Balthazar—former Chairman of the Joint Chief of Staff, General Colin L. Powell, entered into a formal agreement on September 18, 1994 with the Haitian officers in which, for loyal services, they would not be pursued for high crimes and treason, and would regain their frozen personal assets to the tune of $179 million. And the United States promised to rent General Raoul Cédras's princely home for the princely sum of $5,000 a month (Dupuy, 1997: 160).

Little wonder then that the emasculated president would have a contentious relationship with civil society. He was left with little room in which to maneuver, and fewer options still. His relationship with Parliament, political parties, the media, the opposition in general terms, and the business sector continued to deteriorate in the fifteen months remaining in his 5-year mandate. Political assassinations, a standard procedure under the military regimes, slowly started to become more common.

Besides the approximately 5,000 murders that followed Aristide's overthrow in 1991, three well-known individuals had been assassinated: Antoine Izmery (September 11, 1993), a wealthy backer of Aristide and a businessman, Minister of Justice Guy Malary (October 14, 1993), and Roman Catholic priest and political activist Jean-Marie Vincent (August 28, 1994). These murders had taken place under the junta, and the "de facto" governments it had established—President Joseph Nerette with Prime Ministers Jean-Jacques Honorat (October 1991), then Marc Bazin (June 1992); and President Emile Jonassaint (May 1994). After Aristide's return, there were the spectacular assassinations of opposition leader and lawyer Mireille Durocher-Bertin (March 28, 1995), and pro-Aristide legislator, Jean-Hubert Feuille (November 7, 1995). The most famous Haitian reporter, Jean Léopold Dominique, was murdered on April 3, 2000, under the watch of Aristide successor, President René Préval.

The Lavalas movement was transformed into a political party where the overwhelming presence of a "chef" replicates long-standing Haitian traditions. And that party splinters, as many former allies of President Aristide move into the opposition. What was revealed by these permutations was perhaps predictable: the popular movement proved incapable of fostering permanent and profound change that would, in effect, wield a social revolution with attendant political, cultural, economic transformation of the landscape. There were, nonetheless, some changes. The giant had awakened, and unless severe political repression is now applied against the "masses," that giant will never sleep again. And herein lies the fears and the troubles and the sleepless nights of bourgeois and Americans alike. The popular movement remained against the privatization of governmental assets mandated by the United States and the World Bank group. In an "on again, off again" Aristidian dance, the President sacked Prime Minister Smarck Michel, replacing him with Madame Claudette Werleigh who opposed privatization, in October 1995. She had been Secretary of State for External Relations in the Michel cabinet.

The analysis of Robert Fatton, Jr. offers a hopeful stance, though he might disagree with my reading: "... a predatory democracy is not a completely closed system of power; it offers some space for maneuvering. The opposition and its political parties are not completely silenced, civil society is not extinguished, and a free press remains vocal. There is room for popular struggles portending potential alterations in the nature of the state ... many peasant organizations, trade unions, and professional groups have kept their independence and still speak truth to power" (Fatton, 2002: 15). One notes that, since these lines were written, a large number of journalists have been murdered and their murderers have never come to justice. But, in point of fact, this assessment is essentially correct. This represents a change from previous decades from the relatively genteel upper-class rule until 1950, and the horror and mayhem of Duvalierist rule after that. That assessment does not, however, preclude a return to the "past," if the population feels stymied by a lack of progress. I am reminded of a statement made to me by an elderly lady of the Haitian aristocracy, *il n'y a rien de plus laid qu'une classe en formation* ("there is scarcely anything uglier than a class in the process of forming itself"). Things could get ugly. Fatton continued, somewhat optimistically, "[R]epresenting a persistent challenge to the hegemonic pretensions of Fanmi Lavalas [the Lavalas Family political party], these movements make a return to a full dictatorship unlikely. While they cannot guarantee the birth of a functioning polyarchy, they may at least facilitate the transition from a predatory to unconsolidated democracy. Thus, in spite of severe social and material constraints stemming from the existing domestic balance of class power and the external patterns of acute dependence, the future of Haitian society is not entirely foreclosed" (Fatton, 2002: 15).

These are perhaps small steps between predatory and unconsolidated democracy, but significant nevertheless, akin to Aristide's pledge that we would move Haiti from abject misery to mere poverty. As concerns Aristide, his Prime Minister between July and December 1993, Robert Malval, offers a brutal and stinging repudiation of the President, concluding, "[Aristide] had only social rhetoric ... drawn from the well of Liberation Theology doctrines which he brandished constantly and continually to better hide the absence of any real political, social and, particularly, economic thought."[24] Malval specified his meaning further, giving as "proof" of what he asserts that Aristide may not have understood the awesome significance of his election to the presidency, as reflected by "vague," inappropriate and redundant speech that made him appear to be, for some, a simpleton. Premier Malval continued, "... his actions, on the other hand, disconcerted more than one observer. An idea was as easily approved as discarded, thus giving his political acts a contradictory feel which [has] always hindered him in reaching the height of his incredible fate."[25] These are strong words indeed, pronounced by an erstwhile political ally. That judgment defined the "*desarroi*," the distress, the confusion and the anger of those who had given their support to Aristide, then felt the need to disengage from him, and these are legions. There was a sense, not totally justified, of betrayal.

Agronomist René Garcia Préval, a former Prime Minister, was chosen by Aristide to succeed him in the presidency. When one adheres to a mechanistic view of democracy, one often hears that the second free election is more important than the first, since the former solidifies the system. Not necessarily. One cannot ignore the example of the Dominican Republic, for instance, with President Joaquin Balaguer, or Rafael Leonidas Trujillo before him, who may have been a "model" for Haiti's democratic "form" and lack of content. Préval was elected in December 1995, with 87.9 percent from a turnout estimated at 28 percent of the voting population. He took office on February 7, 1996, and would leave office in 2001 when Aristide would reclaim the seat in a fair election. Aristide had considered the idea of extending his first term, ostensibly to "make up the lost years," with the approbation of his electorate, but conditions had changed since this was also done by François Duvalier in the 1960s. And the Americans were watching. U.S. President Clinton had much to lose. All this transpired under the gaze of occupying military forces sponsored by the United Nations.[26]

President Préval, at first, headed over a lackluster administration, but after May 1996, the situation deteriorated considerably, with increases in the rate of political assassinations. Laws favoring privatization were submitted to Parliament in July 1996, and passed in September of that year, under duress and with the desire to acquire foreign loans that would allow the government to pay its bills. Préval was denounced bitterly—even by his party—for his neo-liberal economic policies. Results of parliamentary elections in April 1997 were considered to be fraudulent by the international community, with abysmally low turnouts of below 10 percent. Supplementary elections that followed in July and August 1997 suffered the same fate, with turnouts below 3 percent of the electorate. Prime Minister Rosny Smarth resigned in early June 1997, replaced by Ericq Pierre whose appointment was rejected by the Chamber of Deputies, followed by economist Hervé Denis in early November, also rebuffed by the Chamber in December 1997. None of the proposed premiers had been approved. Lavalas had imploded, and the elites rejoiced. Préval dismissed Parliament, extra-legally, and named Jacques-Edouard Alexis Prime Minister who remained unconfirmed. Haiti remained, formally, without a government for the better part of two years. Meanwhile, the United Nations peacekeeping forces had left Haiti by year's end in 1997.

Elections were held once more on May 21, 2000, with a 60 percent participation rate, and came a few weeks after the assassination of Jean Dominique. The second and third rounds occurred on July 9 and 30, with a decrease in participation at around 30 percent. These elections that gave huge victories to the pro-Aristide forces were seen as illegitimate and fraudulent by the international community and by the internal opposition. Rapid fire elections—form vs. content—were taxing the patience of the electorate and failed to mollify the political parties outside Fanmi Lavalas. The real tragedy, which hid a dangerous reality, is that no fraud need have occurred: the large majority were still supporting the "idea" of Aristide though now in decreasing numbers. Another tragedy resided in the fact that no other political formation had enflamed the electorate, all being divorced from a popular movement that look askance at parties that seemed resurrected from the past—in fact, particules ("particles)" rather than parties, that vehicled the ambitions of one particular man. The socialist parties were no different from the rest. All failed to take into account the organizational structures, the autochthonous paradigms that distance Haitians from the rest of the world. Democracy cannot be spread; it is home grown or it cannot exist at all.

Conclusion

THERE IS NO POSSIBLE DIVORCE BETWEEN THE FORCES OF GLOBALIZATION and Haiti. No isolationist policies, no autarky can provide alternatives, an escape or respite from the stranglehold of engagement. Economic processes are pitiless, and they are experienced around the globe as a "capitalisme sauvage," in all its brutality. The market rules.

Though never isolated from the world, Haiti suffered nonetheless a period of brutal ostracism from the West—Africa and Asia were "non-existent" at that time, Latin America, not yet born—for daring to oppose slavery and colonialism, and Haiti won. It won that particular battle but lost the war, as had done Native Americans before it. Aimé Césaire's famous *cri du coeur, Haiti, ou la négritude s'est mise debout pour la première fois,* ("where negritude stood up for the first time"), is both generous and too optimistic a formulation. That ostracism had been a mere hiatus between colonialism and neo-colonialism—no post-colonialism here—which, not so paradoxically, allowed Haiti to develop some early industries as seen in chapter two. But more significantly, this led also to the maturation of both the Haitian language and the Vodou religion that become the "poto-mitan," the pillars of Haitian culture and markers for its evolving nationality. More than the Citadel itself, Haiti's language and religion were achievements of monumental proportions.

President René G. Préval had taken note in a speech that globalization was not born yesterday, but in the unequal exchange borne by subaltern societies in slavery and in five hundred years of Western imperialism. That speech angered the U.S. ambassador. Haitian society, nationality, culture and language, "race" and poverty, had been birthed in the country's interaction with larger powers, starting in the sixteenth century. Haitian nationalism, contrary to that of the United States or France, is a defensive mechanism, a response to the perceived unfairness of the world.

President Jean-Bertrand Aristide, in his second administration, pursued the logic of Préval's position by asking the French to recognize their debt to Saint-Domingue and other colonized peoples that had allowed France to become a world power with commensurate economic development. Holding "reparations" at bay for the moment, Aristide claimed "restitution" for Haitian payments to former slave owners. The sum owed Haiti, he contended, was $21,685,135,571.48— reparations would come later. The French ambassador was angered. The speech occurred during events commemorating the bicentennial of the death, in France, of Toussaint Louverture, on April 7, 2003. As if rising from the grave, Louverture's statement resonated: "the peoples misled and raging [from the offense] know in their anger how to find the necessary means, even at the enemy's doorstep, to defend their liberty and avenge their honor" (*Les peuples dechainés et trompés, savent dans leur colère, trouver les moyens nécessaires même chez l'ennemi pour défendre leur liberté et leur honneur*). Some children inherit their parents' wealth, others only have their anger to transmit to their "generations." There seems to exist in the world, an inverse relationship between work and wealth.

Haitian history and Haitians' life remain inconsequential in the greater scheme of things. The country no longer commands the hope of blacks worldwide, but brings forth shame and disillusionment for those who misunderstand the causes of underdevelopment and the ravages of self-hatred. Haiti remains the poorest country in the Americas, having gone from riches to rags for the benefit of its masters. Remittances from the one million Haitians abroad—for about 8 millions residing in Haiti—is approximately $1 billion yearly, accounting for 17 percent of Gross Domestic Product. The Dominican Republic weighs in at 10 percent of GDP, with 25 percent of its population residing abroad. Migration and exile are permanent features of the social landscape in late capitalism.

The second Aristide administration (2001), "admits" defeat. Policies, such as they are, cannot contradict the demands of money-lenders. It seems to have little choice but to revert to the status quo ante, one in which widespread and generalized corruption, increased and systematic repression of political opponents of every ideological stripe, is the one "tried and true" Haitian systemic imperative in which too many chase too few spoils: *men anpil, kòb la kout*, ("many hands [in the till], few resources"). The revolution devours its own children! Like in pre-revolutionary Cuba (1959), the only source of enrichment when facing the stranglehold of foreign capitalists domestically is the state apparatus, making corruption endemic and "necessary." Europe went through similar stages in past centuries. In societies where few channels exist for the continued enrichment of the already rich, government corruption becomes a fine art. Nonetheless, progress—if it is progress—is that a different social class commands the spoils, as in the transitions inaugurated by Emperor Faustin Soulouque in mid-nineteenth century, President François Duvalier in mid-twentieth century, and then, President Aristide. Meanwhile, Aristide became largely ineffectual but remained resilient, accepting U.S. diktats and resisting them, a perfect *nèg mawon* ("[Negro] maroon"), in a country whose existence and survival was a supreme act of marronage. Marronage is a refusal to accept defeat even in defeat, or masking that refusal with a grin and ostensible acceptance. Westerners are baffled by Haitians refusing to become "modernized, westernized, civilized, or simply white." Aristide, in office, remained a leader in opposition, though men and women, once in power, need to devise new stratagems and develop a new mien.

One asks the question, *Aristide peut-il gérer la crise?* ("Can Aristide manage the crisis?") Non. No one else might either. Aristide retained the sympathy, the adulation, and the affection of few in the electorate. In a land where easy explanations are sometimes sought, one might hear that the "fauteuil présidentiel" is jinxed, that the seat of power—metaphorically, where the President seats his derrière—brings "madichon," bad luck to all those who achieve the presidency. To insure that this did not take place, children in the woodshop of Aristide's orphanage gerrymandered an ugly seat on which he sat on February 7,

1991. To no avail. The job remained jinxed. Easy answers might also lead some to argue that Aristide is a "chimera," that rare condition that allows someone to have biologically two complete sets of chromosomes without ill-effects—by extrapolation, of having a Jekyll and Hyde personality. Efforts to amend the constitution in September 2003 and other grave incidents would seem to indicate that power corrupts and that the leadership reverts back to type. The "chimères" are also the political thugs who have arisen to beat down all opposition to Lavalas, and seem at once connected and apart from the executive branch, perhaps uncontrolled and uncontrollable, reminiscent of the politicized gangs in Jamaica that served similar functions for the two national parties. The President's lack of a social imagination and political skills may be formidable, but one is not rewarded for going against the grain, as it were, and against superpowers; there are *coups d'état* and murder at the end of that road. African rulers who had conspired with Europe to enslave other Africans knew that there were costs for not going along.

The years have not been kind to Haiti from 1990 to the present. How does one write contemporary history when one lacks distance? Perhaps by staying away from minutiae and by anticipating the broad brush strokes that will be revealed to be significant later? This is my attempt here. As the country commemorates the start of its third century (on January 1, 2004), it faces severe odds, political crises, incessant economic downturns, and social anomie. Its culture remains embattled on all fronts in ways Quebécois and the French may recognize. The world shifts in its orbit. Haiti is not Africa, yet maintained or created a "classic" form of creolization, neo-African institutions, structures, and ideological frameworks, and judicious and assimilated blends of Western elements that aliment the lives of citizens and visions of selves and collectivities.

Occupying forces—in Haiti in 1916 or Iraq in 2003—have a vested interest, for their own safety, in establishing a constabulary that would shield them and control the "natives" ("locals," American soldiers are now taught to say). President Aristide's most recognized achievement, if allowed to stand, may be the outright elimination of the Armed Forces whose sole function had been to police Haiti. And contrarily to the Dominican Republic, Nicaragua, and Panama where the United States established armies, the Haitian bourgeoisie had taken command of the army, except for the hiatus of middle-class control under the Duvaliers, from Commandant Demosthènes Calixte in the 1930s to General Raoul Cédras in the 1990s.

As in the first edition of this book where I remarked, to the horror of some, that Haitian scholars have been remarkably sage, wise, and balanced in their analyses of what ails Haiti, I make the same assertion again. Alex Dupuy, Robert Fatton, Jr., Michel-Rolph Trouillot, Claudine Michel, and others, have continued that tradition by their judicious views of the country. They are passionate, detached, and fair. Haitian scholars seem to appreciate the complexities of an argument. Those interested in Haiti and the Caribbean would be well advised to take note.

History tells us that revolutions can be countermanded, e.g. the Haitian Revolution was essentially overturned by 1806. In contemporaneous terms, the revolution was not the overthrow of the Duvalier dynasty in 1986, not the election of Aristide in December 1990. All these were stages in a process that, in time, may lead to outcomes considered later to have been revolutionary. At present, these are significant but mere defining moments.

Massacres of political activists throughout Haiti, widespread abuse against the media, general strikes in December 2003, the dissolution of Lavalas political structures, raise the distinct possibility that President Aristide may not be allowed to complete his term of office which is scheduled to end in February 2006. He loses ground every day in all social classes, though he retains some political support in some sectors, raising the prospect of a civil war. Meanwhile, the world tires of watching.

In mid-January 2004, the embattled President—deserted by a large segment of the masses from which he had drawn his support—struggled to survive. His non-consecutive second term runs until February 7, 2006. But already, the term of office of 18 senators out of 27, and all members of the Chamber of Deputies expired on January 18, 2004. The unpopular President, once elected democratically in December 1990 with overwhelming support, now must govern by executive decree in the absence of a legislature. The government had failed to hold legislative elections due to its own intransigence, and hampered by the recalcitrance of the opposition.

In that oppositional constellation, the stars and the planets are aligned perfectly. All are demanding "regime change," while most had demanded the restoration of Aristide to power in 1991–1994. The French adage, "plus ça change, plus c'est la même chose," indicated a generalized malaise affecting Haitian society. Neither state structures nor national institutions had been transformed in that short span of time, and neither was the insidious impact of the international system upon Haiti as it affects policies and politics of subaltern societies. Facing similar systemic ordeals, how would have U.S. President George W. "Baby" Bush or U.K. and Canada Prime Ministers Tony Blair and Paul Martin fared in the absence of a democratic framework? One wonders. One was reminded of Jamaica and Guyana rejoining the political orthodoxy mandated by the paramount powers in the second "incarnations" of Premier Michael Manley and President Cheddi Jagan. The terms of the discourse were altered similarly between Aristide I (1991) and Aristide II (1994 and 2001). And if a street woman was overheard to mutter in February 1991, "we put him there, we can remove him," in January 2004, a young man, rendered old and skinny by hunger, muttered to himself, "he must go for the revolution to take place. We must have a revolution." Indeed, revolutionary conditions may exist objectively, never giving rise to revolutions. And when they do? They may not last!

The international community—as distinct from the international system—seems "stumped" by events in Haiti. President Thabo Mbeki of South Africa, forging a new international role for his country, in a grand gesture of Pan-African solidarity, tried vainly to effect a rapprochement between the Haitian government and its opposition. He was the only chief of state to have attended the ceremonies commemorating the Haitian Bicentenary on January 1, 2004. Neither the Organization of American States (OAS), nor the Caribbean Community (CARICOM), despite energetic efforts spent in that direction, seem able to construct a framework to resolve Haiti's tangled "mess." Meanwhile, in a reversal, turning a positive act into a negative outcome perhaps, Aristide's dismantling of the Armed Forces may signal his survival in office ... for a while. A typical course taken by events since the 1940s, had been that the military would depose the president after students had demonstrated and business had gone into a general strike. The mold was broken. The U.S. had opposed the scuttling of the Haitian army it had coddled for eighty years, seeing it as a counterveiling force. In the same vein, in Brazil, the Brazilian army was seen as the "arbiter" of Brazilian politics.

Hundreds have died over the past year in the streets of Haitian cities, towns, and hamlets. Reporters and media outlets were attacked repeatedly by groups supporting the government. Day after day, tens of thousands demonstrated and were fired upon by armed goons who conceal their identity. General strikes by the commercial sector, schools, hospitals, and radio stations brought national life to a standstill. The cities and towns of Port-au-Prince, Gonaïves, Cap Haitien, Jacmel, Saint-Marc, Léogane ... erupted in massive demonstrations repeatedly. Armed Duvalierists entered the fray, invading from the Dominican Republic, routing the National Police in their wake.

> Chimè nan bounda m
> gran gou nan bounda m
> m pap negosye
> fò Aristide ale!
> (Chimeras [armed thugs] on my ass
> hunger in my ass [body]
> I'm [we] are not negotiating
> Aristide must go!)

With armed thugs representing various factions approaching Port-au-Prince, and with the French government insisting that Aristide resign, the President tendered his resignation on February 29, 2004. This French action was the last straw. After all, France had very possibly saved Aristide's life against the wishes of powerful forces both in and outside Haiti, when his government had been overthown by a military coup in September 1991. President Aristide and French President Francois Mitterand, then, were both socialists. Mitterand is now dead, and France has moved to the "right." Much has changed, yet—as the French proverb goes—much also stays the same.

Provincial armies marched South, and aimed to oust a chief of state. These events evoked recollections of nineteenth-century Haiti. There was a sense of painful betrayal felt by this author and millions of Haitians in terms of awesome possibilities that were squandered after the fall of Duvalierism in 1986. Jean-Bertrand Aristide, "un fils du peuple," a man from the peasantry, acceded to power in February 1991. It had to have been a new day. The "peuple" had arrived as full participants in the body politic as had done the middle-classes in 1946 and 1957. It was not to be.

Jean-Bertrand Aristide may well become a martyr—with huge costs to, and political consequences for Haiti—to that still significant minority that remains loyal to him. Michele Montas—the widow of that sainted journalist Jean Dominique—had expressed the desire that "Aristide completes his term." She had made her declaration on American radio, that medium to which she has dedicated her life. Perhaps, in allowing Aristide to complete his remaining two years, the constituents that still support him could be assuaged. Maybe. But significant political changes in the governance would have had to take place nonetheless. This was the desire expressed by CARICOM, the Caribbean Community, and the plan it proposed as a solution for the political crisis.

If conservative forces, as expressed by upper-class and elite sectors and their foreign allies prevail; if Duvalierism is resurgent, and if the Haitian army is re-established (as is desired by the United States and some sectors in Haiti), then Haiti will have rejoined the orthodoxy of Caribbean politics, that of mildly reformist regimes with "apparent" democracy, and no real structural reforms. And that would be a mistake from which most Haitians would suffer dearly.

The first popularly and democratically elected president—outside of those elected by votes of the Assemblee Nationale—came to an ignominious end.

Late on Saturday night, on February 28, 2004—in a time-honored tradition of late night calls from U.S. ambassadors to Haitian chiefs of state who have fallen from favor—U.S. Secretary of State Colin Powell and Aristide spoke, with the suggestion made by Powell that the President leave. He did so early on Sunday morning, February 29, surrounded by U.S. Marine Corps soldiers armed to the teeth. That Sunday, on the CNN network, U.S. Representative Charles Rangel declared that the "U.S. had abetted the coup." Later, on the same network, U.S. Senator Bob Graham said that "the degree of involvement of the United States in that coup" remains unknown. Meanwhile, American commentators stated that the safety of 20,000 American citizens hung in the balance, hence the immediate deployment of U.S. troops in Haiti. Twenty-thousand Americans in Haiti—most in privileged positions of authority in the beleaguered republic—for a population of 8,000,000 would be the equivalent of 720,000 foreigners in the United States in a powerful position to effect change or stymie it in a country not their own. Meanwhile, the new provisional constitutional president, the President of the Cour de Cassation, Haiti's supreme court, Judge Boniface Alexandre, took the oath of office surrounded by armed American soldiers.

There is a sense of *déjà-vu* in the process that disposed of Aristide, as one seemed transported back in time to the end of the Duvalier regime, in February 1986. But this time, it was Aristide who was deposed. Once more, Haiti will have to try again, try to re-invent itself. But will it be permitted to do so with the dearth of allowable models of development under hegemonic globalization?

Selected Orisha/Vodoun/Lwa/Oricha/Orixa and Roman Catholic Equivalents

Dahomey or Nigeria	Haiti	Cuba	Brazil	Catholic Saints	Functions
Legba Eshu Elegbara Avlekete	Legba Avlekete	Ellegua	Exu	St. Anthony St. Peter St. Michael	Crossroads, gates, doorways
Dan Obatala	Danbala Ayida Wedo Gran Batala	Obatala	Oxala	St. Patrick Jesus Christ Lady of Mercy Moses Immaculate Conception St. Ann	Wisdom
Hevioso Shango	Hevioso	Chango	Xango	St. Jerome St. Barbara St. Anthony	Storms, fire, winds

Dahomey or Nigeria	Haiti	Cuba	Brazil	Catholic Saints	Functions
Ezili Oshun Yemoja Olokun	Ezili Freda Ezili Dantò Lasirenn Agwe	Ochun Yemaya	Oxum Iemanja	Mater Salvatoris Mater Dolorosa Czestochowa Mt. Carmel Caridad del Cobre Star of the Sea St. Ulrick	Love, sensuality, sexuality, beauty, motherhood, warrior, sea, oceans, rivers, lakes
Ogou Ogun	Ogou	Oggun	Ogum	St. James St. Philippe St. George St. Peter St. Barbara	Justice, family of Warriors
Ibeji	Marasa	Ibeyi	Ibegi	St. Cosme and Damien St. Nicholas	Twins, duality, children, ancestors

Dahomey or Nigeria	Haiti	Cuba	Brazil	Catholic Saints	Functions
Oshossi	Azaka Gran Bwa Klermezinn	Ochossi	Oxossi	St. Isidor St Sebastian St. Andrew St. Claire	Agriculture, hunt forests, harvests, fields
Oya	Gran Brigit Bawon Samdi Gede Family	Oya	Iansã	St. Brigitte St. Theresa St. Barbara Candelaria St. Gerard St. Expedit	Death, cemetaries, ancestors, children, storms, winds....
	Loko Ayizan			St. Joseph Altagarcia St. Ann	Patrons of the priesthood

Notes

Chapter 1

1. Georges Anglade, *Atlas critique d'Haiti* (Montreal: ERCE and CRC, 1982), p. 7. All translations are the author's unless indicated otherwise.

2. There are numerous spellings for the name of Haiti's religion, even though only whites try to give it a name. In Haiti, in typical African fashion, the religion has no name; adherents are "those who serve the spirits." Originally, "voodoo" referred only to a dance. Consensus now established for "Vodou."

3. This and the following extract are from Jean-Marie Jan, *Collecta: Compilation de documents pour servir à l'histoire du diocèse du Cap*, 3 vols. (Port-au-Prince: Editions Henri Deschamps, 1955–1956), vol. 3, pp. 340–344.

4. Ibid., pp. 350–351.

5. *Life* magazine (August 1987), p. 62.

6. Frederick J. Conway, "Sex Roles and the 'Modernization' of a Religious System" (Paper presented at the 77th annual meeting of the American Anthropological Association, Los Angeles, November 18, 1978).

7. M. B. Bird, *The Black Man or Haitian Independence* (London, 1869), cited in Madeleine Sylvain-Bouchereau, *Haiti et ses femmes: Une étude d'évolution culturelle* (Port-au-Prince: Imprimerie des Presses Libres, 1975), p. 75.

8. Sylvain-Bouchereau, *Haiti et ses femmes*, p. 75.

Chapter 2

1.   See the useful works by Robert W. July, *A History of the African People* (New York: Charles Scribner's Sons, 1974); Walter Rodney, *How Europe Underdeveloped Africa* (Washington, DC: Howard University Press, 1974); and Irving Leonard Markovitz, *Power and Class in Africa* (Englewood Cliffs, NJ: Prentice-Hall, 1977).

2.   Georges Anglade, *Atlas critique d'Haiti* (Montreal: ERCE and CRC, 1982), p. 14.

3.   John Stuart Mill, *Principles of Political Economy* (London: Routledge and Sons, 1900), p. 454.

4.   Cited by André Teulières, *L'Outre-Mer français: Hier, aujourd'hui, demain* (Paris: Berger-Leurault, 1970), p. 214.

5.   Cited by Rodney, *How Europe Underdeveloped Africa*, p. 75.

6.   Dantès Bellegarde, *Histoire du peuple haitien* (Port-au-Prince: Collection du Tricinquantenaire, 1953), p. 30.

7.   See B.R. Burg, *Sodomy and the Pirate Tradition* (New York: New York University Press, 1983), for the role of homosexuality in these relationships.

8.   Jean Fouchard, *Les Marrons de la liberté* (Port-au-Prince: Henri Deschamps, 1972), p. 117.

9.   Georges Sylvain cited in Dantès Bellegarde, *La Nation haitienne* (Paris: J. de Gigord, 1938), p. 312; italics added.

10.   Fouchard, *Marrons*, p. 529; in translating these lines, I have rearranged them slightly.

11.   Bellegarde, *Histoire*, p. 59. Carbonarism refers to an Italian secret society that met in the woods to plot for Italy's unification.

12.   J.C. Dorsainvil, *Manuel d'histoire d'Haiti* (Port-au-Prince: Procure des Frères de l'Instruction Chrétienne, 1949), pp. 71, 80.

13.   Louis-Joseph Janvier, *Les Constitutions d'Haiti* (Paris, 1886), p. 32.

14.   Ibid., pp. 28–29.

15.   Celso Furtado in Richard P. Schaedel, ed., *Research and Resources of Haiti* (New York: Research Institute for the Study of Man, 1969), p. 14.

16.   Bellegarde, *Histoire*, p. 116.

17.   Rodney, *How Europe Underdeveloped Africa*, p. 3.

18. Cited in M.A. Lubin, "Les Premiers rapports de la nation haitienne avec l'étranger," *Journal of InterAmerican Studies* 10 (April 1968), p. 282.

19. Cited in N. Andrew N. Cleven, "The First Panama Mission and the Congress of the United States," *Journal of Negro History* 13, no. 3 (1928), p. 237.

20. Ibid., p. 240.

21. Proclamation of the general-in-chief, January 1, 1804; italics added. Much of Haitian history is oral history and is subsequently reprinted time and again in all basic texts.

22. Bellegarde, *Histoire*, p. 134.

23. Message dated February 12, 1870; 41st Congress, Senate Document 17.

24. Mercer Cook, "Dantès Bellegarde," *Phylon* (Atlanta) 1, no. 2 (1940), p. 128.

25. Quoted in Mercer Cook, ed., *An Introduction to Haiti* (Washington, DC: Federal Security Agency, 1948), pp. 93–94.

26. Edmund Wilson, *Red, Black, Blond, and Olive—Studies in Four Civilizations: Zuni, Haiti, Soviet Russia, Israel* (New York: Oxford University Press, 1956), p. 110.

27. Cook, *An Introduction*, pp. 101, 110. Stanza translated from the French by P. Bellegarde-Smith.

28. R. Piquion, "Préface," in Roussan Camille, *Assaut à la nuit* (Port-au-Prince, 1940), p. 10.

29. A. Viatte, *Histoire littéraire de l'Amérique française* (Paris: Presses Universitaires de France, 1954), p. 466.

30. Rayford W. Logan, interview with author, Washington, DC, November 21, 1975.

Chapter 3

1. Oswald Durand, *Rires et pleurs* (Port-au-Prince, 1896), p. 109. The French original reads:

> Ecoutez! écoutez! C'est le bronze homicide!
> Fils de mil huit cent quatre, est-ce que l'étranger
> Revient fouler le sol où fleurit l'oranger

Et nous montrer encor son bras liberticide?
Levez-vous donc alors! Et, la torche à la main,
Brûlez comme autrefois et les bourgs et les villes!
Peuple, reste debout! et leurs cohortes, viles
T'admireront le lendemain!

2.   From his memoirs, quoted in E. Galeano, *Open Veins: Five Centuries of the Pillage of a Continent* (New York: Monthly Review Press, 1973), p. 122.

3.   J.C. Dorsainvil, *Manuel d'histoire d'Haiti* (Port-au-Prince: Procure des Frères de l'Instruction Chrétienne, 1949), p. 199.

4.   In French, *doublure* is the lining of a garment.

5.   President Dartiguenave, "Proclamation," *Le Moniteur*, April 8, 1916.

6.   Quoted in Roger Gaillard, *Les Blancs débarquent*, 7 vols. (Port-au-Prince: Le Natal, 1973–1983), vol. 2, p. 154.

7.   Sténio Vincent, *En Posant les jalons*, vol. 1 (Port-au-Prince: Imprimerie de l'Etat, 1939), pp. 278–279.

8.   Georges Sylvain, *Dix Années de luttes pour la liberté, 1915–1925* (Port-au-Prince: n. d.), p. 6.

9.   Butler to Wright, USMC-HC, PC54, October 13, 1916.

10.   Butler to John McIlhenny, USMC-HC, PC54, June 23, 1917, and Butler to McIlhenny, USMC-HC, PC54, December 31, 1917.

11.   Quoted in John Allen, "An Inside View of Revolution in Haiti," *Current History* 32 (1930), p. 325.

12.   Knapp to Sec. of Navy Denby, "Supplementary Report on Haiti," January 13, 1921, NA-RG 45, Box 632.

13.   [Illegible] to Butler, USMC-HC, PC54, July 13, 1916.

14.   Quoted in Huntington Wilson, "The Relation of Government to Foreign Investment," *AAASPS* 68 (1916), p. 307.

15.   Farnham to Butler, USMC-HC, PC54, January 21, 1918.

16.   Long to Smoot, USMC-HC, May 21, 1920.

17.   Butler to McIlhenny, USMC-HC, PC54, December 31, 1917.

18.   K. Millet, *Les Paysans haitiens et l'occupation américaine, 1915–1930* (Montreal: Collectif-Paroles, 1978), pp. 30–31.

19.   U.S. Senate, *Hearings*, 67th Congress, 1st session (1922), p. 398.

20. Georges Anglade, *L'Espace haitien* (Montréal: Presses Universitaires du Québec, 1974), p. 33, and Hans Schmidt, *The United States Occupation of Haiti, 1915–1934* (New Brunswick, NJ: Rutgers University Press, 1971), p. 103.

21. U.S. Senate, *Hearings,* 67th Congress, 1st session (1922), pp. 13–14, 19.

22. Ibid., p. 19.

23. Millet, *Les Paysans haitiens,* pp. 100–101, 105.

24. G. Pierre-Charles, *L'Economie haitienne et sa voie de développement* (Paris: G.-P. Maisonneuve et Larose, 1967), pp. 45–46.

25. Ibid.

26. R. Depestre, "Jean Price-Mars et le mythe de l'orphée noire," *L'Homme et la société* (Paris) 7 (January–February 1968), p. 175.

27. Robert D. Heinl, Jr., "Bailing Out Duvalier," *New Republic* 156 (January 14, 1967), p. 15.

28. Quoted in *Le Nouvelliste,* September 5, 1957.

29. J. Price-Mars, *Lettre ouverte au Dr. René Piquion* (Port-au-Prince, 1967), pp. 20–21.

30. See Allan Ebert, "The Days of 'Baby Doc' Are Numbered," *Newsday* (Long Island, NY), February 4, 1986.

31. "Haitian Dictator Heeds Washington's Aid Signals," *Washington Report on the Hemisphere* 4, no. 6 (December 13, 1983), p. 1.

32. Frederick J. Conway, "Pentecostalism in Haiti: Healing and Hierarchy" (Paper presented at the American Anthropological Association, November 30, 1977), pp. 5, 7.

33. World Bank, *Memorandum on the Haitian Economy* (Washington, DC, May 13, 1981), p. 6.

34. Organization of American States, OEA/Ser.L/V/ II.57, 20, September 1982.

Chapter 4

1. *New York Times,* June 11, 1987.

2. See Chapter 2, "Postindependence Crises: Structures, Institutions, and Development," for specifics.

3. Quoted in R. Schaedel, ed., *Research and Resources of Haiti* (New York: Research Institute for the Study of Man, 1969), p. 14.

4.   See Tom Barry, Beth Wood, and Deb Preusch, *The Other Side of Paradise: Foreign Control in the Caribbean* (New York: Grove Press, 1984), p. 240 for a wealth of information on this topic.

5.   See the article on Taiwan by Sam Wynn, *Monthly Review* (April 1982), pp. 30–40.

6.   Cited in the *New York Times*, June 15, 1986, p. 3.

7.   E. Tardieu, "Nous importerons de l'eau," *Le Nouvelliste*, May 4, 1987, citing U.S. congressional estimates.

8.   Joseph Grunwald (Untitled) (Paper presented at Wingspread Conference Center, Racine, Wisconsin, in 1982), p. 38.

9.   Barry, Wood, and Preusch, *Other Side of Paradise*, p. 336.

10. Richard Barnet and Ronald Muller, *Global Research: The Power of Multinational Corporations* (New York: Simon and Schuster, 1974), p. 89.

11. Michael Parenti, *Inventing Reality: The Politics of the Mass Media* (New York: St. Martin's Press, 1986), p. 244.

12. Greg Chamberlain, "Up by the Roots," *NACLA Report* 21, no. 3 (May–June 1987), p. 21.

13. Barry, Wood, and Preusch, *Other Side of Paradise*, p. 338.

14. Ayisyen Rasambleman Fanm, *Femmes Haitiennes* (Montreal, 1980), pp. 13, 14, 50.

15. Ibid., p. 49.

16. Ibid., p. 52.

17. Michael S. Hooper, "Model Underdevelopment," *NACLA Report* 21, no. 3 (May–June 1987), p. 33.

18. Ibid.

19. Barry, Wood, and Preusch, *Other Side of Paradise*, 336.

20. Ibid., p. 87.

Chapter 5

1.   *Guardian* (New York), April 15, 1987, p. 17.

2.   *New York Times*, January 17, 1988, p. 15.

3.   Greg Chamberlain, "Up by the Roots," *NACLA Report* 21, no. 3 (May–June 1987), p. 23.

4.   Richard Barnet and Ronald Muller, *Global Reach: The Power of Multinational Corporations* (New York: Simon and Schuster, 1974), p. 86.

5.   Tom Barry, Beth Wood, and Deb Preusch, *The Other Side of Paradise: Foreign Control in the Caribbean* (New York: Grove Press, 1984), p. 336.

6.   Michael S. Hooper, "The Monkey's Tail Still Strong," *NACLA Report* 21, no. 3 (May–June 1987), p. 28.

7.   I heard the broadcast; also quoted in *Haiti-Observateur*, July 31– August 7, 1987, p. 6.

8.   Caribbean Council of Churches, *Mission to Haiti: Official Report*, August 24–31, 1987, quoting from a report of the Haitian Ministry of Information, pp. 53–54.

9.   *Haiti-Observateur*, July 31–August 7, 1987, p. 25.

10. Quoted in Caribbean Council of Churches, *Mission to Haiti*, p. 11.

11. The manioc plant, from which a flour is made, has poisonous parts that must be avoided. The second part of the statement, *bay tè a blanch*, translated literally is "give the land back white"— white meaning nothingness.

12. Jean-Marie Jan, *Collecta: Compilation de documents pour servir à l'histoire du diocèse du Cap*, 3 vols. (Port-au-Prince: Editions Henri Deschamps, 1955–1956), vol. 3, pp. 350, 351.

13. Caribbean Council of Churches, *Mission to Haiti*, p. 14.

14. Ibid., p. 14.

15. Chamberlain, "Up by the Roots," p. 17.

16. *Newsweek*, May 26, 1986, p. 43.

17. *Haiti-Observateur*, May 22–29, 1987, p. 3.

18. Chamberlain, "Up by the Roots," p. 18.

19. Hooper, "The Monkey's Tail Still Strong," p. 31.

20. *Guardian* (New York), July 29, 1987, p. 18.

21. This extract and the following quotations are from Caribbean Council of Churches, *Mission to Haiti*, pp. 8–9.

22. *Haiti-Observateur*, November 27–December 4, 1987, p. 35.

23. Quoted in *Haiti-Observateur*, December 4–11, 1987, p. 6.

24. *New York Times*, December 22, 1987, p. 3.

25. *Haiti-Observateur*, December 4–11, 1987, p. 23.

26. Ibid., December 11–18, 1987, p. 11.

27. *Guardian* (New York), December 23, 1987.

28.   *New York Times*, December 27, 1987.
29.   *Guardian* (New York), December 23, 1987.
30.   *Caribbean Contact* (Barbados) (February 1988), p. 1.
31.   *New York Times*, September 6, 1987, p. 37.
32.   National Public Radio broadcast, "Morning Edition," January 7, 1988.
33.   *New York Times*, February 8, 1988, p. 3.
34.   *Caribbean Contact* (February 1988), p. 6.
35.   *New York Times*, December 3, 1987.
36.   *New York Times*, February 7, 1988, p. 1; italics added.
37.   *Haiti-Observateur,* January 20–February 5, 1988, p. 14.
38.   *Caribbean Contact* (February 1988), p. 6.
39.   Quoted in Mats Lundhal, "Population Pressure and Agrarian Property Rights in Haiti," Nationalekonomiska Institutionen vid Lunds Universitet, Lund, Sweden, Reprint no. 46, p. 280.
40.   Lundhal, "Population Pressure," pp. 280–281.
41.   Ibid.
42.   Ibid.
43.   Harold Cruse, *The Crisis of the Negro Intellectual* (New York: William Morrow and Company, 1967), p. 12.
44.   Maulana Karenga, *Introduction to Black Studies* (Los Angeles: Kawaida Publications, 1982), p. 206.
45.   See Aldon Morris, *The Origins of the Civil Rights Movements: Black Communities Organizing for Change* (New York: Free Press, 1984).
46.   Quotation given to me by a Zairian scholar; source unknown. My translation from the French original.
47.   Cruse, *Crisis of the Negro*, p. 475.
48.   Karenga, *Introduction to Black Studies*, p. 207.

Chapter 6

1.   Tim Weiner, "Key Haitian Leaders Said to Have Been in CIA's Pay," *The New York Times*, November 1, 1993; Allan Nairn, in *The Nation*, October 14, 1994, pp. 458–461, and *The Nation*, October 31, 1994, pp. 481–482. On the CIA, see Fatton (2002), pp. 89, 95, 104 and Dupuy, (1997), pp. 69 n. 7, 152.
2.   There were psychological effects on the colonizers as well. See Mary A. Renda (2001), and Albert Memmi, *Portrait du colonisé*

précédé du portrait du colonisateur (Paris: Editions Buchet/Chastel, Correa, 1957).

3. Georges Fauriol, Prepared Statement before the Subcommittee on Western Hemisphere Affairs, U.S. House of Representatives, March 8, 1988, pp. 10, 2 and 3.

4. Patrick Bellegarde-Smith, "Resisting Freedom: Cultural Factors in Democracy—The Case for Haiti," in Robert I. Rotberg, ed., *Haiti renewed: Political and Economic Prospects* (Washington, DC: Brookings Institution Press, 1997), pp. 27–46.

5. Anne Fuller, "Revolt Weakens Avril, But U.S. Rushes To Rescue," *The Guardian* (New York), April 19, 1989, p. 15.

6. Rénald Clérismé, Ph.D. Yale University in anthropology, at a lecture at the University of California, Santa Barbara, October 16, 1993.

7. Sabine Manigat, *Les Partis politiques* (Port-au-Prince: CRESDIP-Dossiers, 1990), p. 204.

8. Jacky Dahomay, "Qui a peur de la democratie en Haiti?" *Chemins Critiques*, vol. 2 no. 3 (May, 1992), pp. 10–11. Translations mine unless indicated otherwise.

9. Fauriol, op. cit.

10. *New York Times*, "Book Review" (September 6, 1992), p. 21. "Before Allende was elected [in 1970], Mr. Kissinger himself has revealed, he told the U.S. Ambassador, Edward Korry, to 'reinforce with the [Chilean] military the serious consequences of an Allende presidency' and to 'reiterate the assurances of continued American military assistance' if the military moved against him."

11. In mid-1970s, I argued that a disconnect existed between state and nation. See P.D.B. Bellegarde-Smith, "Haiti: Perspectives of Foreign Policy; An Essay on the International Relations of a Small State," *Caribbean Quarterly* (September/December, 1974), p. 32.

12. Steven Horblitt, "Multilateral Policy: The Road toward Reconciliation," in Georges A. Fauriol, ed., *The Haitian Challenge: U.S. Policy Considerations* (Washington, DC: The Center for Strategic & International Studies, 1993), p. 70.

13. Dahomay, op. cit., 13–15.

14. See the analysis by Michel S. Laguerre, *The Military and Society in Haiti* (Knoxville: The University of Tennessee Press, 1993).

15. Ernest H. Preeg, "Introduction: The Haitian Challenge in Perspective," in Fauriol, op. cit., p. 3.

16. Ibid., pp. 3–4.

17. Revealed in a conversation with a principal actor who attended the Governors Island talks who wishes to remain anonymous.

18. See Patrick Bellegarde-Smith, "Class Struggle in Contemporary Haitian Politics: An Interpretative Study of the Campaign of 1957," *Journal of Caribbean Studies*, Vol 2, No. 1 (Spring, 1981), pp. 109–127.

19. Terry Rey, "Junta, Rape, and Religion in Haiti, 1993–1994," *Journal of Feminist Studies in Religion*, Vol. 15, No. 2 (1999), pp. 73–99.

20. Richard J. Barnet and Ronald Mueller, *Global Reach: The Power of the Multinational Corporations* (New York: Simon & Schuster, 1976) p. 86.

21. Allan Nairn, *The Nation* (October 3, 1994). FRAPH is the French acronym for the "Front for the Advancement and Progress of Haiti." On August 11, 2003, on the McLehrer Report on National Public Television, an American scholar declared with reference to Liberia, that that country "needed adult supervision," and that it was unlikely to get it from the ECOWAS troops presently on the ground. See also, Tim Weiner, "CIA Formed Haitian Unit later Tied to Narcotics Trade," *The New York Times*, November 11, 1993.

22. Lawrence E. Harrison, "Voodoo Politics," *Atlantic Monthly* (June 1993), pp. 101–107, cited in Fatton, 2002: page 71.

23. John Canham-Clyne and Worth Cooley-Prost, "Haiti to the Haitians?" *The Progressive* (September 1995), Vol 59, No. 9, p. 24. Italics mine.

24. Robert Malval, *L'Année de toutes les duperies* (Port-au-Prince: Editions Regain, 1996), p. 51. Translation by the author.

25. Ibid.

26. For a thoroughly competent and readable account of United Nations Forces on Haitian soil, see David M. Malone, *Decision-Making in the UN Security Council: The Case of Haiti* (Oxford: Clarendon Press, 1998).

Bibliographical Essay

A PRIMARY OBJECTIVE OF THIS BOOK IS TO PRESENT HAITI AS HAITIANS SEE it, a fairly novel approach in the scheme of things. I do not argue that Haiti and Haitians are necessarily unique. On the contrary, they share much with the rest of the world in regard to economic circumstances and the historical processes through which nations on the planet form, if not a community, at least a system.

The premises of the one versus those of the other are largely formed as the result of one's position in the hierarchy, although there is some effort to "homogenize" the world into a situation where some cultures, some languages, some religions are more equal than others. Haiti found itself at the bottom of the hierarchy after it challenged this state of affairs two centuries ago, and it continues to be punished. Prejudice dies hard. Alongside these "premises," I have opted for Haitian biases rather than U.S. ones—a calculated risk with an audience that sees its biases as objectivity personified. I hope to widen the discourse.

In a real sense, Haitian scholars and intellectuals—whose work is written mostly in the French language—were pioneers, but their contributions in the fields of social and economic development, national integration, race relations, and small-state foreign relations are generally unrecognized in the West and unknown in the Third World because the educational linkages established by colonialism are West/South.

Because Haiti was the first modern state of African origin and the first Latin American territory to gain independence in 1804 through revolution, the country is a useful link between Africa and Latin

America. The Caribbean itself was the first area to suffer from colonization, and it has oftentimes been a laboratory for social, economic, and political experimentation. Although culturally Afro-American, it also has European and lesser Asian, Amerindian, and Middle Eastern cultural aspects.

Haiti needs to be placed in its proper contexts, and some works do so particularly well. In this essay I leave aside Haitian books written in French or Kreyol and emphasize modern and contemporary works published in the English language. For a listing of Haitian authors whose work is in French, the reader may consult Michel S. Laguerre, *The Complete Haitiana: A Bibliographic Guide to Scholarly Literature, 1900–1980*, 2 vols. (New York: Kraus International Publications, 1982). For Kreyol items, consult the ongoing work by Robert Lawless, "Bibliography on Haiti," University of Florida at Gainesville.

For Haiti's African context, one may wish to consult Cheikh Anta Diop, *The African Origin of Civilization* (Westport, CT: Lawrence Hill and Company, 1974), and Ivan van Sertima, ed., *Blacks in Science* (New Brunswick, NJ: Transaction Books, 1983). These two texts by noted scholars give a brief and succinct overview of the contributions of African civilization to world culture. In the area of art as it intersects with religion and society, see Jan Vansina, *Art History in Africa* (London: Longman, 1984). An interesting work that studies Black women across boundaries is Filomina Chioma Steady, *The Black Woman Cross-Culturally* (New York: Schenkman, 1981). Some of the interaction between Africa and pre-Columbian America is explored in a controversial work by Ivan Van Sertima, *They Came before Columbus* (New York: Random House, 1976).

There are many useful works detailing the interaction between Africa and Western Europe. In the area of colonization and colonialism, Irving Leonard Markovitz, *Power and Class in Africa* (Englewood Cliffs, NJ: Prentice Hall, 1977), gives a general introduction, and the topic is dealt with more specifically by A. Adu Boahen in *African Perspectives on Colonialism* (Baltimore, MD: Johns Hopkins University Press, 1987). The psychology and pathology of colonialism and neocolonialism are handled superbly in Frantz Fanon, *The Wretched of the Earth* (New York: Grove Press, 1968), Fanon, *Black Skins, White Masks* (New York: Grove

Press, 1967), and Aimé Césaire, *Discourse on Colonialism* (New York: Monthly Review Press, 1972).

The economic dimension among Western Europe, Africa, and the Caribbean is the subject of a number of works, including Walter Rodney, *How Europe Underdeveloped Africa* (Washington, DC: Howard University Press, 1982), and George L. Beckford, *Persistent Poverty: Underdevelopment in Plantation Economies of the Third World* (London: Oxford University Press, 1972). See Manning Marable, *How Capitalism Underdeveloped Black America* (Boston: South End Press, [1983] 2001), for an analysis that parallels the view of many Haitian and Caribbean scholars. Another truly classic work by Eric Williams, *Capitalism and Slavery* (New York: Capricorn Books, 1966), shows the role of slavery in producing the capital necessary for the development of the industrial revolution. Another such book is Sidney W. Mintz, *Sweetness and Power: The Place of Sugar in Modern History* (New York: Penguin Books, 1985).

A good historical introduction to the Caribbean is Franklin W. Knight, *The Caribbean: The Genesis of a Fragmented Nationalism* (New York: Oxford University Press, 1978). For material on the slave revolts and political structure, one may look at, among other works, Eugene D. Genovese, *From Rebellion to Revolution: Afro-American Slave Revolts in the Making of the New World* (New York: Vintage Books, 1979), and Richard Price, ed., *Maroon Societies: Rebel Slave Communities in the Americas* (New York: Anchor Books, 1973). For information about modern-day political repression and the economy, see a book by a West Indian author, Clive Y. Thomas, *The Rise of the Authoritarian State in Peripheral Societies* (New York: Monthly Review Press, 1984).

Decried in the nineteenth and early twentieth centuries by foreign authors, the reputation of Haiti has fared better in the latter part of the twentieth century. Although filled with empathy, early works by Haitians remain rather "objective," particularly when compared with those by English and French writers of the same period. A work that remains the classic on Haitian history is by a West Indian author, C.L.R. James, *The Black Jacobins: Toussaint Louverture and the San Domingo Revolution* (New York: Vintage Books, 1963). If only one book on early Haitian history is read, this must be it. A more recent work on the country's early history is Alfred N. Hunt, *Haiti's Influence on Antebellum*

America (Baton Rouge: Louisiana State University, 1988). This latter work is useful in terms of Haiti's influence abroad and the country's early international relations.

A work by a top Haitian historian on Haiti before independence, translated into English, is Jean Fouchard, *The Haitian Maroons: Liberty or Death* (New York: Blyden, 1981). A most fascinating compendium of primary sources is the correspondence between the Haitian king Henri Christophe and a famous abolitionist published in Earl Griggs and Clifford Prator, eds., *Henry Christophe and Thomas Clarkson: A Correspondence* (New York: Greenwood Press, 1968); equally interesting is a translation of Moreau de Saint-Mery's work by Ivor D. Spector, ed., *A Civilization That Perished: The Last Years of White Colonial Rule in Haiti* (Washington, DC: University Press of America, 1986).

All the works listed above contrast sharply with much of the literature published in English in the nineteenth century and the first half of the twentieth century, such as books by T. Lothrop Stoddard, Edward Long, and Bryan Edwards. This earlier mainstream perspective found its promulgation in early twentieth-century authors, from the virulently to the mildly racist, from John H. Craige, *Cannibal Cousins* (New York: Minton, Balch and Company, 1934), to Edmund Wilson, *Red, Black, Blond and Olive—Studies in Four Civilizations: Zuni, Haiti, Soviet Russia, Israel* (New York: Oxford University Press, 1956). In the middle, and still quite useful for their details, are such books as Harold P. Davis, *Black Democracy: The Story of Haiti* (New York: Biblio and Tanner, 1936), Arthur C. Millspaugh, *Haiti under American Control, 1915–1930* (Boston: World Peace Foundation, 1931), and William A. MacCorkle, *The Monroe Doctrine in Its Relation to the Republic of Haiti* (New York: Neale Publishing Company, 1915). A work edited by Emily Green Balch, *Occupied Haiti* (New York: Writer's Publishing Company, 1927), stood out so much that she was nominated by a Haitian diplomat for the Nobel Peace Prize. A contemporary work of utmost significance that transcends Haiti in its scope is Mary A. Renda, *Taking Haiti: Military Occupation and the Culture of U.S. Imperialism, 1915–1940* (Chapel Hill: University of North Carolina Press, 2001). Unfortunately, the anti-Haiti tradition also continues to this day in such works as Robert D. Heinl and Nancy G. Heinl, *Written in Blood: The Story of the Haitian*

People, 1492–1971 (Boston: Houghton Mifflin, 1978), Robert I. Rotberg, *Haiti: The Politics of Squalor* (Boston: Houghton Mifflin, 1971), and Elizabeth Abbott, *Haiti: The Duvaliers and Their Legacy: The First Inside Account* (New York: McGraw-Hill, 1988).

Two social scientists wrote excellent studies in the late 1930s and early 1940s, Melville J. Herskovits, *Life in a Haitian Valley* (New York: Anchor Books, 1971), and James G. Leyburn, *The Haitian People* (New Haven, CT: Yale University Press, 1966). At that time, Haitian scholars, too, were being awakened to their roots, and the creation by the Haitian novelist and ethnologist Jacques Roumain of the Bureau d'Ethnologie in 1941 served Haiti well, and many social scientists were trained there. The genesis of this Haitian scholarly development was anchored in the wounds of the U.S. occupation and its blatant racism, as is illustrated in the voluminous scholarly production of Haitian social thinker Jean Price-Mars and other writers.

African-American scholars have long had a strong sympathetic interest in Haiti. Rayford W. Logan, a noted historian and an associate of W.E.B. DuBois, wrote the classic study of early Haiti-U.S. relations, *The Diplomatic Relations of the United States with Haiti, 1776–1891* (Chapel Hill: University of North Carolina Press, 1941), and a much shorter introduction, *Haiti and the Dominican Republic* (New York: Oxford University Press, 1968). Another African-American historian, Brenda G. Plummer, in *Haiti and the Great Powers* (Baton Rouge: Louisiana State University Press, 1988), based on her Cornell University dissertation, shows the collapsing of two discrete categories, national and international conditions, through her analysis of Haitian socio-economic evolution and international relations. Two of her articles are cited in this book, "Race, Nationality, and Trade in the Caribbean: The Syrians in Haiti, 1903–1934," *International History Review* 3 (1981), pp. 517–539, and "The Metropolitan Connection: Foreign and Semiforeign Elites in Haiti, 1900–1915," *Latin American Research Review* 19, no. 2 (1984), pp. 119–142.

Still within the context of "new" scholarship, there is David Nicholls's *From Dessalines to Duvalier: Race, Colour, and National Independence in Haiti* (Cambridge: Cambridge University Press, 1979) and his more recent *Haiti in Caribbean Context: Ethnicity, Economy, and*

Revolt (New York: St. Martin's Press, 1985). Michel-Rolph Trouillot's *Haiti, State against Nation: The Origin and Legacy of Duvalierism* (New York: Monthly Review Press, 1988) is an analysis of some aspects of Haitian history. A memoir by a Haitian politician, Lyonel Paquin, *The Haitians: Class and Color Politics* (New York: Multi-Tyler, 1983), is useful for consideration of the "color question."

The economy of Haiti has elicited a number of useful books, and the flow of printer's ink for such books is more voluminous than the flow of Haiti's drying rivers. An edited work based on a conference held at the Johnson Foundation at Wingspread Center in Racine, Wisconsin, is Charles R. Foster and Albert Valdman, eds., *Haiti Today and Tomorrow: An Interdisciplinary Study* (Washington, DC: University Press of America, 1984). This work attempts to study Haiti as a totality, being a compendium of studies from a variety of ideological perspectives on the country's economy, rural development, culture, politics, and society. Another good work is Alex Dupuy, *Haiti in the World Economy: Class, Race and Underdevelopment Since 1700* (Boulder, CO: Westview Press, 1988). See also later work, Alex Dupuy, *Haiti in the New World Order: The Limits of Democratic Revolution* (Boulder, CO: Westview Press, 1997). A very useful article by a Haitian economist is Monique Paul Garrity, "The Assembly Industries in Haiti: Causes and Effects," *Journal of Caribbean Studies* 2 (1981), pp. 25–37.

A more specifically "technical" volume, co-edited by Derick W. Brinkerhoff and Jean-Claude Garcia-Zamor, *Politics, Projects, and People: Institutional Development in Haiti* (New York: Praeger, 1986), is useful for its details of a few USAID-sponsored projects that dot the Haitian landscape. An overall and highly readable "primer" on Caribbean political economy is a work by Tom Barry, Beth Wood, and Deb Preusch, *The Other Side of Paradise: Foreign Control in the Caribbean* (New York: Grove Press, 1984). A short but fairly complete introduction is Rod Prince's *Haiti: Family Business* (London: Latin America Bureau, 1985), and Maurice Lemoine's *Bitter Sugar: Slaves Today in the Caribbean* (Chicago: Banner Press, 1985) is an instructive narrative of Haitian cane cutters in the Dominican Republic—their lives, big business, and politics. The latter reads (and grips) like a novel. Another useful work is Mats Lundhal, *The Haitian Economy: Man, Land, and Markets* (London:

Croon Helm, 1983). A pioneering work is that of Vera Rubin and Richard P. Schaedel, eds., *The Haitian Potential: Research and Resources of Haiti* (New York: Teachers College Press, 1975).

There is an obvious overlap among all "discrete" categories, e.g., among economics, politics, international relations, ideology, and social thought, and it is by pure convention that these are defined as separate entities. One work that specifies this overlap is by former President Leslie F. Manigat, "Haiti: The Shift from French Hegemony to the American Sphere of Influence at the Beginning of the 20th Century: The 'Conjoncture' of 1910–1911," published in his *Caribbean Yearbook of International Relations* (Leiden: A. W. Sijthoff, 1976) and in another volume, co-edited with Jorge Heine, *The Caribbean and World Politics: Cross Currents and Cleavages* (New York: Holmes and Meier, 1988). An earlier small piece by Manigat is quite useful for the viewpoints of a public person, *Haiti of the Sixties: Object of International Concern* (Washington, DC: Washington Center of Foreign Policy Research, 1964). Of course, many of the works listed previously fit into interdisciplinary analyses that imitate life itself so well.

The U.S. occupation (1915–1934) was the watershed event that introduced Haiti's modern history, and the Duvalier era introduced contemporary history. With reference to the first, an excellent work in the English language is that of Hans Schmidt, *The United States Occupation of Haiti, 1915–1934* (New Brunswick, NJ: Rutgers University Press, 1971), and one would hope that a translation of Roger Gaillard's seven-volume work, *Les Blancs débarquent* [The Whites land] will appear someday since he is Haiti's foremost historian of that epoch. Making an exception to the rule of listing mostly English-language works here, I want to mention the book by a Haitian social scientist, Suzy Castor, *La Ocupación norteamericana de Haití y sus consecuencias, 1915–1934* (Mexico City: Ediciones siglo veintíuno, 1971), particularly because of its description of the role of the Roman Catholic church and its collaboration with the invader. A book that presents ample knowledge and is useful for comparisons and contrasts to Haiti is Bruce J. Calder's *The Impact of Intervention: The Dominican Republic During the U.S. Occupation of 1916–1924* (Austin: University of Texas Press, 1984).

No book, as of yet, has been written whose primary focus is the role of Vodou in the guerrilla war against the United States or, for that matter, the role of Haiti's religion during the wars of independence. One work that could fairly easily be emulated is David Lan, *Guns and Rains: Guerrillas and Spirit Mediums in Zimbabwe* (Berkeley: University of California Press, 1985), which describes the role of traditional priests and beliefs against the white Rhodesians in the Marxist guerrilla movement that led Rhodesia to independence. A short work, consisting of two essays by distinguished social scientists, one American and the other Haitian, is a first step toward such a book. Harold Courlander and Rémy Bastien, in *Religion and Politics in Haiti* (Washington, DC: Institute for Cross-Cultural Research, 1966), discuss Vodou in Haitian culture and Vodou and politics in Haiti, and do so admirably.

Haiti's national religion is slowly being lifted from the opprobrium with which it is considered in Europe and the United States, and by extension, in the Westernized and schizophrenic Haitian social groups. An excellent background on the origins of the religion can be acquired from texts that cover West and Central African religions in general. Because of inherent prejudice, practitioners have been slow to couch the tenets of the religion in writing, and those who have done so are often white. An excellent crossnational approach is Robert Farris Thompson, *Flash of the Spirit: African and Afro-American Art and Philosophy* (New York: Random House, 1983), now in a paperback version. Two other works, by a nonpractitioner, give a sense of the marvelous continuity between Africa and the African diaspora: Roger Bastide's *African Civilizations in the New World* (New York: Harper Torchbooks, 1971) and *The African Religions of Brazil: Toward a Sociology of the Interpenetration of Civilizations* (Baltimore, MD: Johns Hopkins University Press, 1978). The personal journey of a Puerto Rican devotee is found in Migene Gonzales-Wippler, *The Santeria Experience* (New York: Original Publications, 1982). A Dominican "version" is found in a work in Spanish by a U.S. anthropologist, Martha E. Davis, *La otra ciencia: El vodú dominicano como religión y medicina populares* (Santo Domingo: Editora Universitaria, 1987). A useful comparison with Cuba can be had from Mercedes Cros Sandoval, *La Religión Afrocubana* (Madrid: Playor, 1975). Readers might well look at Leonard Barrett, *The Sun and the Drum: African Roots in Jamaican Folk Tradition* (Kingston:

Sangster's Book Stores, 1976). Also quite useful are John S. Mbiti, *African Religions and Philosophy* (New York: Anchor Books, 1970), a work by Janheinz Jahn, *Muntu: The New African Culture* (New York: Grove Press, 1961), and another by Judith Gleason, *Oya: In Praise of the Goddess* (Boston: Shambhala, 1987).

Clearly, in my mind, one of the most useful books ever written on Vodou is that of Maya Deren, *Divine Horsemen: The Living Gods of Haiti* (New Paltz, NY: McPherson and Company, 1983), with a preface by Joseph Campbell. Originally published in 1953, it remains an excellent work by a non-Haitian initiate. Other works by initiates include one book, more narrowly focused on the performing arts, by Katherine Dunham, *Dances of Haiti* (Los Angeles: Center for Afro-American Studies, UCLA, 1983), and another by a Haitian "aristocrat," Milo Rigaud, *Secrets of Voodoo* (San Francisco: City Lights Books, 1985). Rigaud's work is both significant and difficult, and it and Deren's book are the classics. Interesting as historical curiosities, but faulty in their vision, are the works of African-American anthropologist Zora Neale Hurston, *Tell My Horse* (Berkeley, CA: Turtle Island, 1981), and French anthropologist, Alfred Metraux, *Voodoo in Haiti* (New York: Schocken Books, 1972). A fascinating photographic study is that of Melita Denning and Osborne Phillips, *Voudoun Fire: The Living Reality of Mystical Religion* (St. Paul, MN: Llewellyn Publications, 1979).

The Haitian anthropologist Michel S. Laguerre has published a number of ethnographic monographs on Vodou. One that details the ritual at one Port-au-Prince temple is *Voodoo Heritage* (Beverly Hills, CA: Sage Publications, 1980), and another of his monographs is located at the junction of medicine and religion, *Afro-Caribbean Folk Medicine* (South Hadley, MA: Bergin and Garvey Publishers, 1987). Two controversial works by a Canadian ethnobotanist, Wade Davis—one a popular book, the other scholarly—should be consulted. These are *The Serpent and the Rainbow* (New York: Warner Books, 1985) and *Passage of Darkness: The Ethnobiology of the Haitian Zombie* (Chapel Hill: University of North Carolina Press, 1988). Another important new contribution to the research on Vodou is Reginald Crossley's *Teh Vodou Quantum Leap: Alternate Realities, Power and Mysticism* (St. Paul, MN: Llewelyn Publications, 2000).

Within the area of folklore, religion, and the arts, an important book to consult is that of Harold Courlander, *The Drum and the Hoe: Life and Lore of the Haitian People* (Berkeley: University of California Press, 1985), and his voluminous *A Treasury of Afro-American Folklore* (New York: Crown Publishers, 1976) covers all peoples of African descent in the Americas. For architecture, one would be remiss not to consult Anghelen Arrington Phillips, *Gingerbread House: Haiti's Endangered Species* (Port-au-Prince: Henri Deschamps, 1975), and Suzanne Slesin et al., *Caribbean Style* (New York: Clarkson N. Potter, 1985).

There are good works published about Haitian painting, and among those in English I note Marie-José Nadal-Gardère and Gérald Bloncourt, *La Peinture Haitienne/Haitian Arts* (Paris: Nathan, 1986), Ute Stebich, *Haitian Art* (New York: Harry N. Abrams, 1978), and a classic by Selden Rodman, *The Miracle of Haitian Art* (New York: Doubleday and Company, 1974). The Milwaukee Art Museum in Wisconsin has one of the world's best collections of Haitian paintings, the Flagg Collection, and has published *The Naive Tradition: Haiti* (Milwaukee, 1974).

Translations of Haitian poetry and novels, despite an extraordinarily large production of quality work, are still scarce. Among the works that have been translated, one notes Jacques Roumain, *Gouverneurs de la rosée; Masters of the Dew*, trans. Langston Hughes and Mercer Cook (London: Heinemann, 1978), Haiti's best-known novel translated into seventeen languages. Another, Philippe Thoby-Marcelin and Pierre Marcelin, *The Beast of the Haitian Hills* (San Francisco: City Lights Books, 1987), is by two protégés of the U.S. literary critic Edmund Wilson, and several of their novels have been translated into English largely because of their friendship with Wilson. One collection of tales is Diane Wolkstein, ed., *The Magic Orange Tree and other Haitian Folktales* (New York: Schocken Books, 1980). Two foreign novels about Haiti are Graham Greene's *The Comedians* (New York: Penguin Books, 1966)—not the author's best novelistic effort—and a book by a German of Haitian descent, Hans Christoph Buch, *The Wedding at Port-au-Prince* (New York: Harcourt Brace Jovanovich, 1986). Much remains to be done in this area, and it would be particularly good to see translations of works by Jacques Alexis, René Depestre, Jean Metellus, and Marie Chauvet.

Works about Haitian intellectual production are equally scarce. A good overall work by a Caribbeanist is Gordon K. Lewis, *Main Currents in Caribbean Thought: The Historical Evolution of Caribbean Society in Its Ideological Aspects, 1492–1900* (Baltimore, MD: Johns Hopkins University Press, 1983). Other works of some merit include an aforementioned book by David Nicholls, *From Dessalines to Duvalier*, and Michael J. Dash, *Literature and Ideology in Haiti, 1915–1961* (Totowa, NJ: Barnes and Noble, 1981).

A "primary" work found in English is Jean Price-Mars, *So Spoke the Uncle*, trans. Magdaline W. Shannon (Washington, DC: Three Continents Press, 1983), but a book about Price-Mars, Jacques C. Antoine, *Jean Price-Mars and Haiti* (Washington, DC: Three Continents Press, 1981), is inadequate. An analytical study of Price-Mars's antagonist, Dantès Bellegarde, is P. Bellegarde-Smith, *In the Shadow of Powers: Dantès Bellegarde in Haitian Social Thought* (Atlantic Highlands, NJ: Humanities Press International, 1985). Besides being an intellectual biography, the work analyses Haitian intellectual life in the nineteenth century, including contacts with contemporary thought in Western Europe and Latin America. A book that is still useful is Carolyn Fowler's *A Knot in the Thread: The Life and Work of Jacques Roumain* (Washington, DC: Howard University Press, 1980). A gifted novelist and poet, Jacques Roumain was an ethnologist, a cofounder of what became the Haitian Communist party, and the grandson of President Tancrède Auguste.

A number of significant works were published on Haiti in the last decade. Many scholars with access to university training and to publishers, have produced increasingly sophisticated and sensitive books on the subject. Non-Haitians from various fields seem to have learned from the anthropological discourse to distance themselves from their own cultural milieux to attain a more balanced (rather than objective) view. The emic perspective remains useful when added to the symphony of voices, and Haitians, increasingly, are being heard. Their academic credentials and their positions as insiders add to assessment, re-assessment, and prescription for what ails Haiti. The barbarians have breached the gates and they do speak odd thoughts perhaps, but in recognizable western languages.

Writing largely for a North American and Caribbean anglophone audience, I bemoan still the absence of wholesale translations from the French and Haitian languages into English, or for that matter, into Spanish and Portuguese, these other languages of the Americas. I have selected the works below, those written in English, that extend our knowledge of Haitian society, culture and politics in marvelous and wondrous ways.

What accounts for the renewed interest in the subject matter since the early part of the twentieth century during the U.S. occupation, 1915–1934? Certainly the commemoration of the bicentennial of the Haitian Revolution, the most neglected and forgotten of the world's major revolutions, is a factor. The bicentennial of Haiti's independence in 2004 follows in close order. But the country's endemic political crises that hark back to unresolved societal issues about class, color, economic exploitation, violent repression, and cultural ambivalence, and a world environment inimical to small nation-states demand urgent study. Additionally, a large Haitian diasporic presence in the United States and Canada, the rest of the Caribbean, and in Western Europe, has an increasing impact on host societies—racially, economically, and socially. New hyphenated groups are being formed. Then, there is interest generated from benign and not so benign intervention from multinational organizations: political bodies, lending agencies, from churches bent on conversions, liberals in search of causes. The interest is genuine, mostly well-meaning, leading to renewed interest in research and publications.

A remarkable book on Haitian revolutionary history, adding new perspectives to new research, is Carolyn E. Fick, *The Making of Haiti: The Saint-Domingue Revolution from Below* (Knoxville: University of Tennessee Press, 1990). Other helpful works are those by David Patrick Geggus, *Haitian Revolutionary Studies* (Bloomington: University of Indiana Press, 2002), and his recently edited book, *The Impact of the Haitian Revolution in the Atlantic World* (Columbia: University of South Carolina Press, 2001). It is noteworthy that historians and politicians have had little to say about the Louisiana Purchase and Haiti that occurred in 1803. See Thomas O. Ott, *The Haitian Revolution, 1789-1804* (Knoxville: University of Tennessee Press, 1993). Other works include Doris Y. Kadish, ed. *Slavery in the Caribbean Francophone World: Distant Voices, Forgotten Acts, Forged Identities* (Athens, GA: University of Georgia Press, 2000), Stewart R. King, *Blue Coat or Powdered Wig: Free People of Color in Pre-Revolutionary Saint Domingue* (Athens, GA: University of Georgia Press, 2000).

Helpful reflections upon the fate and continuing underdevelopment of small states, are the late Jamaican's Premier's book, Michael Manley, *Poverty of Nations: Reflections on Underdevelopment and the World Economy* (London: Pluto Press, 1991), and William I. Robinson, *Promoting Polyarchy: Globalization, U.S. Intervention, and Hegemony* (Cambridge: Cambridge University Press, 1996) who devotes chapter 6 to the Haitian case. See also Sing C. Chew and Robert A. Denemark, eds., *The Underdevelopment of Development* (Thousand Oaks, CA: Sage Publications, 1996). Still current in terms of its analysis, is the classical work by Manning Marable, *How Capitalism Underdeveloped Black America* (Boston: South End Press, 2000 [1983]). A book that clearly transcends Haiti is by Haitian anthropologist Michel-Rolph Trouillot, *Silencing the Past: Power and the Production of History* (Boston: Beacon Press, 1995). Another good book is James M. Blaut, *The Colonizer's Model of the World* (New York: Guilford Press, 1993) and his earlier work as editor, *1492: The Debate on Colonialism, Eurocentrism, and History* (New York: Africa World Press, 1992). An intriguing book in terms of conceptualization is found in Joan Dayan, *Haiti, History, Gods* (Berkeley: University of California Press, 1995). A remarkable recent book on Haitian political processes is Robert Fatton, Jr., *Haiti's Predatory Republic: The Unending Transition to Democracy* (Boulder, CO: Lynne Rienner Publishers, 2002).

The Haitian religious system clearly transcends religion to encompass profound paradigmatic inquiries in all fields and realms of human endeavor. It is difficult to compartmentalize. Called "Vodou" by many, the nomenclature is useful only if one needs to differentiate it from other religions found on the ground with which it now "competes." The reader is asked to follow the work of the Congress of Santa Barbara (KOSANBA), a scholarly association for the study of Haitian Vodou, formed in 1997. For the West African trajectory of that faith, see Susan Preston Blier, *African Vodun: Art, Psychology, and Power* (Chicago: University of Chicago Press, 1995). The reader may want to consult Mary H. Nooter, ed., *Secrecy: African Art that Conceals and Reveals* (New York: The Museum for African Art, 1993). Quite significant is the work done by Reginald O. Crosley, *The Vodou Quantum Leap: Alternate Realities, Power and Mysticism* (St Paul, MN: Llewellyn Publications, 2000), and, published under the aegis of the U.S. National Black Catholic Clergy Caucus, Guerin Montilus, *Dompim: The Spirituality of African Peoples* (Nashville: Winston-Derek, 1989).

At the intersection of culture, religion, and history, consult Jan Vansina, *Oral Tradition as History* (Madison: University of Wisconsin Press, 1985); Judy Rosenthal, *Possession, Ecstasy and Law in Ewe Voodoo* (Charlotteville: University of Virginia Press, 1998), and Paula Gushick Ben-Amos, *Art, Innovation, and Politics in Eighteenth Century Benin* (Bloomington: Indiana University Press, 1999). Overall views of neo-African spirituality in the Western hemisphere are found in Patrick Bellegarde-Smith, ed., *Fragments of Bone: Neo-African Religions in a New World* (Urbana: University of Illinois Press, 2004). An excellent volume that accompanied an exhibition of the same name is Donald Consentino, ed., *Sacred Arts of Haitian Vodou* (Los Angeles: Fowler Museum of Cultural History, 1995).

The articulation between Vodou and Christianity is expressed in Leslie G. Desmangles, *The Faces of the Gods: Vodou and Roman Catholicism* (Chapel Hill: University of North Carolina Press, 1992). On politics, see Michel S. Laguerre, *Voodoo and Politics in Haiti* (London: Macmillan, 1990). See also Anne Greene, *The Catholic Church in Haiti: Political and Social Change* (East Lansing: Michigan State University Press, 1993), Terry Rey, *Our Lady of Class Struggle: The Cult of the Virgin Mary in Haiti* (Trenton, NJ: Africa World Press, 1999), and Paul Brodwin, *Medicine and Morality in Haiti: The Contest for Healing Power* (Cambridge: Cambridge University Press, 1996).

The production of Laennec Hurbon is very significant in the areas of theology, but it mostly remains untranslated from the original French. A small book of his, *Voodoo: Search for the Spirit* (New York: N. Abrams, 1995), appears in French, English, and Spanish versions. A most significant work that will see an English translation soon, is Claudine Michel, *Aspects educatifs et moraux du Vodou haitien* (Port-au-Prince: Editions Le Natal, 1995). The Haitian diaspora is represented by Joel James, Jose Millet, and Alexis Alarcon, *El vodú en Cuba* (Santiago de Cuba: Editorial Oriente, 1998), and the extraodinary work by Karen McCarthy Brown, *Mama Lola: A Vodou Priestess in Brooklyn* (Berkeley: University of California Press, 2001 [1991]). Transnationalism is also a main scholarly interest for Elizabeth McAlister, *Rara: Vodou, Power, and Performance in Haiti and Its Diaspora* (Berkeley: University of California Press, 2002).

On music, one finds Gage Averill, *One Day for the Hunter, One Day for the Prey: Popular Music and Power in Haiti* (Chicago: University of Chicago Press, 1997), Gerdès Fleurant, *Dancing Spirits: Rhythms and Rituals in Haitian Vodun; the Rada Rite* (Westport, CT: Greenwood Press, 1996), and Lois Wilcken, *The Drums of Vodou* (Tempe, AZ: White Cliffs Media, 1992). Folkorists have documented the "drapo," among them are Patrick Arthur Polk, *Haitian Vodou Flags* (Jackson: University Press of Mississippi, 1997), and Phyllis Galembo, *Vodou: Visions and Voices of Haiti* (Berkeley: Ten Speed Press, 1998).

More often than not, art forms are viscerally connected to religion as in medieval Europe. The Cuban painter Wilfredo Lam (1902–1982), connected in innumerable ways to Haitian painting, described his art as "an act of decolonization." This description is also true of Haitian creative artists, where art is attached to other domains of culture. The Haitian genius reveals itself in art. The Milwaukee Art Museum via the late collector Richard Flagg and his friend, Milwaukee-born Anglican Bishop of Haiti Alfred Voegeli, has positioned itself as the repository of Haitian paintings of the "classical" age. See Ute Stebich, *A Haitian Celebration: Art and Culture* (Milwaukee: Milwaukee Art Museum, 1992). See also Jean-Marie Drot, *La Rencontre des deux mondes vue par les peintres haitiens* (Paris: Carte Segrete, 1992), and the excellent volume, in separate French and English versions, Gérald Alexis, *Peintres haitiens* (Paris: Editions Cercle d'Art, 2000). A long-standing friend of Haitian art has issued yet another book on painting, Selden Rodman, *Where Art is Joy/Haitian Art: The First Forty Years* (New York: Ruggles de Latour, 1988). The full Caribbean context is revealed in Veerle Poupeye, *Caribbean Art* (London: Thames and Hudson, 1998). For architecture, see Andrew Gravette, *Architectural Heritage of the Caribbean* (Kingston: Ian Randle Publishers, 2000), which devotes a large number of pages to Haiti.

At another end of the spectrum, perhaps, in terms of Haitian creativity, one finds Haiti's written literature. There exists a vast production of works written by Haitians since 1804, the bulk of which has never been translated from the original French. That literature is unique in the context of Latin America since it is in French and written by blacks.

The last decade has seen the translation of some of Haiti's best novels. Some were written directly in English (and subsequently translated into French), a sign of the growing significance of a large diaspora of western-educated Haitians. Among those persons, we cite the important opus of Edwidge Danticat: *Krik? Krak!* (New York: Random House, 1996 [reprinted edition]), *Breath, Eyes, Memory* (New York: Random House, 1998), *The Farming of Bones* (New York: Penguin, 1999). She has edited a number of books showcasing young Haitian diasporic talents, particularly women.

Other women whose works have found translation are Lilas Desquiron, *Reflections of Loko Miwa* (*Les chemins de Loco-Miroir*), translation by Robin Orr Bodkin (Charlottesville: University of Virginia Press, CARAF Books, 1998); and Marie Chauvet, *Dance on the Volcano* (*Danse sur le volcan*), translation by Salvator Attanasio (New York: William Sloan, 1959). One hopes that her masterpiece, *Amour, Colère, Folies* will soon be translated in its totality. The only novel translated from the Haitian (Creole) is Maude Heurtelou, *The Bonplezi Family: The Adventures of a Haitian Family in North America* (*Lafami Bonplezi*), translated by John D. Nickrosz (Coconut Creek, FL: Educa Vision, 1998). The novels and short stories by Paulette Poujol-Oriol urgently need translation. One finds only a large and sophisticated production awaits translation, that of physician and Paris resident Jean Metellus. See Metellus, *The Vortex Family: A Family Saga Set in Haiti* (*La famille Vortex*), translation by Michael Richardson (London: Peter Owen; Paris: UNESCO Publishing, 1995). A contemporary Haitian novelist residing in Canada, Dany Lafferière, has had seven of his novels translated. Some are:, *How to Make Love to a Negro* (*Comment faire l'amour à un nègre sans se fatiguer*), translation by David Homel (Toronto: Coach House, 1987); *An Aroma of Coffee* (*L'odeur du café*), translation by David Homel (Toronto: Coach House, 1993); *Dining with the Dictator* (*Le goût des jeunes filles*), translation by David Homel (Toronto: Coach House, 1994); *A Drifting Year* (*Chronique de la dérive douce*), translation by David Homel (Toronto: Douglas & McIntyre, 1997); and *Down among the Dead Men* (*Pays sans chapeau*), translation by David Homel (Toronto: Douglas & McIntyre, 1997).

Some "classical" works are being translated at long last, notably, Jacques-Stephen Alexis, *General Sun, My Brother* (*Compère Général Soleil*), translation by Carrol F. Coates (Charlottesville: University of Virginia Press, CARAF Books, 1999); *In the Flicker of an Eyelid* (*L'espace d'un cillement*), translated by Carrol F. Coates and Edwidge Danticat (Charlotesville: University of Virginia Press, CARAF Books, 2002); and René Depestre, *Festival of the Greasy Pole* (*Le mat de cocagne*), translation by Carrol F. Coates (Charlottesville: University of Virginia Press, CARAF Books, 1990). See also Pierre Clitandre, *Cathedral of the August Heat* (*Cathédrale au mois d'août*), translation by Bridget Jones (London: Readers International, 1987).

I do not pretend that the books listed in this essay represent all the works about Haiti. I have largely limited the list to works in English and to works that are recent and available. The majority of the books listed are available in paperback form. Despite a growing interest in Haiti, owing largely to the recent political upheavals and to an economic destitution that has few parallels in the world, books about the country are uneven in quality. On the other hand, Haitian perspectives, available in books in French and Kreyol, have a short run, and the supply "dries up" before it reaches the sea of world intellectual and literary discourse. That sea is more shallow as a result, and we are the poorer for it.

Index

A

Abraham, Hérard, 229
Acaau, Jean-Jacques, 96
Acquired Immune Deficiency
    Syndrome (AIDS), 35, 168–169
Adolphe, Rosalie, 37
affranchis, 66–67, 69
    discrimination against, 56–57
    and independence wars, 18, 62, 95
    racial composition, 56
Africa, 3, 9, 17, 43, 49, 58, 60, 62,
    66, 79, 105, 144, 168, 216, 257,
    260, 262
    ancient civilizations, 22, 49
    culture and religion, 25–26, 28–
        29, 37, 42–44, 49, 54, 59,
        82, 95, 103, 125, 224, 250
African swine fever, 207–208, 213
Agency for International
    Development (USAID), 126,
    146, 164–166, 208, 250
agribusiness, 105–106, 108, 165,
    207, 226
agriculture, 16, 36, 44, 68–69, 106,
    144, 146, 148–151, 162, 164,
    166, 170, 177, 186, 208
AIDS. See Acquired Immune
    Deficiency Syndrome

AISLD. See American Institute for
    Free Labour Development
Alexandre, Boniface, 265
Alexis, Jacques Stephen, 84
American Institute for Free Labour
    Development (AISLD), 188
Amerindians, 48–49
    genocide of, 18
Anti-Slavery Society, 163
Archin-Lay, Luce, 40
Ardouin, Beaubrun, 2, 7, 79
Argentina, 38, 205, 221
Aristide, Jean-Bertrand, 191–192,
    223, 226–227, 230, 233–241,
    243–248, 251–256, 258–265
army, 115, 117, 119, 125–128, 131,
    142, 150, 157–159, 177–179,
    181–184, 189, 199–202, 205,
    207, 221–223, 226–229, 232,
    238–240, 243–244, 246, 248–
    249, 263–264
    see also militarization
Athis, Louis-Eugène, 163, 183, 198
Avril, Prosper, 180, 226–229, 240

B

Bahamas, 160, 162, 187
Bastien, Rémy, 125

Batraville, Benoît, 108
Bazelais, Boyer, 114
Bazin, Marc, 198, 204, 234, 247, 253
Bélair, Suzanne Sanite, 41
Belgium, 7, 156
Beidelman, T.O., 211
Bellegarde, Argentine, 40, 202
Bellegarde, Dantès, 49, 55, 62, 70, 82, 97, 124, 212
Bellegarde, Fernande, 39
Belley, Mars, 57
Bemis, Flagg, 114
Bennett, Michèle, 37, 139
Bergeaud, Emeric, 81
Bergson, Henri, 83
Besse, Martial, 57
Biassou, 60
Black Power. See negritude
boat people, 141, 146, 161, 168, 186, 194, 241, 245
Boisrond, Isidore, 40
Boisrond-Tonnerre, Félix, 64
Bolívar, Simon, 7, 72, 224
Bonheur, Claire-Heureuse, 37
Borno, Louis, 101, 114–115
Boyer, Jean-Pierre, 37, 68, 74
brain drain, 151
Brazil, 25–26, 54, 146, 221, 263
Brierre, Jean F., 84–85
Bush, George W., 228, 262
Butler, Smedley D., 93, 102–103, 105, 108

C

cacoism, 97, 230
caco wars, 79, 97, 104, 107–108, 115, 118
    see also uprisings
Canada, 142, 160, 165, 199, 204, 230, 233, 249, 262
capitalism, 69, 78, 90, 98, 251, 258

Caribbean, 3, 5, 8, 18, 20, 35, 73, 76, 78–79, 114, 126, 132, 145, 211, 223, 230–231
Caribbean Basin Initiative (CBI), 133, 146, 153, 183
Caribbean Community (CARICOM), 204, 262, 264
Caribbean Council of Churches (CCC), 193, 201
CARICOM. See Caribbean Community
Carter, Jimmy, 134, 137, 154, 252
Castor, Suzy, 83
caudillism, 53, 67, 89–90, 94
Cayo Lobos incident, 141
CBI. See Caribbean Basin Initiative
CCC. See Caribbean Council of Churches
Chanlatte, Juste, 79
Chauvet, Marie, 40, 84
Chavannes, Jean-Baptiste, 57
China, 147
Christianity, 21–22, 24, 26, 36, 216–217, 224
    and slavery, 33, 48, 59
Christophe, Henry, 37, 57, 66, 69, 74
church
    Protestant, 21, 34, 41, 59, 80, 135, 165, 174, 187, 189, 192–195, 211, 213, 226, 250–251
    Roman Catholic, 21, 26, 34–35, 75, 80, 95, 100, 125, 129, 133–136, 142, 158, 174, 178, 181, 184, 186–187, 190–192, 194–195, 210, 213, 233–234, 250
    see also Christianity
Cinéas, Jean-Baptiste, 84
citizenship laws, 69, 93–94, 144
Clarkson, Thomas, 74

class structure
    Haiti, 7, 20, 31, 54–55, 65, 95,
        97, 115–116, 130, 159, 171,
        173, 181, 218, 223–224,
        235, 243, 246, 248
    Saint-Domingue, 54
Claude, Jean, 96
Claude, Sylvio, 140, 198, 204
Clinton, Bill, 255
Clitandre, Pierre, 84
Code Noir, 56
coffee, 20, 43, 69, 91, 144, 149
Coidavid, Louise, 37
Colimon, Marie-Thérèse, 39, 84
colonialism, 7, 19, 24, 35, 42, 66–67,
    81, 87, 93, 116, 144, 214, 237,
    251, 257
colonial period
    culture, 33–35, 49
    economy, 18, 53, 69
    politics, 52–53
    society, 52, 55
Columbus, Christopher, 24, 47–48,
    159
communism, 35, 105, 126, 134–136,
    174, 186, 194–195, 200, 225,
    236
Comte, Auguste, 80
Concordat, 233
Congolese, 25
congressional Black caucus, 137,
    201, 228
conservatism, 80
constitution of 1987, 22, 36, 173–
    176, 179–181, 184–185, 196,
    214, 218, 224–225, 228, 231,
    237, 241–242
constitutions, 2, 42, 65, 69, 73, 106,
    140, 173, 182, 235
    and the peasantry, 174, 177,
        180–181
Cook, Mercer, 77, 83
Creole, 54–55, 58–59, 73, 79

La Crête-à-Pierrot, Battle of, 41
Cruse, Harold, 211
Cuba, 16, 25–26, 54, 100–101, 111–
    112, 131–132, 153, 157, 162,
    164, 185–186, 223, 259
currency, 50
Cyprien, Augustin, 96

D

Dahomay, Jacky, 241
Dahomean, 24
Danticat, Edwidge, 84
Dartiguenave, Phillipe-Sudre, 101,
    114
debt, 98, 161, 247
Déjean, Yves, 84
Déjoie, Louis, 124–125, 138, 140,
    198, 204
Delatour, Leslie, 165, 208
Delorme, Demesvar, 80
Denby, Edwin, 192
Depestre, René, 84, 116
de Ronceray, Hubert, 198
Dessalines, Jean-Jacques, 37, 64–66,
    69, 72–73, 95, 131
Désulmé, Thomas, 198
Désyr, Luc, 196
de Vastey, Valentin, 79
Dévieux-Dehoux, Liliane, 84
Dévot, Justin, 81
Diaz, Porfirio, 114
Dominican Republic, 14–15, 73, 75–
    77, 93, 98, 112, 115, 122–123,
    126, 131, 146, 152, 160, 162,
    163, 200, 223, 230–231, 246,
    255, 258, 261
Dominique, Jean Léopold, 84, 253,
    256, 264
Dorsainvil, J.-C., 96
Dorsinville, Roger, 84
Dubois, W.E.B., 85
Dupuy, Alex, 222, 225, 251–252, 261

Durand, Oswald, 92
Durocher-Bertin, Mireille, 253
Dutty, Boukman, 40, 59–60, 62
Duvalier, François, 35, 37–38, 83,
    117, 119, 125–126, 129, 136–
    137, 139–140, 152–153, 159,
    178, 190, 198, 206, 212, 227,
    230, 233, 255, 259
duvalierism, 175, 182, 192, 195,
    199–200, 205, 223, 235, 244,
    249, 250, 254, 264
see also macoutism
Duvalier, Jean-Claude, 37, 119, 130,
    136–137, 139, 142, 147, 152,
    161, 223, 229, 244
Duvalier, Marie-Denise, 37–38
Duvalier regime, 5, 9, 21, 37–38, 45,
    123, 128–131, 134, 136, 141,
    151, 159, 161, 165, 179, 185,
    194, 216, 225, 234, 265
    constitutions, 140, 199
    overthrow of, 5, 21, 88, 130,
        155, 159, 181, 196
    terrorism within, 9, 140, 151

E
ecology, 150
economic development, 16, 52, 66,
    71, 239
economy
    colonial period, 20, 70
    contemporary period, 20, 118,
        130, 152, 155, 156–157,
        166, 170–171, 201, 208–
        209, 241, 246
    modern period, 67, 69, 90
education policy. See Haitian,
    education
elections, 123, 126, 180, 182, 199–
    200, 202–206, 229–230, 234,
    236, 238, 255–256, 261–262
England. See United Kingdom

Estimé, Dumarsais, 37, 117–119,
    121–122, 125, 159, 230, 249
Eugène, Grégoire, 139, 140, 198
exile, 9, 16, 86, 122, 127, 131, 134,
    140, 146, 151, 160, 234, 240–
    241, 246, 258
    see also migration

F
Farnham, Roger L., 99, 104
fascism, 96, 115, 236
Fatiman, Cécile, 40, 59
Fatton, Robert, 254, 261
Faubert, Ida, 40
Faubert, Pierre, 81
Feminine League for Social Action,
    38
Feuille, Jean-Hubert, 253
Fignolé, Daniel, 126–127, 140, 198
Firmin, Anténor, 81, 87
Ford, Gerald, 226, 242
foreign aid (loans), 9, 141, 143, 163,
    165, 169, 185, 255
foreign investment (capital), 9, 98,
    101, 104, 118, 141–143, 163,
    169
foreign ownership, 69, 90, 94, 162
foreign policy. See Haiti, foreign
    policy
Fouchard, Jean, 55, 83
France
    as a colonial power, 5, 18, 34–
        35, 50, 53–54, 63–64, 65,
        67, 81, 144, 193, 223, 231,
        258
    economic development, 6, 20,
        50, 92, 97, 142, 199, 230,
        249
    trade with Saint-Domingue and
        Haiti, 6, 50–53, 77, 90
    see also language, French;
        revolution

freemasonry, 24
free trade (market), 54, 70–71, 175, 251
French language. *See* language, French
Furtado, Celso, 69, 91

G
Gaillard, Roger, 83
Garoute, Alice, 39
Garvey, Marcus, 85
Gayot, François, 190
Geffrard, Fabre-Nicolas, 76, 96, 124
Génération de La Ronde, 40, 82, 84
génération de l'occupation, 83
Germany, 77–78, 90, 92, 94, 97, 142, 223
Gérome, Pétion, 79
Gilles, Serge, 198
globalization, 251, 257, 265
Gomez, Vincente, 114
Gourgue, Gérard, 83, 140, 182, 196, 198, 204
Grant, Ulysses S., 76–77
Grenada, 147
Guerilla warfare. *See* Cacoism, Caco wars, Piquet revolt
Guérin, Mona, 84

H
Haitian
    agricultural policy, 16, 20, 69, 91
    culture, 9, 13, 19, 22, 31, 35, 36–37, 42–43, 54, 59, 80, 85, 90, 129, 169, 194, 210, 219, 224, 232, 242, 257–258, 260
    economic policy, 6, 9, 19–20, 91, 93, 143, 148, 217
    education, 34, 38–40, 75, 80, 90–91, 135, 144, 148, 175, 177, 213, 218, 225

flag, 64, 73
foreign policy, 9, 70, 73, 78, 91, 159
government, 67–68, 98–99, 106, 117, 121, 124, 147, 151, 163, 166, 222, 232, 262
health care, 16, 144, 148, 175, 177, 218, 225
independence, 1, 7, 19, 33, 41, 57, 64, 66–67, 69, 71, 74, 78–79, 81, 95, 142, 249
industrial policy, 6
international relations, 7, 13, 18, 63, 74, 79
language policy, 7, 177, 196, 214, 257–258
legal system, 42, 45, 91, 149
rural policy, 177, 207
social pyramid, 54, 58
Haitian-American Sugar Company (HASCO), 112
Haitian Communist party (PUCH), 84, 119, 174, 247
Harlem resistance, 85–86
Heubreux, Joseph, 226
Heurtelou, Lucienne, 37
Hibbert, Fernand, 82
Holland, 63, 71
homosexuality, 26, 35, 42, 168
Honorat, Jean-Jacques, 253
Hudicourt, Max L., 84, 197
Hudicourt, Thérèse, 39
Hughes, Langston, 83
Hypolite, Florvil, 90

I
IDB. *See* Interamerican Development Bank
Igbo, 24
ILO. *See* International Labour Organisation
illiteracy, 8, 80, 116, 134, 170, 196

IMF. *See* International Monetary
   Fund
income
   disparity, 9, 156, 210
   rural/urban, 68, 79, 94, 147,
      177
   standard of living, 143–144,
      161
indigenism, 31, 84, 103, 135, 218
   see also negritude
industrialization, 6, 81, 103, 145,
   151, 165
industry, 50, 164, 166, 169, 225,
   232, 257
Inginac, Joseph-Balthazar, 74
Innocent, Antoine, 82
Inter-American Commission on
   Human Rights, 140
Interamerican Development Bank,
   163
International Monetary Fund, 143–
   144, 251
international relations. *See* Haiti,
   international relations
interracial unions, 56
Iraq, 260
Islam, 24, 216
Israel, 142, 158, 182, 200
Izmery, Antoine, 253

J
Jagan, Cheddi, 251, 262
Jagan, Janet, 251
Jamaica, 25, 119, 147, 157, 204,
   208, 251, 260, 262
James, C.L.R., 70
Jan, Jean-Marie, 193
Janvier, Louis-Joseph, 66, 81
Japan, 33, 142, 147
Jean-François, 60
Jeannot, 60
Jean-Rabel massacre. *See* massacre,
   Jean-Rabel

Jeanty, Lydia O., 37
Jefferson, Thomas, 63, 71
John Paul II, 136, 190, 233
Jonassaint, Emile, 253
Judaism, 21
judiciary, 68, 175, 185, 215, 240
Jumelle, Clément, 126–127

K
Kennedy, John, 131
Kissinger, Henry, 226, 242
KNG. *See* National Council of
   Government
Karenga, Maulana, 218

L
labour
   force, 105, 153, 210, 225
   policy, 170
   unions, 154–155, 160, 163, 174,
      182–184, 188, 199, 213,
      243, 254
Lachennais, Joute, 37, 68
Laferrière, Danny, 84
Lafontant, Roger, 234, 244
Laguerre, Michel S., 228
Lahens, Yanick, 84
Laleau, Léon, 84–85
Lamartinière, Marie-Jeanne, 41, 63, 68
land
   distribution, 13–14, 19, 144,
      149, 210
   reform, 68–69
   tenure system, 187
   transfers, 162
language
   Kreyol (Haitian), 8, 22, 31, 49,
      82, 95, 127, 134, 177–178,
      210, 214–215, 217, 239,
      257
   French, 7, 21, 31, 95, 127, 177–
      178, 210, 214

policy, 54
Latin America, 2–3, 7, 24, 49, 55, 68–70, 72, 144, 168, 206
Latortue, François, 182, 196
Latortue, Régine, 39
League of Nations, 78, 231
Leclerc, Charles, 63, 65
Le Petit Samedi Soir, 134
Lépine, Belmour, 40
Lescot, Elie, 114–115, 117, 122
Lespès, Anthony, 84
Lespinasse, Beauvais, 80
Lhérisson, Justin, 82
liberalism, 80
liberalization, 133, 169, 200
Liberia, 7, 75
Lincoln, Abraham, 75
literature, 40, 78–79, 81–86, 96
Logan, Rayford W., 87, 121
Louisiana Purchase, 2, 63, 71
Louis-Phillippe, King, 74
Louverture, Toussaint, 2, 37, 60, 62–64, 67, 69–71, 258
Lucas, Rémy, 188
Lundhal, Mats, 211

M

macoutism, 191, 223, 235
Madiou, Thomas, 80
Madison, James, 71
Magloire, Nadine, 84
Magloire, Paul-Eugène, 117, 122, 124, 126, 230
Maitland, Thomas, 70, 71
Makandal, François, 54, 60, 62
Malary, Guy, 253
Malval, Robert, 247, 254
Manifest Destiny, 114
Manigat, Leslie F., 121, 125, 198, 205–206, 221, 223–224, 226, 228
Manigat, Myrlande Hyppolite, 37

Manigat, Sabine, 235
Manley, Michael, 251, 262, 293
manufacturing, 151, 153
Marcelin, Frédéric, 82
maroons, 48, 54, 59, 68, 223, 248, 259
massacre
    Dominican, 76
    Jean-Rabel, 184–186, 188–191, 194, 196, 208, 213
    of November, 202–203
Mathon, Alice, 39
media (press), Haitian, 131, 133–134, 136, 163, 183–184, 189, 195, 224, 243, 252, 254, 261
Ménos, Solon, 78
Métellus, Jean, 84
Mexico, 85, 114
Michel, Claudine, 3, 86, 261, 294
migration, 9, 16, 147, 149, 161, 164–165, 170, 210–211, 233, 245, 258
    see also exile
militarization, 65, 67–68, 221
    see also army
Mintz, Sidney W., 222–223
Miranda, Francisco, 66, 72
Missionaries. *See* Christianity; church; religion
Mitterrand, François, 137, 231, 263
modernization, 89, 208, 218, 259
Môle Saint-Nicolas, 77, 98
Moline, Jeannot, 96
Monroe Doctrine, 72, 75, 78, 92
Montas, Michele, 264
Moravia, Adeline, 84
Morisseau-Leroy, Félix, 84, 214
Murray, Gerald F., 210–211

N

Namphy, Henri, 180–181, 188, 203, 206, 226, 228, 242

Napoleon, 1, 19, 63, 65
Napoleonic Code, 42
National City Bank, 93, 98–99, 103–
    104
National Council of Government
    (KNG), 156, 181–182, 184,
    189, 191, 195, 200–201, 203–
    205
National Railroad, 98–99, 106
national security policy, 75, 131
    see also army; militarization
Nau, Emile, 48
Nau, Ignace, 81
negritude, 80, 83–84, 87, 103, 116,
    119, 126, 128, 224, 257
Nerette, Joseph, 253
Nicaragua, 93, 115, 123, 223, 261
Nicolas, Louise, 41, 96
Nixon, Richard, 126, 249
Nkrumah, Kwame, 85

O

OAS. See Organization of American
    States
occupation of Haiti
    censorship, 102
    economic policy, 18, 106, 129,
        144, 250
    national unity, 87–88, 224
    resistance, 9, 21, 41, 81–82, 90,
        98, 101–102, 104–105,
        107–112, 215
    social policy, 34–35, 100, 250
    support for, 100
    terrorism, 111
    women, 41
OECS. See Organization of Eastern
    Caribbean States (OECS)
Ollivier, Emile, 84
Oreste, Michel, 90
Organization of American States
    (OAS), 244–245, 252, 262

Organization of Eastern Caribbean
    States (OECS), 204
Ovide, Simone, 37

P

Pamphile, Léon, 88
Pan-Africanism, 86–87, 213, 262
Pan-Americanism, 87
Pan-Caribbeanism, 87, 119
Panama, 72, 75, 164, 261
Pascal-Trouillot, Ertha, 39, 229–230,
    234, 239–240
Paul, Jean-Claude, 227
Paul, Max, 194
peasant uprisings. See Caco wars,
    uprisings
Péralte, Charlemagne, 108, 241
Pétion, Alexandre, 37, 66, 68–69, 72,
    223
Phelps, Anthony, 84
Pierre, Antoine, 96
Pierre-Charles, Gérard, 112
Pierre-Louis, Joseph Nemours, 123
Piquet revolt, 41, 79, 96–97
plantation economy (plantocracy),
    20, 53–55, 57–59, 62, 69, 74,
    104, 144, 151
Plummer, Brenda, 92
Plymouth, 54, 60
Poitevien, Marie-Thérèse, 39
political
    culture, 8, 18, 54, 130
    development, 66, 92
    parties, 119, 127, 139–140, 176,
        182, 197–198
    system, 68, 97, 119, 196, 222,
        228
politique de doublure, 96–98, 100
Pompilus, Pradel, 83
population, 16, 17
    colonial, 55
    ethnic composition, 8, 18–19
    foreign, 18–19

Port-au-Prince, 15, 37, 67, 76, 94–
    95, 99, 108, 115, 121, 129, 136,
    141–142, 148, 152, 155, 162,
    164–165, 168, 170, 183, 185–
    186, 188, 191, 196, 203, 216,
    237–238, 246–247
Portugal, 50
positivism, 80, 103
Poujol-Oriol, Paulette, 84
Powell, Colin L., 252, 264–265
Préval, René G., 223, 238, 241, 253,
    255–257
Price, Hannibal, 81
Price-Mars, Jean, 76, 80, 83, 87, 128
prostitution, 168
    see also women
Protestantism, 31, 33, 210
Provisional Electoral Council (KEP),
    181–182
PUCH. See Unified Party of Haitian
    Communists
Puerto Rico, 25, 85, 145–147, 153

R
racism, 7, 22, 38, 57, 64, 79, 80–81,
    85, 87, 102–103, 115, 139, 166,
    170, 193, 224
Reagan, Ronald, 134, 146, 154, 249
Régala, Williams, 188, 200, 203
regionalism, 89, 95
religion, 21, 34, 36, 54, 95, 217
    see also church; Vodou
resistance. See uprisings
resources,
    human, 8, 13, 18, 20
    natural, 8, 13, 16, 18, 90
revolution
    American, 50, 57, 66
    assistance to American, 57
    French, 50, 55, 57, 66, 173
    Haitian, 2, 41, 57, 69, 71–72,
        95, 104, 173, 223, 261

Richard, Yves, 195
Riché, Jean-Baptiste, 96
Rigaud, André, 57, 62
Rochambeau, Donatien, 64–65
Rochambeau, Jean-Baptiste, 57
Rockefeller, David, 181, 249
Rockefeller, Nelson, 152
Rodney, Walter, 70
Romaine the Prophetess, 60
Roman Catholicism, 21, 31
see also church
Romanticism, 40, 81
Romélus, Willy, 190–191
Roosevelt, Franklin D., 99, 212
Roumain, Ernest, 76
Roumain, Jacques, 83–84, 197

S
Saint-Amant, Edris, 84
Saint-Domingue, 2, 6, 50, 52, 54–55,
    57–59, 62–63, 75, 151, 258
Saint-Marc, Henriette, 41
St-Méry, Moreau de, 59, 72
Saint-Rémy, Joseph, 80
Salomon, Lysius-Félicité, 40, 90
Sam, Vilbrun Guillaume, 99
Sampeur, Virginie, 40, 81
Sandino, Augusto César, 108
Santo Cerro, Battle of, 48
Sartre, Jean-Paul, 85
Scandinavia, 71
schools. See Haitian, education
Schultz, George, 8, 205, 218
Seaga, Edward, 204
Senghor, Léopold Sédar, 83, 117
Seward, William H., 76
Simon, Suzanne, 37
slave revolts, 62, 71, 73, 215
slavery, 6–7, 42, 48, 50, 57–59, 62–
    65, 67, 69, 71, 75, 85, 105, 144,
    163, 173–174, 224, 251, 257
    life expectancy, 58

profitability, 18, 50
see also Anti-Slavery Society
Social Darwinism, 103
socialism. See communism
Sonthonax, Leger-Félicité, 62
Soulouque, Faustin, 95, 97, 230, 259
South Korea, 142, 200
Soviet Union, 225
Spain,
   during colonization, 18, 20, 47–
      49, 62–63, 66
   contemporary, 20
   at independence, 73, 76
sugar, 18, 20, 50, 52, 69, 91, 144,
   149, 162, 182, 208, 232
Sylvain, Bénito, 81, 87
Sylvain, Georges, 84, 101, 214
Sylvain, Madeleine, 39, 44
Syrians, 18, 77, 91, 94

T

Taino/Arawak, 14, 24, 47–48
Taiwan, 142
Talleyrand, Charles, 71
technology, 16, 67, 70
terrorism, 1, 9, 64, 200, 202, 221,
   243, 249
Tet Ansanm, 184, 186–189, 194
Théodore, René, 197, 247
Thoby-Marcelin, Phillipe, 84
Thoby-Marcelin, Pierre, 84
Ti Légliz, 136, 190, 213, 234, 243
Tontons Macoutes (Volunteers for
   National Security), 37, 131,
   157–158, 188–189, 194–195,
   200, 202–203, 212, 226, 251
tourism, 151, 160, 166, 168, 170
trade, 50–53, 70–71, 74, 77, 90, 144,
   148, 160, 163, 184, 215
   exports, 50, 77, 91, 147, 149,
      151, 153, 164, 169, 245
   imports, 50, 143, 147

transportation, 16, 186
Treaty of Basel, 62, 75
Treaty of Ryswick, 50
Trinidad, 25, 119, 204
Trouillot, Lyonel, 84
Trouillot, Michel-Rolph, 261
Trujillo, Rafael Leonidas, 76, 115,
   117, 123, 162, 223, 255
Turnbull, Wallace, 193–194

U

unemployment, 106, 116, 146–147,
   153, 155, 165
Unified Party of Haitian
   Communists (PUCH), 140, 197
United Kingdom, 52, 54, 63–64, 70–
   71, 73, 74, 77, 79, 97, 157, 223,
   262
United Nations, 5, 131, 163, 244–
   246, 252, 255
United States
   colonial policy, 33–34
   corporations, 146, 152–153,
      162, 164–165, 168, 221,
      226
   early relations with Haiti, 66, 71,
      73–76, 139, 226
   economic interests, 8, 77, 90,
      97, 117
   economic policy for Haiti, 94,
      132, 145, 230, 249
   foreign aid, 34, 99, 126, 131–
      133, 135, 137, 142, 146,
      161, 199–201, 204, 208,
      224, 245
   industrial policy for Haiti, 20,
      230
   interests, 15, 17, 77, 104, 194,
      221–222
   interventions, 63, 82, 87, 96, 99,
      114–115, 122–123, 125–
      126, 145, 159, 181, 204,

206, 222, 242, 244, 249,
  261
investments, 100, 133, 152,
  158–161, 163, 166, 230
Marine Corps, 19, 93, 95, 102,
  108, 114–115, 125, 129,
  131–132, 158, 178, 221,
  241, 245, 265
media and Haiti, 127, 139, 152,
  161, 168, 175, 190, 204,
  265
military assistance, 129, 131–
  133, 142, 158, 183,
  200–201, 221, 227–228
presidential support, 131–132,
  142–200, 230–231, 248
see also trade, occupation
uprisings (resistance), 60, 64, 155,
  180, 222, 247
see also slave revolts; Caco Wars
urban centers, 17, 68, 154, 164
USAID. See Agency for International
  Development

V

Vatican, 40, 75, 135, 190, 230, 233,
  244
Venezuela, 114, 199–200, 205, 230–
  231, 246–247, 249
Verna, Paul, 72
Viatte, Auguste, 87
Vincent, Jean-Marie, 253
Vincent, Sténio, 101, 114
Virgin Islands, 76, 126, 147
Vodou
  and the arts, 31
  cosmology, 25, 30
  culture, 21, 59, 82, 100, 125,
    250, 257
  decriminalization of, 178, 224,
    233
  definition of, 24–25

and language, 21–22
and national identity, 33, 36
persecution of, 22, 34–35, 59,
  75, 134, 194–195
and resistance, 21, 59, 62, 213,
  216, 250
scholarship, 86
and science, 30–31
tradition, 26, 28–29, 37
and U.S. occupation, 33–35
and wars of independence, 21
Western perceptions of, 35, 217
Voegeli, Alfred, 192
Volel, Yves, 183
Volunteers for National Security. See
  Tontons Macoutes
Voodoo. See Vodou

W

wars of independence, 19, 21, 37,
  41, 68, 97, 215, 244
West Indies, 54, 70
Wilson, Edmund, 8, 83
Wilson, Woodrow, 104
Wolff-Ligondé, François, 136, 190
women
  access to resources, 17
  and agriculture, 40, 43, 150
  and commerce, 40, 44, 68, 150
  and education, 38–40
  in industry, 40, 154
  and the law, 39, 42, 44
  and literature, 40, 68
  organizations (women's
    movement), 37–40
  and politics, 37–38, 44, 68, 239–
    240
  and prostitution, 168
  and religion, 26, 37, 41–42, 68
  and resistance, 41, 60
  and sexual division of labour, 43
  in slavery, 58

voting, 39, 45, 124, 175
and westernization, 40–42
Women's International League for
    Peace and Freedom, 111
World Bank, 137, 143, 163, 198,
    234, 251, 253
Wright, Butler J., 102

Y
Yoruba, 24

Z
Zamor, Dugué, 96
Zyphir, Flore, 88